The Baker's Four Seasons

Baking by the Season, Harvest, and Occasion

Marcy Goldman

RIVER HEART PRESS
Montreal, Canada

The Baker's Four Seasons
Baking by the Season, Harvest, and Occasion

First Edition
Copyright 2014
Text and recipes © 2014 by Marcy Goldman
River Heart Press
www.RiverHeartPress.com
Montreal, Canada

Library and Archives Canada in Publication
ISBN 978-0986572494 (Print edition)
ISBN 978-0-9865724-1-8 (eBook edition)

Goldman, Marcy
The Baker's Four Seasons/Marcy Goldman
1.Baking l.Title
Printed in the United States of America

Cover Photo: Free Form Apple Tart, Fall Chapter, Ryan Szluc
Book Cover Design: Damon, Damonza.com
Book Interior Design: Benjamin Carrancho, Damonza.com
Book Indexer: Karen Griffiths
Author Photo: Wanda Malfara

Other Books by Marcy Goldman
When Bakers Cook, 2013 River Heart Press (Print, eBook)
A Passion for Baking, 2014 River Heart Press (Print, eBook)
A Treasury of Jewish Holiday Baking, 2007 Whitecap Books (Print, eBook)
The New Best of BetterBaking.com, 2007 Whitecap Books (Print, eBook)
A Passion for Baking, 2005 Oxmoor House (Print)
Love and Ordinary Things, 2014 River Heart Press (Print, eBook)

Marcy Goldman is a cookbook author, master baker, and host of the baking website, www.Betterbaking.com, Est. 1997. Inquiries may be sent to editors@betterbaking.com or marcygoldman@bell.net.

With love to my sons, Jonathan, Gideon and Benjamin

*With affection and appreciation to my caring circle of friends and
readers. I am honored to share the seasons with all of you.*

Table of Contents

A Note from the Baker

To Everything There is a Season
(Ecclesiastes)

Welcome to The Baker's Four Seasons and welcome to my kitchen. We're about to embark on a journey as old as time because this baking adventure is all about time as it unfolds by the seasons. Through recipes and companion notes, you'll taste the seasons, enjoying and sharing the flavor palate of the harvest on each and every page.

The four seasons are an integral part of a special clock and it's Nature's gentle tick-tock pulse that frames our lives. As a baker, I am especially attuned to the seasons, for they speak to me in a visceral way. Through my five senses, particularly those of taste and smell, the seasons remind me of my calling as a baker and writer. Unlike like wheat from the chaff, I can't easily separate what and who I am from the recipes I create and

share. Similarly, I can't separate the seasonal offerings from those on my table; both are part and parcel of each other; the former is the impetus for the latter.

How do I measure the seasons? I measure them in vistas of wheat, mountains of apple peelings, vanilla raindrops, followed by dustings of walnuts and the mellow warmth of a chocolate dew. I gather and hold the seasons and revel in my appetite for life. I take it all in swigs with a gusto born of well-being and a deep-rooted appreciation. I'm sure it's the same with you.

On any given day in any given season as I stand at my kitchen sink window, I glance outside. In winter, the trees are clad in white and offset a pair of red cardinals who visit me daily. In spring, I cherish the sight of the lilac blossoms and am thrilled to witness the return of Canadian geese. In summer, there's a frenzy of rhubarb in the corner garden, the tall pink shoots asking to be part of a tart and sweet pie. In autumn, I'm captivated by the maple trees as they turn from green to red, enjoying the pervasive scent of apple in the spicy harvest breeze. In fall, I confess, I get giddy just thinking of the huge baking season ahead! Nothing brings me back to the kitchen quite like the first frost of September when I happily anticipate both familiar, beloved baking and the new recipes I'll create.

It doesn't really matter what month it is, my kitchen and heart rev in synch, just by looking around me and always finding a culinary resonance. There's this song I hear; it's music born of love and memories. The tune weaves its way into my rolling pins and cookie cutters; the sweet refrain whispers in canisters of flour, sugar and fragrant spice jar and the seasons themselves are a four-part melody, caroling at our doors, asking us to join in.

Like Demeter, the goddess of grain, those of us who are culinarily attuned hear that that clarion call, courtesy of the harvest at hand. We respond baking by the season – something we've always done. Baking-in-season was a trend that began in California, as part of the 1970's culinary movement and it soon spread all over the continent. But baking (or cooking, for that matter) 'by the harvest' is not new. Good chefs, home or professional, have long relied and made the most of ingredients that are fresh, local or native. The Slow Food movement, the Green movement, the economy and global climate change have only emphasized the wisdom of this approach. More than that, seasonal baking is not about being a "foodie"; it's far more real, innately authentic, intimate and close to our hearts than that. When we head to the kitchen, it's just second nature for us to think in terms of the seasons.

How to Use This Cookbook

This book is divided into four major seasonal chapters, starting with Fall, as it is the prime baking season and features so many holidays and occasions. Still, as you turn the pages, all recipes being equal and totally tempting, you can mix and match recipes, no matter what the season. Feel free to take inspiration from one season to the next, changing the spices, or adding a different fruit, nut or extract.

In addition, in each chapter, as an overview of what's ahead, I offer some notes on the baking themes for each season. This is to put you in the mood! You'll also notice an emphasis on 'seasonal perfume' wherein I describe the scented 'notes' of each season. I've long dabbled in perfumes and potions and this will be more apparent when you read about the Fragrance Notes of the season and then later on in the bonus Chapter Nine, a collection of my favorite tea and coffee blends. Chapter Ten is where you'll find Baking Techniques you are sure to find most helpful.

Little and Big Baking, Recipes: both small and grand

I've also sub-divided each season into 'little" or "big" (which includes special occasion and holiday) baking. I did this because I feel we all generally know when we want or need to bake something small-ish or need something larger, especially if we are hosting or want something for a larger gathering. Little baking includes things like muffins, cookies, scones, and other casual baking. "Big" baking includes crowd-pleasing recipes for entertaining or holidays, such as luxurious cakes and tortes. These are not only larger recipes but recipes that are meant to celebrate whatever the occasion with their more elaborate appeal. In short, these are traditional or innovative showstoppers.

One note about the seasonality of this book: never feel contained or limited to bake what you want, when you want it! A Pumpkin Cheesecake doesn't need to wait for Thanksgiving to be appreciated, nor does a decadent chocolate torte, befitting Easter or Passover, need be held back from those who pine for chocolate at any time of year.

The Baking of Fall

When asked what their favorite season is, most people will vote for summer or spring but a disproportionate number of bakers will always choose fall. Short and sweet, fall provides the best baking months of the year. Fall is baking's homecoming queen, the princess of B&B, old-fashioned baking. It's the homey baking you grew up with (or wished you did!). Harvest-oriented, fall is all about the hunker-down flavors of nuts, spice, honey, brown sugar. It's all things gold and amber: butterscotch, toffee and caramel with healthy lashings of cinnamon. At midpoint, fall segues from autumnal hospitality baking to the gateway of the festive holiday season. When you think of fall, think muffins, cookies, after-school sheet cakes, hefty scones, hospitable slicing cakes; then switch gears and think of the majesty of the Thanksgiving dessert bounty.

The Baking of Winter

Winter baking is majestic. This is the no-holds-barred celebration of the flour arts. It's the perfect time to showcase your baking prowess as well as your generous, giving spirit. So pull out the chocolate and double up the vanilla; there's company coming and gifts to bake. Winter is the most buttery-baking time, replete with elegant, fussy cookies or the simplicity of old-fashioned shortbread. To me, winter baking is all about our revered traditions which is why this chapter features both more elaborate recipes as well as the much-loved treats that have been passed down through the generations.

What makes winter baking particularly special is the collective energy in the kitchen as so many people, the globe over, all get involved in baking, because baking is a treat and it always makes the perfect gift.

Once the major December holidays have gone, it's still winter and the chilly air is incentive enough for more cozy baking times. You'll find the post-holiday section of the Winter Chapter is chock full of temptations to keep your spirits up in that no-man's land between winter holidays and Valentine's Day, which in itself, is yet another time to indulge in some decadent baking.

The Baking of Spring

Spring is all about freshness, exemplified by berries and a lighter touch, especially after the rustic recipes of fall or the rich desserts of the winter special occasions. Holidays such as Easter and Passover exemplify the mood of renewal in the kitchen, which revels in lighter coffeecakes, flavors of maple, apricot, and a lot of strawberry and rhubarb baking, all to celebrate the change of seasons. Expect 'pretty' baking in this chapter, recipes designed to lighten your mood as well as your palate.

The Baking of Summer

For summer, I've created a bouquet of recipes that are rife with a heady warmth yet flirtily casual. This is a time for treats that are both sweet and easy - recipes that fit easily into the rhythm of our summer lives. Summer is outdoorsy and active; no one wants to be in the kitchen for too long. Happily, the summer recipes are at once refreshing, exotic, fruity and fun and generally are 'short bakes'. In the Summer Chapter, you'll find the perfect baking to pack into brown bag lunches, picnic hampers to bring to the beach or cottage, or to offer with a July barbecue. Pies figure in much of summer baking and you'll also find some of my best creamy, luxurious cheesecakes in this section.

Chapter Ten, A Bonus Recipe Chapter

Teas and Coffees

Looking for something nice to drink to go with all that baking? You've come to the right place. In this special tea chapter, I've included many of the original recipes I've first created in my own kitchen as I've hosted family, friends, colleagues, and guests. Many of those recipes have appeared on my website, www.BetterBaking.com. There's over 40 unique tea recipes to suit the time and occasion or your taste. Like the baking recipes, they're all arranged by season.

I also pride myself in being a tea and coffee 'intuitive', that is, I can usually tell at a glance what someone will be partial to – who is a coffee drinker or tea drinker, or both. At any rate, this baking book is also an occasion to offer my best concoctions in teas, as well as a cocoa or two, a white sangria and fresh, old-fashioned lemonade to go with summer recipes.

Chapter Eleven, Baking Techniques

Great baking needs great, foundational techniques. This is the chapter where you'll find all the information on those techniques, as well as my best baking tips and tricks and some insights into ingredients and bakeware I recommend.

Before you're Off to Bake

This hand-picked, original recipe collection is a mindful nod to how we bake, whether it's for ourselves and our families, or for friends and work mates. It's a cookbook I've created just for you but it's also a salute to our collective, global table. As we bake, we're are also experiencing the seasons together, no matter where we are. I hope you'll feel the energy waft from my kitchen to yours as you make these recipes, knowing I'm probably doing the same. There's a good chance however, that when it's spring in my neck of the woods, it more likely already fall where you are. But still, when it comes to food, we are all one.

Your kitchen is and always should be an oasis that brings you back to the table, to break bread with those we love. The calendar days and years swirl around us, making us cleave, connect, scatter like leaves and then once again, reunite, as occasion and time permits. We gather at the table but it's the kitchen that is the anchor of our families and our lives. That anchor makes a house not just

shelter, but a home. In this special domain, you're the keeper of the keys. You have the unique power to make home, homey. What better way to do this than with baking that's as old-fashioned as a bib apron and as contemporary as a text message on your smart phone saying: *The bake sale is tomorrow!*

Whatever the time of year, whatever the weather: rain, snow or balmy sunshine, it's always a good time to bake. I wish you special times, both in your kitchen and in life. No matter what the season or the reasons – may it all be sweet.

Marcy Goldman

Author & Master Baker

www.BetterBaking.com

Fall Baking

The Harvest Season
Spice, Brown Sugar, Comfort and Hospitality

Fall in the Bakery

Close your eyes and envision the red and gold leaves of fall as they tumble and swirl. Imagine the sound as you walk and rustle through those leaves, in your garden, a park or through an apple orchard. There's a scent of wood smoke in the air; someone has lit a fire. Is it hickory, maple, or perhaps a touch of mesquite? In days gone by, native people could easily tell who (whether other tribes or settlers) were near or how far they were, simply by the smell of smoke. Given the vibrant colors and its heady scents, I'm not surprised that special feeling of fall seems more timeless than any other season.

After Labor Day, we bakers renew our baking vows with floury fervor. That first crisp morning is impetus enough and our baking creativity is ignited. We almost hunger to return to the kitchen after a leisurely summer. This is the time of harvest and homecomings and there's a distinct sweetness of mood and a sense of anticipation. I delight in every season, but as a baker I confess, I'm *in love* with fall.

Fall showcases baking in a way few seasons can, whether you hail from New England or sunny California or the Canadian Prairies, for it touches a collective soul in a unique way. September conjures up the smell of Crayolas on the first day of school; in October, you remember the ghosts of Halloweens and carved pumpkins past, the treasures you found at an autumn antique show, the sight of U-pick apples in the car trunk, or the groaning bounty of a Thanksgiving table. Breathe in the heady aroma of any fall day and tell me it doesn't take much to bring you back to someplace in time or memory.

The Perfume of Fall

Fall's perfume is like a warm, friendly girl - bounteous, hospitable, and hardly bashful. Years ago, with this same inspiration, I even created a perfume with a fragrance company and called it *Wheat Siren*. It was a heady mix of honey, vanilla, jasmine, and orange blossom. Similarly, in baking, the thematic note of fall is just as warm and inviting. Unlike my perfume foray, it forgoes the floral notes and instead, features spice, brown sugar, along with copious lashings of other uplifting, festive spicy notes. As with all the seasons of baking, fruit is pivotal to fall's perfume. Think of a plethora of ripe apples and mellow pears, all laced with the grapey harvest of the vines and a final hint of luscious buttery nutmeats and you have fall's theme down pat.

Base Notes

Brown sugar, caramel, apples, new wheat and new harvest wine

Heart Notes

Cinnamon, nuts, golden raisins, dried fruits

Top Notes

Spice and honey

Theme Mood

Nostalgia and gratitude

Theme Colors

Orange and gold

Fall Baking Style

Fall Flavor and Ingredient Palate

Sugar and spice, fresh nuts, pears and plums, the last of peaches and stray berries all tumble together into September. Fall is the beginning of the apple season and the cue to haul in the new crop of cranberries, black walnuts and golden Southern pecans. Pie-bound pumpkins, on display at the farmer's market are another seasonal cue; the gorgeous orange orbs remind us to refresh the cinnamon, clove and allspice jars and stock up on sweet butter for baking.

Fall is replete with baking occasions both large and small but it's also always an occasion for exceptionally, heartwarming baking. This includes the back-to-school bake sale, the sports team snack, the coffee klatch with friends, the apple-picking fest, the preserving party, as well as the many holidays—from Halloween to the Jewish New Year and of course, Thanksgiving. Country-style breads rule, as do quick breads, muffins, scones, and sheet cakes. This is a major brown sugar and apple oasis, a flavor combination that turns up in Fall's recipes.

Fall, Small Baking

Fall, Small Baking
Recipes

Raspberry Scuffins

Sweet Maple Crisp Scones

Chewy Crumble Buttermilk Spice Cake

Caramel Apple Bagels

Sweet Potato Apple Butter Muffins

Old-Fashioned Giant Snickerdoodles

General Store Oatmeal Cookies

Peanut Butter and Jam Cookies

McIntosh Honey Apple Compote

Vermont Apple Cider Doughnuts

Granny Smith Sour Cream Apple Muffins

Multi-Grain All Purpose Baking Flour

Home Blend Pumpkin Pie Spice Mix

Pumpkin Millet Muffins

Greek Yogurt Blueberry Banana Muffins

Orange Pecan Brown Sugar Scones

Canadiana Buttertart Squares

Crop Circle Trail Bars

Buttermilk Cinnamon Biscotti

Shoebox Brownies

Nutella Banana Bread

Weekend in New England Brown Bread

Pumpkin Caramel Sticky Buns

Dried Pear and Cranberry Strudel

Pecan Pie Biscotti

Cheddar Fig Buns

Raspberry Scuffins

Cross a muffin with a scone and what do you get? Scuffins! Big, beautiful crusty scones and muffin hybrid that features a pastry-crisp outside with a cake-like interior, and a surprise cache of raspberry preserves. Whipping cream makes them especially tender and high-rising.

SCONES

4 cups all-purpose flour

2/3 cup sugar

4 teaspoons baking powder

1 teaspoon baking soda

1/2 teaspoon salt

2 teaspoons orange zest, finely minced

3/4 cup unsalted butter, very cold, diced into 1/2 inch cubes

2 eggs

1 cup whipping cream mixed with 2 teaspoons lemon juice

2 teaspoons pure vanilla extract

1/2 cup raspberry preserves

FINISHING TOUCHES

Fresh raspberries

Unsalted butter, melted

Sugar

Place the oven rack in the middle of the oven position. Preheat the oven to 400°F. Line a baking sheet with parchment paper. Line 12 muffin cups with large muffin cups or tulip style parchment muffin cups.

In a food processor, place the flour, sugar, baking powder, baking soda, salt and orange zest. Blend ingredients for 10-20 seconds. Add the butter and pulse to cut up the butter into the dry mix until you have fine crumbs or a mealy mixture. (You can also so this by hand in a large bowl). In a small bowl, blend the eggs, whipping cream/lemon juice mixture and vanilla together.

Add the dry ingredients to a large bowl and make a well in the center. Add in the egg and cream mixture and blend with a spoon or by hand to bring mixture together, adding more cream as required to make a soft batter (stiffer than muffins, less stiff than roll-out scones).

Scoop muffin cups two-thirds full of batter, top with a tablespoon or so of raspberry preserves and top with some batter. Brush with melted butter, top with a fresh raspberry and dust with sugar.

Bake 22-27 minutes or until scuffins are well-browned all over.

Makes 9-12

Sweet Maple Crisp Scones

Rustic-with-flair best describes these scones, made with whipping cream and pure maple syrup. Brush these with butter before baking or glaze them afterwards with the decadent maple glaze. I'm very fond of glazing scones; it fussies them up and also keeps them a bit fresh.

3 cups all- purpose flour

1/3 cup brown sugar, firmly packed

4 teaspoons baking powder

¼ teaspoon cinnamon

3/4 teaspoon salt

3/4 cup cold unsalted butter

1/2 cup finely chopped walnuts

1 egg

1/3 cup pure maple syrup

1 teaspoon pure vanilla extract

3/4 cup whipping cream, approximately

MAPLE BUTTER

3 tablespoons unsalted butter, melted

1/4 cup pure maple syrup

1/4 cup brown sugar, firmly packed

MAPLE FONDANT GLAZE

2 cups confectioners' sugar

1 teaspoon pure vanilla extract

½ teaspoon pure maple extract, optional

2 tablespoons pure maple syrup

Whipping cream, as required

FINISHING TOUCHES
Chopped walnuts

Preheat the oven to 425°F. Line a double-up baking sheet (two sheets stacked together, one inside the other) with parchment paper.

In a food processor, place the flour, brown sugar, cinnamon, baking powder, salt and cinnamon. Pulse to combine. Add butter and pulse to cut or break butter into flour mixture. Mix to make a sandy mixture. Place mixture in a large bowl. Fold in walnuts. Make a well in the center and add the egg, maple syrup, vanilla and most of the cream. Stir with a fork to make a soft dough.

Turn out onto a lightly floured board and knead briefly; drizzling on a bit more cream to ensure dough holds together. Shape the dough into a round, about 1 inch thick and 10 inches wide. Cut in half and then each half into 4-5 wedges each. Place them on the baking sheet.

For the Maple Butter, in a small bowl, blend the melted butter and maple syrup. Brush each wedge with this mixture and then dust with brown sugar. (If you are using the Maple Fondant, this step is optional; they are richer with it but it's up to you).

Bake until nicely browned, 18-22 minutes.

For the Maple Fondant, in a small bowl, blend the confectioners' sugar, vanilla and maple extracts, maple syrup and as much cream as required to make a soft fondant or glaze. Smear over scones and dust with walnuts; let the glaze set.

Makes 8-12, depending on size

Chewy Crumble Buttermilk Spice Cake

Mouth-watering, buttery and tender, this cake reminds me of breakfast at a New England B&B. Everything in this recipe depends on using the finest of simple things, such as the best quality cinnamon you can find.

CHEWY CRUMBLE TOPPING

1 1/2 cups all-purpose flour

1 cup sugar

1/2 cup unsalted butter, melted

CAKE

2 1/2 cups all-purpose flour

1 ½ cups sugar

2 ¼ teaspoons baking powder

1/2 teaspoon baking soda

¼ teaspoon salt

1 teaspoon cinnamon

1/8 teaspoon nutmeg

1 cup unsalted butter, cold, diced small cubes

¾ cup buttermilk

¾ cup whipping cream, approximately

2 eggs

2 teaspoons pure vanilla extract

1 cup raspberries or blueberries, optional

Preheat oven to 350°F. Stack two baking sheets together and line the top one with parchment paper. Spray a 9-by-13 inch pan with non-stick cooking spray and place on baking sheet.

For the Chewy Crumble Topping, place the flour and sugar in a bowl and mix well. Then stir in the butter and mix with a wood spoon or knead by hand to combine to make a crumble topping.

For the cake, in a larger mixer bowl, combine flour, sugar, baking powder, baking soda, salt, cinnamon and nutmeg. Add the butter and pulse to make a grainy mixture. Add buttermilk, most of the cream, eggs and vanilla. Blend to make a thick batter. If batter appears very thick, drizzle in more cream (about 1 ½ cups liquid in all, if it's needed). Fold in the fruit by hand. Spread batter in pan and distribute reserved crumb topping evenly over top.

Bake until the cake seems set, about 45-50 minutes, until the topping is golden brown. Cool well (this cake is delicate of crumb; give it a good hour to cool); then cut into squares to serve.

Serves 10-14

Caramel Apple Bagels

Homemade bagels are so good, especially when it's these autumnal versions. Bagels are fast, easy and the varieties are unlimited- there's so much potential! In fall, when you have a hankering for a something sweet but totally toast-able, this is just the ticket.

2 cups warm water, preferably spring water

2 3/4 teaspoons instant yeast

5-6 cups bread flour

2 tablespoons honey

3 tablespoons brown sugar

2 tablespoons canola oil

2 teaspoons salt

1 teaspoon malt powder, optional

Pinch cinnamon

3/4 cup butterscotch chips

4 cups diced (peeled) apples

1 cup diced caramels (such as Kraft)

KETTLE WATER
Water

2 tablespoons honey

2 teaspoons salt

FINISHING TOUCHES
1/3 cup oatmeal

½ cup brown sugar, firmly packed

Stack two baking sheets together and line the top one with parchment paper.

In a mixer bowl, hand whisk the water and yeast; let stand 1 minute, and then briskly add in a cup of the flour, the honey, brown sugar, oil, salt, malt powder, cinnamon and blend well. Fold in most of the flour (all but 2 cups) to make a stiff dough. Attach dough hook and knead, adding more flour as required to make a very tough, slick dough, 6-10 minutes. Let rest 20 minutes, lightly covered in plastic.

Meanwhile, heat an 8 quart pot with water (two-thirds full) to which you have added the honey and salt. Allow to come to a medium boil.

Press dough down and knead in the butterscotch chips, apples and caramels. If mixture gets wet and slack, dust in more flour. Let dough rest, lightly covered with plastic wrap, 15 minutes. Gently deflate and then divide dough into 10-14 sections. Form each into an 8-10 inch rope. Press two ends together, and roll back and forth on a work surface to "lock" them, and form a ring or bagel. In a small bowl, mix the brown sugar and oatmeal.

Preheat oven to 450°F.

Place bagels in simmering water a few at a time and simmer, turning once, for a total of 3 minutes. Place bagels on parchment-lined baking sheet. When they are all done, dust the tops with brown sugar/oatmeal mixture. Place bagels back on baking sheet.

Bake until nicely browned on top side, turning once to brown undersides (which are now the tops), about 15-20 minutes. Cool well before serving or bag up to freeze.

Makes 12-14

Sweet Potato Apple Butter Muffins

This combination of sweet potato and apple butter (or regular applesauce) and cranberries make for a harvest extravaganza. Pureed pumpkin or squash can be swopped for the sweet potato. This also makes a great quick bread recipe for potluck suppers or Thanksgiving.

GINGERSNAP STREUSEL

15-20 gingersnap cookies (or graham)

¼ cup brown sugar, firmly packed

½ teaspoon cinnamon

6-8 tablespoons cold butter, cut in bits

MUFFIN BATTER

1/2 cup brown sugar, firmly packed

½ cup white sugar

3/4 cup canola oil

2 eggs

1 1/2 teaspoons pure vanilla extract

1 cup cooked sweet potato puree

1/3 cup apple butter *(or sweetened applesauce)

2 ¼ cups all-purpose flour

1 1/2 teaspoons baking powder

1/2 teaspoon baking soda

1 teaspoon cinnamon

1/8 teaspoon cloves

1/8 teaspoon allspice

1/8 teaspoon salt

1/2 cup finely chopped walnuts, optional

1 cup plumped raisins or cranberries

Preheat oven to 350°F. Line a baking sheet with parchment paper. Line a 12-cup muffin tin with regular or tulip style muffin papers. Place muffin tin on baking sheet.

For the Gingersnap Streusel, place the cookies in a food processor and pulse to break into coarse crumbs. Add in the sugar, cinnamon and butter and pulse to make a coarse streusel. Set aside. (If it doesn't quite hold together, add 1-2 tablespoons more butter)

In a mixer bowl, blend the white sugar, brown sugar, oil, eggs, vanilla extract, sweet potato puree and apple butter. Fold in the flour, baking powder, baking soda, cinnamon, cloves, allspice and salt; blend well. Fold in the raisins (or cranberries) and nuts; mix thoroughly. Scoop batter into muffin tin. Top with equal portions of Gingersnap Streusel.

Bake until muffins spring back when touched with fingertips, about 30-35 minutes.

Makes 12 regular muffins

Old-Fashioned Giant Snickerdoodles

The trick to Snickerdoodles is using this old-fashioned leavener, a combination of cream of tartar and baking soda. It makes for a light, crisp cookie, characteristic of a classic Snickerdoodle. The fragrance of the old-fashioned spice quartet (cinnamon, nutmeg, allspice, and cloves) is as old as a pioneer mother's cookie jar.

COOKIE DOUGH

1 cup unsalted butter

1¼ cups white sugar

¼ cup brown sugar, firmly packed

2 eggs

1 tablespoon pure vanilla extract

3 cups all-purpose flour

1 teaspoon baking soda

2 teaspoons cream of tartar

¼ teaspoon salt

SPICE SUGAR

1/2 cup sugar

4 teaspoons cinnamon

1/2 teaspoon nutmeg

1/4 teaspoon allspice

1/8 teaspoon cloves

Stack two baking sheets together and line the top one with parchment paper.

In a mixer bowl, cream the butter, white sugar and brown sugar until fluffy and pasty. Blend in the eggs and vanilla. Fold in the flour, baking soda, cream of tartar and salt to make a soft dough. Refrigerate the dough for 15 to 20 minutes.

Preheat the oven to 375°F.

For the Spice Sugar, in a bowl, mix the sugar, cinnamon, nutmeg, allspice and cloves. Roll balls of dough the size of golf balls and roll them in the spice-sugar mixture. Place the balls on the baking sheet 3 inches apart, and flatten them slightly.

Bake until cookies rise, fall, and wrinkle up, about 16 to 18 minutes. Let cool on the baking sheet for 15 minutes before removing.

Makes 15 to 20 large cookies

APPLE BUTTER, A TASTE OF EDEN

Butter always sounds nice and something called fruit butter sounds positively ambrosial. Better yet, nothing tastes as good as apple butter. Fruit butter and specifically apple butter are intense reductions of fruit, cooked down from stewed to sauce to finally, fruit butter, which is the thickest, most flavorful essence of the fruit. You can make apple butter at home, in a stovetop preserving kettle and slowly reduce it down to butter. It just takes a great recipe, a lot some pot-watching and some patience. In bygone days, making apple butter was an all-day affair and in Amish country in particular, apple butter making still endures. Food mills, heavy duty Dutch ovens and even crock pots, figure in the mix of apple butter making. Apple butter can be used in baking by adding it to scones, cookies, on top of pancakes or English muffins. I like adding it to apple pie, baked apples or apple strudel filling. Just a touch of apple butter intensifies the orchard-fresh, tart sweet flavors of any apple recipe.

General Store Oatmeal Cookies

Reminiscent of a Chunky © Chocolate Bar, these cookies are crisp and chewy, with nuggets of chocolate and raisins studding the butterscotch-scented cookies. To make these 'General Store' huge, use 6 to 7 ounces of batter; extra-big cookies bake up with more dense, chewy centers.

1 cup unsalted butter, at room temperature

1 1/2 cups brown sugar, firmly packed

1/2 cup white sugar

1 egg

2 teaspoons pure vanilla extract

1 teaspoon baking soda mixed with 1 tablespoon hot water

1 cup all-purpose flour

1/4 teaspoon salt

4 cups old-fashioned oatmeal

1 cup dark raisins, plumped and dried

1 cup milk or semi-sweet chocolate chips

1/2 cup coarsely chopped walnuts or pecans, optional

Preheat the oven to 350°F. Line a baking sheet with baking parchment, and lightly spray it with non-stick cooking spray.

In a large mixer bowl, cream the butter and sugars. Mix in the egg and vanilla. Stir in the baking soda/water mixture. Mix in the flour, salt and oatmeal. Fold in the raisins and the chocolate chips and nuts.

Roll the dough into 2-inch balls and place them on the sheet. Dip your hands in

some water and press the cookies down to flatten very slightly. (For large cookies, use 6 to 7 ounces of dough.)

Bake the cookies until golden brown, about 12 to 15 minutes. For large cookies, bake 16 to 20 minutes. Do not overbake these cookies; they may seem a little underdone, but they will set up as they cool.

Makes about 18 cookies

Peanut Butter & Jam Cookies

Buttery, crisp but with dense centers, this is a superb peanut butter cookie. Use organic or all-natural peanut butter in this recipe (it's both healthier and more flavorful). Regular peanut butter makes these spread too much.

1 cup unsalted butter

½ cup sugar

1 ½ cups light brown sugar, firmly packed

1 ½ cups crunchy-style, natural peanut butter

2 eggs

2 teaspoons pure vanilla extract

2 ½ cups all-purpose flour

½ teaspoon baking powder

1 teaspoon baking soda

¼ teaspoon salt

1 cup roasted, salted chopped peanuts

FINISHING TOUCHES
1/3 cup raspberry jam

Preheat the oven to 350°F. Stack two baking sheets together and line the top one with parchment paper.

In a mixer bowl, cream the butter with the white and brown sugar. Blend well and then fold in the peanut butter, eggs and vanilla, adding in a touch of flour to bind it together. Fold in flour, baking powder, baking soda and salt. Fold in peanuts. Wrap the dough and refrigerate 20 minutes.

Shape a golf-ball-sized hunk of dough into a ball. Place on the cookie sheet and press down very slightly and then crisscross the top surface of the cookie with a fork.

Bake 14-16 minutes. Let the cookies set up on baking sheet 5-10 minutes before removing. Smear jam on the bottom of one cookie and top with another one and press gently.

Makes about 3 dozen single cookies or 18 sandwich style ones

McIntosh Honey Apple Compote

Nothing beats homemade apple sauce for pure nostalgia or for the marvellous, pure taste of farm-fresh apples and honey. I use a food mill for apple sauce which saves peeling time. If you don't have Macs, use Cortland or any other sweet, soft apple you prefer.

12-18 McIntosh apples, well washed and halved (unpeeled)

1/2 cup water, approximately

1/3 cup sugar

Juice of half a lemon

1/4 teaspoon cinnamon

2-4 tablespoons clover or another mild honey

In a large Dutch oven add the apples, water and sugar. Simmer over very low heat until apples are mushy, stirring to break up fruit. Once they are quite softened, add the lemon juice, cinnamon and honey and stir. Adjust sweetening and add more cinnamon, if desired. If mixture seems to be dry or getting sticky on the bottom, add in a bit of water to ensure there's no scorching.

Cool well; then press through a food mill.

Makes 4 cups (Can keep refrigerated 1-2 weeks)

Vermont Apple Cider Doughnuts

Moonlight in Vermont and true, sweet comfort food from New England in the shape of these wonderful doughnuts. These are a cider house treat.

DOUGHNUT DOUGH

1 cup apple cider

1 cup sugar

1/4 cup unsalted butter

2 eggs

1 teaspoon pure vanilla extract

1/2 cup buttermilk

3 1/2 cups all-purpose flour, approximately

2 ½ teaspoons baking powder

1/2 teaspoon baking soda

3/4 teaspoon cinnamon

1/4 teaspoon nutmeg, freshly grated

1/2 teaspoon salt

4 cups canola oil (for frying)

APPLE CIDER GLAZE

2 cups confectioners' sugar

1/4 cup apple cider (or juice)

1/4 teaspoon cinnamon

Pinch fresh grated nutmeg

In a small saucepan over low heat, boil the cider until reduced to ¼ cup, about 10 minutes. Cool to room temperature (or place in the fridge until needed).

In a mixer bowl, cream the sugar and butter until well-combined and mix in the reduced cider. Blend in the eggs, vanilla and buttermilk. Mix in the flour, baking powder, baking soda, cinnamon, nutmeg, and salt thoroughly to make a stiff dough, much like a Tollhouse or oatmeal cookie dough. Wrap and refrigerate 30 to 60 minutes or overnight.

For the Apple Cider Glaze, in a medium bowl, combine the glaze ingredients and stir until smooth.

To make the doughnuts, in a wok, heat the oil to 375°F. Roll out the dough to ½-inch thick and use a doughnut cutter, if you have one, or a biscuit cutter to cut it into 2 1/2 to 3-inch doughnuts (remove the holes by cutting centers out with a smaller cookie cutter or even a bottle top; fry the holes separately). Fry a few doughnuts at a time, turning once, as they puff and brown evenly. Drain on paper towels briefly, and then dip them in the glaze. Let set. You can also opt to double glaze (dip them twice) the doughnuts for an extra decadent finish.

Makes 16 to 20 doughnuts

Granny Smith Sour Cream Apple Muffins

Sour cream, toasted walnuts, chunks of Granny Smith Apples along with and a crunchy topping makes this my favorite muffin. No need to peel the apples for this recipe; just save a few pretty slices to garnish the muffins before baking.

SPICE STREUSEL TOPPING

3 tablespoons unsalted butter

2 tablespoons white sugar

¼ cup brown sugar, firmly packed

½ cup all-purpose flour

1/2 teaspoon cinnamon

2 teaspoons pure vanilla powder, optional

Pinch cloves

Pinch allspice

3 tablespoons unsalted butter

MUFFIN BATTER

½ cup white sugar

1 cup brown sugar, firmly packed

1/2 cup unsalted butter, melted

2 eggs

1 cup sour cream

2½ teaspoons pure vanilla extract

3 cups all-purpose flour

2 ½ teaspoons baking powder

1/2 teaspoon baking soda

1/2 teaspoon ground cinnamon

3/8 teaspoon salt

½ cup toasted, finely ground walnuts

3 cups unpeeled, ½-inch-diced Granny Smith apples

Arrange the oven rack to the middle position. Preheat the oven to 400 F.

Line a baking sheet with parchment paper. Line a 12-cup muffin tin with muffin liners and generously spray it (including the top surface) with non-stick cooking spray. Place the pan on the baking sheet.

For the Spice Streusel Topping, place the white and brown sugar, flour, cinnamon, cloves, and vanilla powder in a small bowl. Add the butter and rub it into the dry ingredients until you have coarse crumbs. You can also make the streusel in a food processor by pulsing all the ingredients together to make a grainy mixture.

For the muffin batter, in a mixer bowl, blend the white and brown sugars, butter, eggs, sour cream and vanilla. Fold in the flour, baking soda, baking powder, cinnamon, salt and walnuts into the wet ingredients together gently. When partially blended, fold in the apples. If the batter seems too loose (it should be a thick batter, not a watery glop), mix in 4 to 6 tablespoons flour.

Using a large ice-cream scoop, deposit batter into the muffin tin. Sprinkle streusel topping evenly over each muffin.

Bake for 15 minutes. Lower the temperature to 350°F and bake another 12 to 15 minutes, or until the muffins spring back when pressed lightly. Allow to cool in pan for 5 minutes before removing.

Makes 9 to 12 muffins

Multi-Grain All Purpose Baking Flour

Baked goods made with multi-grain flours might not be as light, but they are outstandingly wholesome, and tasty. This healthy, home-blend baking mix is a super-convenient way to ramp up the nutrition in your baking. It's perfect for rustic muffins and quick breads.

3 cups organic all-purpose flour (organic unbleached)

2 cups organic stone round whole-wheat flour

1 cup organic spelt flour

1 cup organic kamut flour

1 cup organic quinoa flour

Mix the flours together and store, sealed, in the fridge or freezer.

Use as a 1-cup substitution for all-purpose flour in muffins, brownies, biscotti, breads, and scones.

Makes 8 cups (store in the fridge or freezer)

Home Blend Pumpkin Pie Spice Mix

Gourmet quality pumpkin pie spice is easily available online or found in the supermarket spice section but making your own guarantees absolute freshness (because you use your own freshest spices). You can also customize the blend by adding more or less of one spice or another or a touch of mace or cardamom. The recipe also doubles and triples as you require. I use homemade Pumpkin Pie Spices in my Pumpkin Pie, Pumpkin Bread, Pumpkin Sticky Buns and of course, Pumpkin Eruption Cheesecake in the Fall Chapter. Don't forget to grate fresh nutmeg for a veritable explosion of nutmeg-y soul in the finished spice blend.

4 tablespoons cinnamon

4 teaspoons nutmeg

4 teaspoons ginger

1 tablespoon allspice

Combine all ingredients. If you make extra spice mix, store in an airtight container such as a glass spice jar.

Makes 1/3 cup

Pumpkin Millet Muffins

These honey-tinged, healthy multi-flour muffins are simply resplendent with their orange hue and wholesome goodness. If you don't want to fiddle with the various flours in this recipe, substitute with the Multi-Grain Baker's Flour Mix for the various flours here.

1½ cups pureed pumpkin (not sweetened pumpkin pie filling), canned or homemade

1 cup warm buttermilk

½ cup oatmeal

½ cup millet

½ cup canola oil

¾ cup brown sugar, firmly packed

2 eggs

3/4 teaspoon pure vanilla extract

1 tablespoon honey

1 tablespoon pure maple syrup

1 cup all-purpose flour

½ cup whole-wheat flour

2 tablespoons kamut flour

2 tablespoons spelt flour

2 teaspoon baking powder

½ teaspoon baking soda

3/4 teaspoon cinnamon

3/8 teaspoon cloves

3/8 teaspoon salt

¼ cup unsalted pumpkin (or pepita) seeds

FINISHING TOUCHES
Pumpkin seeds, rolled oats

If you are not using canned pumpkin, prepare the pumpkin first. In a small saucepan, simmer about 2 cups of peeled pumpkin cubes in water, just to cover, until tender; drain and puree. Alternatively, you can roast the pumpkin at 400°F, lightly oiled, on a parchment paper covered baking sheet, in the oven, for 30-45 minutes, until softened.

Arrange the oven rack to the middle position. Preheat the oven to 375°F.

Line a baking sheet with parchment paper. Line a 12-cup muffin tin with muffin liners and generously spray it (including the top surface) with non-stick cooking spray. Place it on the baking sheet.

In a small bowl, stir the oatmeal into the buttermilk and set aside.

In a small non-stick frying pan, over very low heat, toast the millet for 5 to 10 minutes, tossing with a spatula or shaking the pan a bit (so the millet doesn't stick or burn), until lightly, evenly browned. Remove and let cool a few minutes.

In a large mixer bowl, blend the pumpkin puree and oatmeal-buttermilk mixture. Blend in the vegetable oil, brown sugar, eggs, vanilla extract, honey, and maple syrup. Fold in the toasted millet, the flours, baking powder, baking soda, cinnamon, cloves, and salt. Fold in the pumpkin seeds.

Using an ice-cream scooper, deposit muffins into the muffin wells. Sprinkle the tops with some pumpkin seeds and rolled oats.

Bake 20 minutes and then lower the temperature to 350°F and bake until done, another 15 to 20 minutes, or until the muffins spring back when gently touched with fingertips. Cool in the pan 20 minutes before removing.

Makes 9-12 muffins

Greek Yogurt Blueberry Bran Banana Muffins

These muffins have a rough-hewn, rustic, high cap that crowns a moist, flavor-packed muffin that's just sweet enough. You just feel noble when you have one of these plus it also prevents an attack of the nibbles for a few hours.

4 cups all-purpose flour

1 tablespoon baking powder

2 teaspoons baking soda

2 teaspoons cinnamon

1/8 teaspoon salt

3/4 cup canola or unsalted butter, melted

2 tablespoons honey

1/4 cup molasses

1 cup plus 3 tablespoons light brown sugar, firmly packed

1 teaspoon pure vanilla extract

3/4 teaspoon pure maple extract, optional

1 small banana, finely mashed

3 eggs

½ cups Greek yogurt

½ cup water

1/4 cup wheat germ

2 cups natural bran (not the cereal)

½ yellow raisins, plumped in steaming water for 2 minutes and dried on paper towels

1 cup semi-frozen blueberries

1 cup chopped peeled apples, optional

FINISHING TOUCHES
Sesame seeds or sunflower seeds

In a medium bowl, using a whisk, blend the flour, baking powder, baking soda, cinnamon and salt. Set aside.

In a mixer bowl, whisk the oil, honey, molasses, brown sugar, vanilla and maple extracts, and banana. Whisk in the eggs. Stir in the Greek yogurt, water and blend well. Then fold in the wheat germ and bran. Allow to rest 10 minutes.

Mix the dry ingredients into the wet mixture and whisk to blend partially. Using a rubber spatula, stir in the fruit. Blend the batter thoroughly, making sure bottom of bowl does not have undistributed ingredients. Add in more flour, (up to another cup) as required to make a soft batter. Cover the batter with plastic wrap and allow to rest overnight in the fridge or at least 1 hour before baking.

Preheat the oven to 400°F. Line a baking sheet with parchment paper. Line a 12-cup muffin tin with muffin liners and generously spray it (including the top surface) with non-stick cooking spray. Place the pan on the baking sheet.

Using an ice-cream scoop, scoop the muffin batter into the prepared muffin cups. Fill any empty muffin cups halfway with water (this allows the muffins to bake evenly). Sprinkle the tops with sesame or sunflower seeds as a garnish.

Place the pan on the uppermost oven rack and bake for 20 minutes, then lower the heat to 375°F and bake until done, about another 10 to 12 minutes.

Makes about 14 large muffins

Orange Pecan Brown Sugar Scones

These irresistible scones feature a bouquet of buttery pecans, brown sugar and fresh orange zest. They're as satisfying with a drizzle of honey on them as they are with a wedge of sharp white cheddar cheese to offset their sweet, nutty taste.

Zest of 1 large orange, finely minced

3 cups all-purpose flour

1 cup brown sugar, firmly packed

2 1/2 teaspoon baking powder

1/2 teaspoons baking soda

3/8 teaspoon salt

3/4 cup unsalted butter, in chunks

1 cup coarsely chopped pecans

1 egg

1½ teaspoons pure vanilla extract

Juice of 1 large orange

2/3 - 1 cup whipping cream, as required

FINISHING TOUCHES

3-4 tablespoons unsalted butter, melted

Brown sugar

Chopped pecans

Arrange the oven rack to the upper third position. Preheat the oven to 425°F. Stack two baking sheets together and line the top one with parchment paper.

For the scones, in a food processor bowl, add the orange zest, flour, brown sugar, baking powder, baking soda and salt; blend briefly. Add the butter and pulse to make a coarse, grainy mixture. Turn the mixture out into a large bowl and add the pecans. Make a well in the center and add the egg, vanilla, orange juice, and 2/3 cup of the whipping cream. If the mixture seems dry, drizzle in another 1/3 cup cream, and even a bit more if required. It should be a very thick mixture that holds together.

Turn the dough onto a lightly floured board. Knead a few times to make a smooth mass. Divide the dough into 2 portions and flatten them into rounds about 1 inch thick. Cut each round into six wedges. Brush the tops generously with melted butter, dust them with brown sugar, and sprinkle on some chopped pecans. Bake until lightly golden brown on the tops and edges, 18 to 20 minutes.

To store scones, wrap each in wax paper and store in a zip-top bag or on a plate covered with a cake dome for 2-3 days. Alternatively, wrap but freeze for up to 2 months.

Makes 12 to 16 small scones

Canadiana Butter Tart Squares

Forget fiddling with tarts - this easy approach to this decadent sweetie makes for fast finger food. Think of a butter tart square as pecan square but without the nutty crunch.

Pie Pastry for a double piecrust, such as My Favorite All Butter Pie Pastry

FILLING

4 eggs

1 teaspoon pure vanilla extract

2 ¼ cups light brown sugar, firmly packed

2 tablespoons corn syrup

2 tablespoons pure maple syrup

1 tablespoon fresh lemon juice

2 tablespoons flour

¼ teaspoon baking powder

1/2 cup unsalted butter, melted

1 cup raisins, plumped and dried, optional

Preheat the oven to 350°F. Line a baking sheet with parchment paper. Press the pie pastry into a 9 by 13-inch baking dish on the bottom and two-thirds of the way up the sides. Place the pan on the baking sheet. Place a piece of parchment paper, cut to fit, on the dough. Using another similarly sized pan as a weight, press lightly on the parchment paper. Bake 15 minutes. Remove from the oven and remove the extra pan and parchment paper.

For the filling, place the eggs, vanilla, brown sugar, corn syrup, maple syrup, lemon juice, flour, baking powder, and butter in a medium bowl. Using a whisk, stir about one minute. Stir in the raisins and pour into the pastry crust.

Bake 30 to 35 minutes, until just set. Chill 3 hours before cutting into small or medium squares.

Keep refrigerated. These cut nice and neat when cold, but will ooze as they warm up; that is the test of great Canadian Butter Tarts.

Makes 24 to 48 bars/squares, depending on size

Crop Circle Trail Bars

I love granola bars of all sorts, but commercially made bars are often filled with preservatives, fat and too much sugar. Yet it's rare to find a homemade bar that matches that crisp, satisfyingly chewy texture. These bars are it – the best of both worlds- wholesome but chewy and crisp. Feel free to play around with the ingredients as you like. They're perfect for a fall hiking day or an October bake sale table.

4½ cups miniature marshmallows

1/3 cup unsalted butter

½ cup warm honey

2 tablespoons brown sugar

1/8 teaspoon cinnamon

1 cup chopped almonds, toasted

1/4 cup sunflower seeds

3 cups granola (any sort, any brand)

3 cups bran cereal, Rice Krispies, Special K, or your favorite similar cereal

1 cup dried cranberries or cherries

1 cup raisins, plumped

Preheat the oven to 350°F. Line a baking sheet with parchment paper. Generously spray a 9 by 13-inch pan with non-stick cooking spray and line the bottom with parchment paper. Place the pan on the baking sheet.

In a large pot, melt the marshmallows in the butter over lowest heat. Turn off the heat and stir in the honey, brown sugar, cinnamon, almonds, sunflower seeds, granola, cereal, cranberries or cherries, and raisins. Stir with a large wooden spoon or with hands dipped in cold water.

Press the mixture into the pan. Place in the oven and immediately lower the temperature to 325°F. Bake 15 minutes, or just long enough to dry them out. Freeze the bars in the pan for 1 hour or so; then cut the bars to your desired size.

To store the squares, wrap each in wax paper and store in a zip-top bag or on a plate covered with a cake dome. Alternatively, wrap the same way and freeze for up to 2 months.

Makes 20 to 24 bars

Buttermilk Cinnamon Biscotti

These nice and crunchy biscotti whip up in a flash. Once they're in the oven, alert your coffee klatch gals to come by to enjoy! I'm so fussy about cinnamon that I order and blend Cassia, Ceylon, and Vietnamese cinnamon for a special sweet and lively 'custom' cinnamon.

1 cup unsalted butter, melted

2 cups sugar

5 eggs

1 tablespoon pure vanilla extract

1 teaspoon pure almond extract

1/4 cup buttermilk

4 cups all-purpose flour, approximately

2½ teaspoons baking powder

¼ teaspoon baking soda

½ teaspoon salt

FINISHING TOUCHES

2 to 3 tablespoons cinnamon

½ cup sugar, approximately

Preheat the oven to 350°F. Stack 2 baking sheets and line the top one with parchment paper. Generously spray a 9 by 13-inch pan with non-stick cooking spray and place the pan on the baking sheet.

In a mixer bowl, blend the butter and sugar. Blend in the eggs, vanilla, almond extract, and buttermilk. Mix in the flour, baking powder, baking soda and salt. Blend until you have a very thick batter, adding in more flour if required so it is soft but not wet. Spoon two-thirds of batter into the prepared pan.

Dust on two-thirds of the cinnamon and sugar, so that batter is well covered. Top with dollops of the remaining batter. If batter is very thick (it gets thicker as it stands), loosen with some water and spread it out as best you can. It does not have to be perfect; it will still bake properly. Dust with the remaining cinnamon and sugar.

Bake until set to the touch, about 45 minutes. The biscotti should seem a little less solid than a cake or cookie. Cool 20 minutes, then unmold onto a cutting board. Cool another 30 minutes, and then cut into ½ inch sticks.

Place the biscotti on their sides on the baking sheet. Preheat the oven to 325°F and bake the biscotti again, turning once, until crisp, about 20 to 30 minutes.

Makes 2 to 3 dozen, depending on size

Shoebox Brownies

Back-to-school treats should always be this good. Remember crackly topped brownies made with real, melted chocolate, the kind of brownie that was packed up in a shoebox as a gift? These are the real deal. When it comes to chocolate to be used in baking, make sure you love how it tastes for eating out of hand; chances are you'll love how it performs in baking as well, especially in these kid-pleasing brownies.

1/2 cup unsalted butter

1 cup semi-sweet chocolate, chopped

2 tablespoons cocoa

1 1/4 cups sugar

1 teaspoon pure vanilla extract

3 eggs

1 cup all-purpose flour

1/8 teaspoon salt

Preheat oven to 350°F. Line a baking sheet with parchment paper. Generously spray a 7 by 11-inch rectangular pan or 8 by 8-inch pan with non-stick cooking spray and place it on the baking sheet.

Over low heat, in a heavy bottomed 1-quart saucepan, melt the butter and chocolate together, stirring until smooth. Stir in the cocoa. Remove the mixture from the heat and spoon it into a medium bowl. Let cool to room temperature.

Blend in the sugar, vanilla and eggs, mixing until smooth. Fold in the flour and salt; stir to make a smooth batter. Spoon into the pan.

Bake 35 to 38 minutes, or until the brownies seem just set.

Makes about 12 to 16 brownies

Nutella Banana Bread

When you think of it, sliced banana and Nutella sandwiches make perfect sense which means this gorgeous banana bread makes even more sense. This is sublime, featuring the warm, mellow taste of banana along with a swirl of hazelnut chocolate spread.

1 cup mashed very ripe banana

1 cup white sugar

2 tablespoons brown sugar

½ cup unsalted butter, softened

2 eggs

1 teaspoon pure vanilla extract

1/2 cup buttermilk

1 2/3 cup all-purpose flour

1 teaspoon baking soda

¼ teaspoon salt

1/3 cup Nutella

FINISHING TOUCHES

¼ cup chopped, toasted hazelnuts

Coarse or regular sugar

Preheat oven to 350°F. Stack two baking sheets together and line the top one with parchment paper. Generously spray a 9 by 5 inch loaf pan with non-stick cooking spray and place on the baking sheet. Line the bottom of the loaf pan with parchment paper.

In a small bowl, hand mash (using a fork or potato masher) the bananas and set aside. In a mixer bowl, mix or cream the white and brown sugar and butter until well-blended. Add in the eggs, vanilla, buttermilk and bananas. If mixture appears curdled, fold in ½ cup of the flour. Fold remaining flour, baking soda, salt and blend well.

Spoon two-thirds of the batter into the pan and top it with dollops of Nutella, (reserving 2 tablespoons of Nutella). Marbleize the Nutella so that it swirls through the batter. Cover with remaining dollops of batter and the remaining Nutella. Top with chopped hazelnuts and sprinkle the nuts with sugar.

Bake 30 minutes and then lower temperature to 325°F and bake until cake springs back when lightly pressed with fingertips, about 45-50 minutes. Cool well before slicing.

Serves 10

Weekend in New England Brown Bread

This is one of my most favorite breads of all time. Maple, honey, rye, whole wheat, buttermilk, and spice – totally riveting stuff. Serve it with crock pot Boston baked beans and you have a feast. This little bread is also terrific alongside a plate of corned beef for St. Pat's Day. The bread is traditionally made in 1 pound coffee cans, but a regular loaf pan is fine.

1 cup stone-ground cornmeal

1½ cups warm buttermilk

1 cup whole wheat flour

1/4 cup rye flour

1 1/4 cups all-purpose flour

2 teaspoons baking soda

1 teaspoon cinnamon

1/2 teaspoon cloves

1/4 teaspoon allspice

Pinch ginger

1 teaspoon salt

1/2 cup molasses

1/4 cup maple syrup or honey

1 egg, optional

2 tablespoons unsalted butter

1 1/2 cups buttermilk

1 cup dark raisins, plumped and dried

Preheat the oven to 275°F. Line a baking sheet with parchment paper. Line the bottoms of three 1-pound (cleaned and well dried) coffee cans with parchment paper that has been sprayed with non-stick cooking spray. Leave a 1 1/2 inch extension of paper beyond the rims of the cans. Alternatively, use two 9 by 5-inch loaf pans. Line the pans with buttered parchment paper and place them on the baking sheet.

In a medium bowl, stir together the cornmeal and buttermilk and let stand while you assemble the remaining ingredients. In a large mixer bowl, mix together whole wheat flour, rye, white flour, baking soda, salt, cinnamon, cloves, allspice, and ginger and salt. Stir in the cornmeal mixture, then add the molasses, maple syrup or honey, egg, butter, buttermilk, and raisins and stir to combine. You should have a very thick batter, just a bit thicker than muffin batter. If not, stir in 2 to 4 tablespoons more white flour. Spoon the batter into the pans.

Fill a large roasting pan with water and place in the oven. Place the filled pans in the roasting pan. Cover the pans with a large sheet of parchment paper and place a baking sheet on top of it all to hold the paper down. (This will ensure the proper flat, wettish top, not a dry, cracked loaf top.)

Bake 2½ to 3 hours until breads spring back when gently pressed with fingertips. Serve warm with honey or butter.

Makes 2 to 3 loaves

Pumpkin Caramel Sticky Buns

Don't throw out your Halloween pumpkin! Before it turns mushy, roast the pumpkin in hunks, scrape out the flesh and puree for a filling that gets baked up into these ultra-delicious spiced pumpkin cinnamon buns bursting with a sweet, chewy filling and glazed with fondant and spice. This yeasted dough is a beautiful mellow hue, and the combination of brown sugar, spice, and caramel in a sticky bun treatment is worth writing a song about. Canned pumpkin puree also works in non-pumpkin season.

PUMPKIN SPICE DOUGH

1 1/3 cups warm water

2 tablespoons instant yeast

1 cup pumpkin puree

3 eggs

3/4 cup sugar

1 1/2 teaspoons salt

3/4 cup (1½ sticks) unsalted butter, softened

1 tablespoon pure vanilla extract

2 1/2 teaspoons cinnamon

1/2 teaspoon allspice

1/2 teaspoon cloves

1/4 teaspoon pumpkin pie spice

5 to 7 cups all-purpose or bread flour

CARAMEL FILLING

3/4 cup brown sugar, firmly packed

1/2 cup dark brown sugar, firmly packed

1 teaspoon cinnamon

1/2 teaspoon pumpkin pie spice

1/3 cup caramel or butterscotch chips

3/4 cup unsalted butter

3/4 cup walnuts or pecans, chopped, or 12 graham crackers, chopped

1 cup minced caramels (Kraft type)

PAN BOTTOM

1/3 cup unsalted butter, melted

1/2 cup brown sugar, firmly packed

FONDANT

2 cups confectioners' sugar

2 to 4 tablespoons whipping cream

1/2 teaspoon pure vanilla extract

1/2 teaspoon maple or butterscotch extract, optional

Line a baking sheet with parchment paper. Generously spray a 9 by 13-inch pan with non-stick cooking spray and place it on the baking sheet.

For the dough, in a mixer bowl, hand-whisk the water and yeast briefly. Briskly add in the pumpkin puree, eggs, sugar, salt, butter, vanilla, cinnamon, allspice, cloves, pumpkin pie spice and 4 cups of the flour. Mix and then begin kneading (using the dough hook) adding more flour as required to make a soft dough. Depending on how wet the pumpkin is, you might need to add a fair amount of flour; this is okay. Knead on slowest mixer speed, dusting in more flour as required, until soft and elastic, about 8 to 12 minutes. Remove the dough hook, spray the dough with non-stick cooking spray, and cover the entire bowl and mixer with a large plastic bag. Let the dough rise until almost doubled in size, 45 to 60 minutes.

Meanwhile, for the filling, in a food processor, add the light and dark brown sugar, cinnamon, pumpkin pie spice, butterscotch chips, and butter and pulse to make a clumpy mixture that almost but doesn't quite hold together. Set aside.

For the Pan Bottom preparation, mix the brown sugar and butter together over the bottom of the pan.

Gently deflate the dough. On a floured surface, roll it out to a rectangle about 24 by 18 inches. Spread the filling over the dough and then sprinkle on the nuts, graham cracker crumbs and caramels. Roll the dough into a large, snug log and cut it into 12 big slices (or more if you want smaller buns). Arrange the slices cut side up in the baking pan. Cover and let rise 30 to 45 minutes, until almost doubled in size.

Preheat the oven to 350°F. Bake until the rolls are lightly browned, about 40 to 45 minutes. If the buns seem to be browning but do not appear fully baked in the center, lower the temperature to 325°F and bake 10 to 15 minutes more. Let the buns cool in pan for 5 to 10 minutes; then transfer the buns to a large parchment paper sheet on a work surface.

For the fondant, in a medium bowl, whisk together the confectioners' sugar, cream, and extracts until soft and spreadable. Smear, spread, or drizzle on the warm buns; let set.

Otherwise, for cut/individual buns, wrap each bun in wax paper and place in a Ziplock bag.

Makes 12 large buns or 24 medium ones

BOO! IT'S PUMPKIN AND HALLOWEEN TIME

Halloween has its roots in Celtic traditions and is related to the festival Samhaim, held on November 1. Although we celebrate Halloween with treats and costumes, it has, in contrast to holidays which are plainly joyous and positive, a ghoulish shadow to the fun (trick or treat?) part. Some say this is what makes Halloween a 'hoot', since it's a "safe scare"—something like the appeal of suspense novels and rollercoasters. For me, Halloween is all about the kids and the baking. As a baker, I adore working with pumpkin at this time of year—in pumpkin pie, pumpkin biscotti, and especially these gorgeous, gooey, addictive Pumpkin Caramel Sticky Buns. Halloween gives me an occasion to do a ton of pumpkin-based baking.

Sour Cream Mock Puff Dough

For the Sour Cream Mock Puff Dough, in a food processor bowl, place the flour and salt. Add the butter and pulse to create a grainy mixture. Add the sour cream and process only until a ball forms. If a ball doesn't form, remove the mass of dough from the processor and work it on a lightly floured board for a couple of seconds by hand firmly but gently. Shape the dough into a smooth disc, cover, and refrigerate for 30 minutes to an hour.

2 cups all-purpose flour

1/4 teaspoon salt

1 cup unsalted butter, cold, cut into 12 chunks

1 cup sour cream

Pear Cranberry Filling

1 cup finely chopped walnuts

2 to 3 tablespoons sugar

1/2 teaspoon cinnamon

1/2 cup shredded, sweetened coconut

1/3 cup chopped yellow raisins

1 cup dried pears

1/3 cup dried cranberries

3/4 cup diced fresh pears

2/3 cup apricot or peach jam

FINISHING TOUCHES

Unsalted butter, melted

Confectioners' sugar

For the Pear Cranberry Filling, in a medium bowl, combine the walnuts, sugar, cinnamon, coconut, raisins, dried pears, cranberries and diced pears.

Preheat the oven to 375°F. Line a large baking sheet with parchment paper.

Divide the dough in half. Roll the dough out on a lightly floured board to a 14 by 14-inch square. Brush the dough lightly with melted butter. Smear half the jam over the surface, then evenly sprinkle on half the fruit/nut filling, staying at least ¾ inch away from the edges of the dough. Roll the dough half way (to the middle), then cut away the unrolled dough. Cut the rolled/filled dough into 3-inch lengths (each individual pastry should be about the size of an egg roll - perhaps slightly wider).

Transfer to the prepared pan. Repeat with the remaining section of dough—filling, rolling and cutting, and moving strudel pieces to the baking sheet.

Bake until tops of the pastries are golden brown, about 35 minutes, and the fruit filling is beginning to ooze out. Cool well, and then dust with confectioners' sugar.

Makes about 15 to 20 pastries, depending on size, or many more, if you make these extra small.

Pecan Pie Biscotti

This is essentially a ton of pecans and caramel pecan goodness with a minimalist excuse of biscotti batter to hold it together. I think of this as pecan pie but with extra crunch. For a salty-sweet sensation, use salted pecans instead.

2 cups sugar

3 tablespoons dark corn syrup

1 cup unsalted butter, melted and cooled

3 eggs

1 tablespoon pure vanilla extract

2 cups all-purpose flour

1/2 teaspoon baking powder

1/4 teaspoon salt

3-4 cups pecan halves

1 cup butterscotch or caramel chips

½ cup caramel sundae topping or dulce de leche

Preheat the oven to 350°F. Line a baking sheet with parchment paper. Place it on top of another baking sheet (you will need two together as these biscotti are gooey; this extra insulation will prevent burning and over browning even though the biscotti are in a pan).

Generously spray a 9 by 13 inch pan with non-stick cooking spray and place on baking sheet. Line the bottom and sides of the pan with pieces of parchment paper (the batter is sticky and this will help you remove it after baking)

In a mixer bowl, blend the sugar, corn syrup and melted butter. Blend in the eggs and vanilla, then the flour, baking powder, salt and blend a little bit. Fold in the nuts and caramel chips. Drizzle in most of caramel topping. Spoon into prepared pan, drizzling remaining caramel topping on top.

Bake until firm, about 45-55 minutes. Cool 20 minutes and then freeze for 45 minutes. Then turn the biscotti out onto a parchment paper lined work surface with a brisk movement. Using a sharp knife, slice into ¾ inch slices and put back on a baking sheet to dry out in the oven, another 20 minutes, 325°F, turning once. You might find these hard to cut and get uneven shards -that is fine. Refrigerate the biscotti an hour or so to make them 'set up' a bit faster.

(They are sticky even after the second bake but even 1-2 hours at room temperature helps them dry out more and they go from soft/sticky to crispy/sticky)

Makes about 1 ½ -2 dozen

Cheddar Fig Buns

There's a Montreal bakery that bakes up the most unique breads and rolls, such as white chocolate brioche miniatures that look like wee mushroom and all sorts of healthy breads. They also make this incredible bun from a rough-hewn sourdough rolled with oversized chunks of sharp orange Cheddar cheese and hunks of dried or string figs. It's one of the finest recipes I know and had to replicate.

SPONGE OR POOLISH STARTER

1 cup water, preferably spring water

1/2 teaspoon instant yeast

1 1/4 cups unbleached bread flour or organic white bread flour

2 tablespoons organic rye flour

Dough

(all of) starter

1 cup water, preferably spring water

2 1/2 teaspoons salt

2 tablespoons Greek or unpasteurized honey

3 tablespoons light olive oil

1/2 teaspoon instant yeast

3 3/4 to 4 cups unbleached bread flour

2 1/2 cups large chunks of sharp or old cheddar cheese

1 string of dried figs (about 2-3 cups), whole (string removed) *

* If figs are large, cut them in half

The night before or up to 16 hours before: In a small bowl, stir together the water and yeast and let yeast dissolve by briskly whisking.

With a whisk or medium wood spoon, stir in bread flour and rye flour to make a thick mixture. It should be like a thickened, gloppy pudding.

Cover bowl lightly with plastic wrap (leaving a small air space) and let stand at room temperature 8 to 16 hours.

For the dough, first, stir down the starter. Add remaining ingredients while holding back about 1/2 cup of the flour. Knead until dough is smooth and resilient. Then gently but firmly press in the cheddar cheese chunks and figs.

Shape dough into a ball and place in a lightly greased bowl. Insert bowl in a large plastic bag and let rise about 45-60 minutes.

Stack two baking sheets together and line the top one with parchment paper.

After the rise, gently deflate dough and cut into 6-8 pieces. Form each into an oval shape. Place each roll on the prepared baking sheet.

Spray dough lightly with a non-stick vegetable spray. Insert entire baking sheet inside a large plastic garbage bag (this is your "proofing tent"). Let dough rise until rolls are puffy (40% to 55% larger).

Preheat oven to 400°F. Gently press the ovals down a bit and then score each with a knife to make some small slits.

Spritz each roll with some cold water (using a plant atomizer) and dust with flour. Spray oven interior with cold water every five minutes for the first 15 minutes. When 20 minutes remain, reduce heat to 350°F. to finish baking. Loaf should be well browned after 25-35 minutes. Cool well on rack before serving.

Makes 6-8

BOGGED DOWN IN CRANBERRIES

There are only three fruits that can directly trace their lineage to North America. They are Concord grapes, blueberries, and the scarlet darlings of the bog and the baker, cranberries. Almost untenably tart when eaten raw, their flavour shines brilliantly in collaboration with sweeteners and other fruits especially within a baked good. And who doesn't welcome that burst of glorious color? Plus it's all packaged up in a little nutritional powerhouse. And of course, Thanksgiving wouldn't be Thanksgiving without a cranberry offering! Dried cranberries, called Craisins, are good enough to snack on alone and added to cereal, muffins, cookies, squares, scones and biscotti, such as Dried Pear and Cranberry Strudel.

DRIED PEAR AND CRANBERRY STRUDEL

This little strudel is ideal for a casual fall occasion, for the Jewish holiday of Succoth or for Thanksgiving. It's fruity goodness in a buttery pastry. Don't forget to plump the dried fruit in hot water (then drain) for the best flavor. The Sour Cream Mock Puff Dough is easy but if you're in a hurry, use store-bought puff dough. Including Holiday and Occasion

Fall, Big Baking

Including Holiday and Special Occasions

Fall, Big Baking
Including Holiday and Special Occasions Recipes

My Favorite All Butter Pie Pastry

Old-Fashioned Apple Pie

Country Fresh Blueberry Pie with Butter Streusel

Toffee Espresso Cake

Caramel Pumpkin Apple Cider Tart

Shortbread Crumb Country Apple Cake

Cinnamon Baby Babka

Russian Sour Cream Coffee Cake

Indian Summer Pear Cranberry Crisp

After School Yellow Sheet Cake with Milk Chocolate Icing

Free Form Rustic Apple Tart

Carrot Cake Chunk Cheesecake

Carrot Sheet Cake

Free Form Rustic Apple Tart

Caramel Sticky Pudding

Vintage Tollhouse Pie

Cinnamon Vanilla Swirl Sour Cream Kutchen

Golden Butternut Squash Applesauce Bundt Cake

Oregon Vanilla Chai Tea Cake

Zucchini Carrot Bread with Cream Cheese Icing

Holiday Corn Bread

Walnut Crunch Pumpkin Pie

Thanksgiving Cranberry Ripple Biscotti

Country Pumpkin Bread

Pumpkin Eruption Cheesecake

Bourbon Crème Anglaise

Butterscotch Bread Pudding

Cream and Spice Sweet Potato Pie

My Favorite All Butter Pie Pastry

If you want a dough that is a joy to work with, this all-butter, freezes-like-a-charm- pie- dough is a must. This is my go-to pie pastry for almost everything pie, quiche or tart I create. The recipe yields a large batch of easy-to-work with pie dough: flaky but trouble-free rolling and handling. Lemon juice tenderizes the dough. This is a perfect pastry for almost any filling, from apple pie, to pumpkin pie to quiche and it handles like a dream. Makes a big batch for pie now and (freeze) for pie later.

4 cups unbleached all-purpose flour

1 ½ cup unsalted butter

2 1/2 teaspoons sugar

1 3/8 teaspoon salt

1 tablespoon lemon juice

1/2 cup ice water

This can be made in a large food processor if you have one (14 cup capacity); alternatively you can halve the recipe for the butter-in-flour procedure and once you have the flour/butter crumbs, place that in the large bowl and continue on. You can also make this by hand in a big mixing bowl, breaking the fat into the flour with your fingertips to make a grainy mixture.

Place the flour in a large mixing bowl. With a pastry blender or two knives, cut in the butter until the mixture is crumbly – a somewhat lumpy, bumpy mixture of little and larger lumps of flour-covered-butter.

Make a well in center of flour mixture and stir in the sugar, salt, and lemon juice. Drizzle in most of ice water and using a fork or fingers, toss mixture together to moisten flour. Stir to make a soft mass and pat into a rough dough. Add remaining (or additional) ice water as required to make sure dough sticks together.

Turn out onto a lightly floured work surface. Knead very briefly into a smooth, cohesive dough. Divide dough in 2 portions (for two double crusts each) or 4-5 portions (for 4-5 single crusts). Wrap each section well by wrapping first in plastic wrap and then insert into a Ziploc bag. Refrigerate the dough at least one hour or up to two days (or freeze). Dough freezes for 3-4 months.

Makes two 9 inch double pie crusts plus one 8-9 inch single pie crust pies

Old Fashioned Apple Pie

A trio of apples makes this superb and it's the trick behind great apple pies, mixing and matching of different apples: crisp, soft, sweet and tangy. Most often, I choose McInstosh, Cortland and Golden Delicious. I also love retro graniteware pie tins for my best pies or ceramic, pottery pie dishes.

PIE PASTRY

1 cup unsalted butter

3 cups all-purpose flour

1 3/4 teaspoons salt

1/2 teaspoon sugar

1/2 cup, more or less, ice water

APPLE FILLING

10-12 large apples, peeled, cored, pared or diced

1 cup sugar

1/4 teaspoon cinnamon

1/2 teaspoon apple pie spice (or ¼ teaspoon cloves)

2 tablespoons flour

2 tablespoons unsalted butter, in bits

FINISHING TOUCHES

Milk, sugar

Line a baking sheet with parchment paper and set aside.

In a large mixer bowl, cut butter into flour, salt and sugar until it is mealy. Stir in water and make a stiff dough. Wrap, and refrigerate for at least 2 hours. Meanwhile, place prepared apples in a large bowl and toss with sugar, cinnamon and cloves or apple pie spice and flour.

Preheat the oven to 425°F.

Roll out pie dough to make a top and bottom crust (retain extra for another pie or refrigerate to make Pie Dough Cookies). Pile apples high into pie shell and top with butter bits. Place pastry on top, sealing edges well by crimping with a fork. Brush top crust with milk, then cut some air vents. Sprinkle on some sugar.

Place pie on baking sheet and bake for 15 minutes at 425°F. Reduce temperature to 350°F. and bake for another 25 - 35 minutes, until juices are bubbling. Cool 20 minutes before serving.

(Give this pie the time it needs so if it needs longer, just watch the top doesn't brown too much and let it bake until the juices are bubbling over)

Makes 6-8 servings

Carrot Sheet Cake

This is a classic, moist carrot cake and the perfect for Carrot Cake Chunk Cheesecake.

2 cups sugar

1 1/4 cup canola oil

4 eggs

2 tablespoons fresh lemon juice

2 teaspoons pure vanilla extract

3 cups all-purpose flour

2 teaspoons baking powder

½ teaspoon baking soda

2 1/2 teaspoons cinnamon

½ teaspoon salt

3 cups shredded carrots

1 cup yellow raisins, plumped and dried

1/2 cup chopped pecans

Preheat the oven to 350°F. Line a large baking sheet with parchment paper. Generously spray a 9-by-13 inch pan with non-stick cooking spray. Place on the baking sheet.

In a mixer bowl, blend the sugar, oil, eggs and vanilla. Fold in the flour, baking powder, baking soda, cinnamon and salt; blend well. Fold in the carrots, raisins and nuts and mix thoroughly. Spoon into pan.

Bake for 40-45 minutes or until cake springs back when gently touched. Cool well before serving.

Serves 10-12

10,000 APPLES--CHOOSING APPLES, CHOOSING FRIENDS

I choose apples like I choose my friends; I gravitate to friends and apples, both new and those of older vintage, who complement the occasion. In baking, the criterion is based on a triumvirate of my baker's touch, spice, and sweetness. The right apples for the apple occasion, if you pardon the pun: core. Alas, many people, even professional chefs, take apples for granted. Red, green, and yellow apples of indifferent taste, in and out of season, are cut, diced, and unceremoniously dispatched into a cake, pie, cobbler, or pie. But there are so many choices!

In choosing apples for baking, begin with what tastes sublime when you bite into it as a snack apple. Is it juicy and fragrant? Mealy or sour-sweet and crackling with complex apple flavor dimension? I always recommend combining apples: the sweetness of one with the acidic nature of another, or the firmness of one with the softness (which later on forms a nice apple "mush" filling in the crevices in an apple pie) of another. These apple marriages make an average apple pie aspire to new heights. Dedicated apples, like dedicated friends, can make a recipe, or life, sing.

Country Fresh Blueberry Pie with Butter Streusel

This pie is totally country, with its all butter pie dough and a sprinkle of streusel on top, which looks grand, taste swell and bumps this pie up to the next level of dessert goodness.

Pie Pastry for a double-crust pie, such as My Favorite Butter Pie Pastry

STREUSEL TOPPING

1/4 cup flour

1/4 cup sugar

3 tablespoons unsalted butter

1/4 teaspoon pure vanilla extract

COUNTRY BERRY PIE FILLING

2 cups fresh blueberries

2 1/2 cups frozen blueberries

3/4 cup sugar

1 tablespoon lemon juice

1 tablespoon flour

2 tablespoons cornstarch

1 tablespoon unsalted butter, in small bits

FINISHING TOUCHES

Milk

Sugar

Preheat the oven to 400°F. Place a piece of parchment paper on a cookie sheet.

For the streusel, rub flour, sugar, butter and vanilla together to make a grainy mixture. Set aside. Roll out bottom crust to fit pie pan.

For the Country Berry Pie Filling, in a large bowl, toss blueberries with sugar, lemon juice, flour, cornstarch and butter bits; blend gently with a large spoon. Spoon into prepared pie shell. Dab rim of shell with water (this will help glue top crust). Roll out the top pastry crust and arrange over filling. Crimp sides. Brush top and edges with milk and then sprinkle with streusel topping. Make some air vents in top. Place the pie pan on the cookie sheet and place the sheet on the lowest rack in the oven. Brush with milk and dust on some sugar.

Bake 15 minutes at 400°F; then lower temperature to 375°F. Bake until top streusel is golden brown, another 30-40 minutes, covering streusel with foil if it starts to brown too much and pie is not yet done (juices will begin to ooze out when it's nearing doneness) Cool before serving.

Serves 6-8

Toffee Espresso Cake

A simple but decadent little chocolate cake with a smack of bourbon and a toffee espresso sauce that is drizzled over. This is a lip-smackingly good and fussy cake without the fuss.

ESPRESSO CAKE

1 cup semi-sweet chocolate, coarsely chopped

¾ unsalted butter

1 ½ cups espresso or strong coffee

1 ½ cups sugar

¼ cup bourbon

2 eggs

1 teaspoon pure vanilla extract

2 cups all-purpose flour

3/4 teaspoon baking powder

1/4 teaspoon baking soda

1/8 teaspoon salt

TOFFEE SAUCE

1 cup sugar

1/3 cup water

½ cup whipping cream

2 tablespoons espresso or strong coffee

Preheat the oven to 325°F. Line a baking sheet with parchment paper and spray a 10 inch angel food cake pan with non-stick cooking spray. Place pan on baking sheet.

For the cake, in a heavy-bottomed saucepan, over low heat, melt the chocolate, butter, and coffee. Let cool 15 minutes. Whisk in the sugar, bourbon, eggs and vanilla. Mix in flour, baking powder, baking soda and salt. Spoon into prepared pan and bake until cake is set to touch, about 35-45 minutes. Cool 20 minutes in pan and then on cake rack.

For the Toffee Espresso Sauce, in a small saucepan, heat the sugar and water slowly, brushing inner sides of pan with a pastry brush dipped in water until sugar is dissolved. Do this slowly.

As the sugar turns light amber in colour, place pot in the sink and whisk in the cream and espresso. The mixture will bubble and froth so take care. This is a thin caramel sauce you drizzle over (versus a thick one).

Serve each slice of cake with some sauce and additional whipping cream.

Serves 8-12

Caramel Pumpkin Apple Cider Tart

This is one of those recipes that becomes an instant classic the moment you make it. It's the best of both worlds of pumpkin cheesecake and pumpkin pie and is laced with the warmth of caramel, apple cider and a decadence of candied walnuts.

SWEET PIE DOUGH

1 1/2 cups all-purpose flour

1 tablespoon sugar

1 teaspoon salt

½ cup unsalted butter, cut into small chunks

6-8 tablespoons whipping cream

Candied Walnuts

1 teaspoon corn syrup

1 teaspoon sugar

1/8 teaspoon salt

1/2 cup chopped walnuts

PUMPKIN FILLING

8 ounces cream cheese, softened

¾ cup light brown sugar, firmly packed

3 eggs

1 teaspoon pure vanilla extract

1 ¼ cup canned pumpkin puree

1 teaspoon cinnamon

½ teaspoon pumpkin pie spice

2/3 cup whipping cream

CARAMEL APPLE CIDER SAUCE

1/2 cup water

1 cup white sugar

1/4 cup brown sugar

1/8 teaspoon fleur de sel (or flaked salt)

1 cup warm whipping cream

1/4 cup apple cider

For the Sweet Pie Dough, place flour, sugar and salt in a large mixer bowl. Cut in the butter until mixture is crumbly. Make a well in center of flour mixture and stir in most of the whipping cream. Using a fork or fingers, toss mixture together to moisten flour. Stir to make a soft mass and pat into a dough. Add remaining (or additional) whipping cream as required to make sure dough sticks together. Turn out onto a lightly floured work surface. Knead very briefly into a smooth dough. Place the dough in a Ziplock bag and refrigerate at least one hour or up to two day.

Preheat the oven to 350°F. Line a baking sheet with parchment paper. Roll dough out on a lightly floured work surface to fit a 9 or 10 inch, deep fluted tart tin with removable bottom. (If you only have a quiche pan or spring-form pan, use one of those). Trim edges a bit but allow some rustic overhang. Prick the bottom of the pie crust and then cover pie dough with pie weights and bake to brown slightly, 15 minutes. Remove from oven and let cool (but keep oven on)

For the Candied Walnuts, toss ingredients together in a small bowl. Place on the parchment lined baking sheet (you used for pie crust). Bake 5-10 minutes. Let cool and break into smaller pieces (versus a big clump of nuts).

For the Pumpkin Filling, in a food processor or a bowl, blend the cream cheese, sugar, eggs, vanilla, pumpkin puree, cinnamon, pumpkin pie spice and whipping cream. Pour into pie shell. Place pie shell on a parchment paper lined baking sheet. Bake 35-40 minutes or until filling seems set. Refrigerate a few hours or overnight.

For the Caramel Apple Cider Sauce, in a small saucepan, heat the water, white sugar, brown sugar and salt over low heat. For 20-30 minutes, allow to gently simmer, brushing inner sides of pot with a brush dipped in water. Once the mixture turns medium amber, remove from burner and put it in the sink. Pour warm cream slowly into sauce (take care, it bubbles up and is hot!), and the apple cider. Whisk until smooth. Refrigerate until needed and then rewarm.

To serve, remove tart from mold and place on serving platter. Dust edges with confectioners' sugar. Pour warmed caramel sauce over top of pie and garnish tart with the candied walnuts.

Serves 8

HOW TO PEEL AND PARE APPLES

There are old-school apple corers that are as charmingly old-fashioned as Eve herself – farm-styled gizmos that core and peel at the same time. But you need to make sure the apple is of perfect shape and firmness for these things to work well. You also have to align the apple on the corer part at the perfect place to get rid of the core – which always still takes hand trimming at the end as the core is never totally removed (and/or you remove too much core and lose a lot of great apple on the way). I prefer a bird's beak paring knife for peeling apples. It's just the right shape for one thing and the sharpness (especially a Cutco bird's beak knife or a well-honed favorite knife) is unrivaled. Peel the apples first, then quarter them and remove the section of the core from each apple section. Dice or pare as you need. If your apples are lying about for any time, spritz them with a bit of lemon juice to stop them from turning brown.

Shortbread Crumb Country Apple Cake

This is a spice apple cake with a unique shortbread crumb topping that's good as is or with a bit of spice added to it. I suggest a soft apple for this cake such as McIntosh or Golden Delicious or if using Granny Smith, pare very thinly.

VANILLA CRUMB TOPPING

1 cup all-purpose flour

½ cup confectioners' sugar

1 teaspoon pure vanilla extract

½ cup unsalted butter

APPLE SPICE FILLING

5-6 cups sliced, peeled apples

1 tablespoon fresh lemon juice

5 teaspoons cinnamon

¼ teaspoon cloves

2-3 pinches nutmeg

1/4 cup sugar

CAKE

2 cups sugar

1 cup unsalted butter, softened

3 teaspoons vanilla

1/2 cup buttermilk

4 eggs

3 cups all-purpose flour

1 tablespoon baking powder

½ teaspoon baking soda

1/4 teaspoon salt

FINISHING TOUCHES

Cinnamon

Nutmeg

Preheat the oven to 350°F. Line a large baking sheet with parchment paper. Generously grease a 12 cup angel cake pan and place on baking sheet.

For the Vanilla Crumb Topping, in a food processor, blend flour, confectioners' sugar, and vanilla extract briefly. Add in the butter and pulse to create a crumble topping. Set aside.

For the Apple Spice Filling, in a medium bowl, add the apples and add in the lemon juice, cinnamon, cloves, nutmeg and sugar.

For the cake, in a mixer bowl, cream the sugar and butter until well combined. Blend in vanilla, buttermilk and eggs until smooth. Fold in flour, baking powder, baking soda and salt, blending to make a smooth batter. Spoon half the batter into prepared pan. Cover with two-thirds of the Apple Spice Filling, and then top with remaining batter and apples, mixing a bit with a spatula to cover apples with some batter. It won't be perfect but it does bake up just fine. Sprinkle top lightly with a dusting of cinnamon and nutmeg. Then sprinkle on reserved crumb topping.

Bake for one hour or more until done. Cake will appear firm to the touch. If you are not sure, lower temperature to 325°F and bake a little longer until cake appears firm (but not too browned). Keep cake in pan an hour before removing to a wire cake rack to completely cool.

Serves 12-14

Russian Sour Cream Coffeecake

One of those simple, but I-got-to-have-the-recipe cakes and it's a must in anyone's repertoire. Dust with confectioners' sugar or a simple vanilla glaze and then just brew up a huge pot of tea or coffee for this splendid cake.

FILLING

1/4 cup brown sugar, firmly packed

2 teaspoons cocoa

1/2 cup chocolate chips

1 teaspoon cinnamon

1/2 cup raisins, plumped and dried

1/2 cup chopped toasted almonds

1/3 cup apricot jam

CAKE

1 cup unsalted butter

1 cup brown sugar, firmly packed

1/2 cup white sugar

4 eggs

1 teaspoon pure vanilla extract

1 cup sour cream

3 cups all-purpose flour

2 3/4 teaspoons baking powder

1/2 teaspoon baking soda

Pinch cinnamon

Pinch nutmeg

1/2 teaspoon salt

FINISHING TOUCHES

Confectioners' sugar

Preheat the oven to 350 Degrees°F. Spray a 9 or 10 inch tube or angel food cake pan with non-stick cooking spray.

Prepare the filling by mixing all ingredients together and set aside. In a mixer bowl, cream the butter with the brown and white sugar until fluffy. Add eggs and vanilla and mix thoroughly. Stir in sour cream. In a separate bowl, stir together flour, baking powder, baking soda, cinnamon, nutmeg and salt. Fold dry ingredients into batter, scraping down sides and mix well on low speed of mixer 2-3 minutes. Spread one-third of filling in prepared pan. Top with some of the filling mixture. Layer this way until filling is used up.

Bake until done, and cake springs back when gently touched with fingertips, 50-55 minutes. Cool in pan 10 minutes before removing. Dust with confectioners' sugar before serving.

Serves 10-12

Cinnamon Baby Babka

I adore sweet yeast baking, especially homemade babka. It's moist, sweet, buttery and great fresh or toasted. This recipe is not only easy and not overwhelmingly big. It makes a small but jaunty, fragrant loaf, perfect for a weekend's munching or a coffee klatch with friends. It's better-than-any-bakery and features layer after layer of sweet, cinnamon, rippled through a beautiful, butter-vanilla sweet dough.

SWEET DOUGH

¼ cup warm water

2 ½ teaspoons instant yeast

4 cups bread flour

½ cup warm milk

3 eggs

1 yolk

2 ½ teaspoons pure vanilla extract

½ cup sugar

½ teaspoon salt

¾ cup unsalted butter, softened, in chunks

4 cups all-purpose or bread flour

Cinnamon Filling

1 ½ cups brown sugar, firmly packed

1/3 cup all-purpose flour

4 tablespoons unsalted butter, melted

1 cup miniature marshmallows
*

4 teaspoons cinnamon

BUTTER CRUMB TOPPING

4 tablespoons unsalted butter, softened

½ cup confectioners' sugar

1/2 cup all-purpose flour

FINISHING TOUCHES

1 beaten egg

*Marshmallows make for an appealing, gooey cinnamon filling. If you don't have some on hand, use 2 egg whites instead.

For the dough, in a mixer bowl, hand whisk together water and yeast. Let stand a minute and then briskly stir in one cup of the flour, then the warm milk, the eggs, yolk, vanilla, sugar and salt. Fold in softened butter and most of the remaining flour, holding back some until you see if you need all over it (or may have to add a bit). Mix the dough and then, with dough hook, knead on slow speed 8-10 minutes, until smooth and elastic. This is a somewhat soft dough.

Remove the dough hook from the mixer, spray the dough with non-stick cooking spray and cover the entire mixer (bowl, machine and all) with a large plastic bag. Allow to rise until puffy, about 45-90 minutes.

For the Cinnamon Filling, in a bowl or a food processor, blend the sugar, flour, butter, marshmallows and cinnamon to make a paste. Set aside.

For the Butter Crumb Topping, in a small bowl, with your fingertips, rub or cut butter, confectioners' sugar and flour together to make a crumbly topping. Set aside.

When the dough has risen, gently press down and turn onto a lightly floured board. Pat dough into a 12 by 20 inch rectangle. Let rest while preparing baking pan.

Line a baking sheet with parchment paper. Generously spray a 10 by 5 inch loaf pan or 10 inch angel food cake pan with non-stick cooking spray and line bottom and sides with parchment paper. Place on baking sheet.

Pat two-thirds of the Cinnamon Filling all over dough surface, pressing slightly. Roll up dough into a large jellyroll and press down a little bit. Smear with remaining Cinnamon Filling. Bring two ends of the dough into the center (to meet each other) and press slightly. Pick up the whole roll and twist. Place in the prepared pan. Brush with egg wash and sprinkle top with Butter Crumb Topping.

Place the pan on the baking sheet and cover the entire sheet with a large plastic bag. Let rise until bubka is flush or over top of pan, 45-90 minutes. Preheat the oven to 350°F.

Bake 35-45 minutes or until the babka is medium brown. Cool in the pan fifteen minutes before removing to a rack or serving plate.

Makes one babka

MISTRESS OF SPICES, MASTER OF FRESHNESS

"EVERYONE HAS A SPICE....."

The Mistress of Spices, a wonderful novel (also a film) by Chitra Banerjee Divakaruni, is set in a lavish spice store where its mistress/owner Tilo is part spice witch and part spell caster. Her domain is spices and her loyalty to them, in service to administering to others (the lonely, the victimized, and those who suffer unrequited love) is admirable. But the deal-breaker is that the spices ask their mistress to abandon her own desires as she administers spice curatives to others. The bottom line is Tilo can never fall in love herself. Tilo reflects that 'everyone has a spice'. Hers is sesame and the man she loves? His spice is chili, passionate, warm and untamed. You can imagine the heated romance that follows such a premise. What spice are you? Are you warm cinnamon, exotic cardamom, soothing vanilla or perky nutmeg? In fall, you can be a different spice-a-day, such is the inspiration of this season of hospitality and fireside warmth. The only thing you must not do, when it comes to spices, is to use old ones or less than best quality ones in your baking. If you want to be a mistress of spices or a baker-with-the-mostest, start casting your spell in the spice choices you make.

Indian Summer Sweet Pear Cranberry Crisp

Usually we think of apples when we think of an old-fashioned 'crisps' but ripe, sweet autumn pears are wondrous in this recipe. Just use very flavorful pears such as Bosc or Anjou or a combination of a few pear varieties. A touch of cranberries brings some added to color and a light touch of spice makes this a total fall portrait.

FILLING

6 large pears, cored, diced in large chunks

1 cup fresh or frozen cranberries

3 tablespoons light brown sugar

2 tablespoons white sugar

2 tablespoons fresh lemon juice

1 teaspoon pure vanilla extract

1/4 teaspoon cinnamon

Pinch each cloves, allspice, nutmeg, ginger

OATMEAL CRISP TOPPING

1 cup rolled oatmeal

1/3 cup all-purpose flour

1/3 cup light brown sugar, firmly packed

¼ cup white sugar

¼ teaspoon cinnamon

Pinch salt

½ cup unsalted butter, diced

Preheat the oven to 350°F. Line a baking sheet with parchment paper. Generously spray a 3-quart baking pan (such as a ceramic oval or round baking dish that is ovenproof) with nonstick cooking spray or lightly butter the dish. Place on baking sheet.

For the filling, add the pears and cranberries to a large bowl and toss with the brown and white sugars, lemon juice, vanilla extract, cinnamon, cloves, allspice, nutmeg and ginger. Spoon pear and cranberry filling into the prepared pan.

For the Oatmeal Crisp Topping, in a medium bowl, combine the oats, flour, brown and white sugars, cinnamon and salt and mix briefly. Cut the butter into the dry ingredients to make a crumbly topping.

Sprinkle the topping over the fruit. Bake 35- 45 minutes or until the fruit begins to bubble and it the fragrance of baked pears is evident (it might take longer than 45 minutes but it's done when fruit juices bubble and burst out of the oatmeal crisp topping). Serve warm or at room temperature.

Serves 4–6

After School Yellow Sheet Cake with Milk Chocolate Icing

A tender yellow cake is quintessential memory food. A big hunk of this wonderful, moist yellow sheet cake with a swirl of sour cream frosting launches a whole new generation of memories for the after school crowd. It's also a perfect birthday cake recipe or does double duty as cupcakes.

CAKE

1 ¼ cup unsalted butter, softened

2 1/3 cups sugar

4 eggs

1 tablespoon pure vanilla extract

1 3/4 cup warm milk

6 tablespoons sour cream

3 cups all-purpose flour

2 tablespoons cornstarch

1 tablespoon baking powder

1/2 teaspoon baking soda

1/2 teaspoon salt

MILK CHOCOLATE FROSTING

1 ½ cups whipping cream

3 cups milk chocolate, coarsely chopped

2-3 tablespoons unsalted butter

Preheat the oven to 350°F. Line a baking sheet with parchment paper. Generously spray a 9 by 13 inch pan with non-stick cooking spray and place on the baking sheet.

In a mixer bowl or food processor, cream the butter with the sugar until well blended. Blend in the eggs, vanilla, milk and sour cream. Fold in the flour, cornstarch, baking powder, baking soda and salt and blend until smooth, about 3-4 minutes. Spoon into prepared pan. Bake until cake test done when gently pressed with fingertips, 40-45 minutes.

Cool in pan 15 minutes before unmolding to cool completely.

For the Milk Chocolate Frosting, heat the cream until it starts to bubble. Add in the chocolate, turn off the heat, and stir to melt chocolate evenly into cream. Chill 2-4 hours until firm. Place in a mixer bowl and whip on low speed, adding in butter to fluff up the ganache. Spread on cake.

Serves 10-12 or makes 24 medium or about 48 smaller cupcakes

Carrot Cake Chunk Cheesecake

This is the best of both worlds – gorgeous golden chunks of carrot cake, set in a decadent cheesecake batter and topped with a bit of caramel and white chocolate drizzle as the 'cream cheese' icing. A totally stunning cheesecake.

CHEESECAKE CRUST

1 cup graham crumbs

½ cup shortbread crumbs

1/3 cup unsalted butter, melted

¼ cup dark brown sugar, packed

¼ teaspoon cinnamon

Pinch cloves, allspice

CHEESECAKE

2 ½ pounds cream cheese, softened

1 ¼ cups sugar

1/4 cup all-purpose flour

2 ½ teaspoons pure vanilla extract

2 tablespoons fresh lemon juice

5 eggs

½ cup whipping cream

½ cup yellow raisins, plumped and dried

2 1/2 cups loosely packed carrot cake cubes *

1/3 cup caramel sundae topping

½ teaspoon cinnamon

FINISHING TOUCHES

½ cup chopped white chocolate, melted

1/8 teaspoon cinnamon

1/4 teaspoon pure vanilla extract

1/8 teaspoon orange oil or orange extract

* For the Carrot Cake, use your own favourite recipe or use the Carrot Sheet Cake recipe that follows. (Keep half the cake for eating and the other half, cut into carrot cake cubes to use in this cheesecake recipe.)

Preheat the oven to 350°F. Line a baking sheet with parchment paper. Generously spray a 10 inch spring-form pan with non-stick cooking spray and place on the baking sheet.

For the Cheesecake Crust, put all the graham and shortbread crumbs, butter, sugar, cinnamon, cloves and allspice into the bottom of the cheesecake pan, mix and then press crumbs into bottom of pan.

For the Cheesecake, in a mixer bowl, blend the cream cheese with the sugar and flour. Then add in the vanilla, lemon juice, eggs and cream and blend well. Fold in the raisins.

Pour 1/3 of the cheesecake mixture into the cake pan. Top with half the carrot cake chunks, drizzle on half of the caramel topping and dust with the cinnamon. Add more batter and more almost all the carrot cake cubes. Top with remaining batter (this doesn't have to be perfect; you simply want a mixture of batter and cake chunks). Drizzle on remaining caramel topping and dust with cinnamon.

Bake until just set, 45-55 minutes. Turn off oven and let sit in oven 2 hours and then refrigerate 8 hours or up until three days.

For the White Chocolate Drizzle, slowly melt the white chocolate and then whisk in the spice and extracts. Drizzle over cake.

Serves 16-24

Free Form Rustic Apple Tart

This beautiful bistro-style open faced apple tart is so easily put together but looks like a French pastry chef took residence up in your kitchen. I use both Golden Delicious, Granny Smith and Royal Gala apples but feel free to try your own apple combinations. This is the recipe that graces the cover of this cookbook.

DOUGH

2 cups all-purpose flour

2 tablespoons sugar

¼ teaspoon baking powder

1/2 teaspoon salt

1 cup unsalted butter, cold, cut in 1/2-inch pieces

2-6 tablespoons, approximately, ice chilled water

FILLING

5-6 cups or 2 pounds apples (mix of Granny Smith and Golden Delicious), peeled, cored and thinly sliced

1 tablespoon fresh lemon juice

½ cup sugar

¼ teaspoon cinnamon

4 tablespoons unsalted butter, melted

FINISHING TOUCHES

Sugar

2 tablespoons unsalted butter, melted

GLAZE

1/2 cup apple jelly

Stack two baking sheets together and line top one with parchment paper.

In a food processor, blend the flour, sugar, baking powder and salt. Add the butter and pulse until mixture resembles coarse meal. Add in most just enough ice water and mix until dough just holds together. Blend with a fork or fingertips, and gradually bring dough together into a rough ball. Flatten the ball into a thick disc, place in a Ziplock bag and refrigerate 30 minutes.

Preheat the oven to 400°F.

On a well-floured work surface, roll into a 14-inch circle about 1/8 inch thick. Dust excess flour from the dough. Place the dough on the baking sheet. Place apples, lemon juice, sugar, cinnamon and butter in a large bowl and toss to coat the apples. Arrange the apples on the dough concentrically, to 2 inches from edge. Fold the border of any dough into a border onto the apples. Dust apples with 1-2 tablespoons more sugar and brush a touch of melted butter on the edges of the pastry.

Place the pastry in the oven and immediately lower the temperature to 375°F. Bake until the apples are softened and their edges start to brown and the crust has started to turn medium brown, about 45 minutes). Turn pastry to bake evenly.

Warm the apple jelly with a little water. Once tart is done, remove from the oven and let stand 15 minutes before brushing with hot apple jelly.

Serves 6-8

Caramel Sticky Pudding

This Quebecoise treat is the queen of rustic desserts, a poor man's pudding of pantry essentials, whipped together in minutes. The simple cake batter is spooned into a pan and then doused with a homey brown sugar and maple concoction. The magic of the oven transforms it into a golden brown cake that sprawls over a luscious caramel bottom you spoon out over portions of cake.

CAKE

1/2 cup unsalted butter, softened

3/4 cup white sugar

2 eggs

1 teaspoon pure vanilla extract

3/4 cup milk

1 1/2 cups all-purpose flour

2 teaspoons baking powder

1/8 teaspoon salt

BROWN SUGAR SAUCE

1/2 cup boiling water

1 cup whipping cream

1 1/4 cups light or golden brown sugar, firmly packed

3/4 cup pure maple syrup

¼ cup unsalted butter, softened

¼ teaspoon pure vanilla extract

¼ teaspoon pure maple extract, optional

Preheat the oven to 350°F. Line a baking sheet with parchment paper.

Generously spray a 4 quart baking dish or 9 inch layer cake pan with non-stick cooking spray. Place on the baking sheet.

For the cake, in a mixer bowl, cream the butter with the sugar until fluffy, 2-4 minutes and then add the eggs and vanilla and blend well. Stir in the milk and then the flour, baking powder and salt. Spoon into the prepared pan.

For the Brown Sugar Sauce, in the same mixer bowl, (no need to clean it) whisk the boiling water, cream, brown sugar, maple syrup, butter, vanilla and maple extract. Pour this over the batter in the pan. Bake until the top is medium brown and you can see the sauce underneath bubbling through, about 40-45 minutes. Serve warm or room temperature.

Serves 6-8

Vintage Tollhouse Pie

This is a quick and easy, but satisfying pie. It features the wonderful taste of chocolate chips and brown sugar batter, packed into a buttery pie shell.

PREPARED 9 INCH PIE SHELL SUCH AS MY FAVOURITE ALL BUTTER PIE PASTRY RECIPE

1/2 cup white sugar

1/2 cup brown sugar, firmly packed

1 cup unsalted butter, melted and cooled

2 eggs

1 1/2 teaspoons pure vanilla extract

1/2 cup all-purpose flour

Pinch salt

1 cup semi-sweet chocolate chips

1 cup chopped walnuts or pecans, optional

Preheat the oven to 325°F. Line a baking sheet with parchment paper.

If using homemade pie dough, use an 8 inch quiche or tart dish and line with pastry. Place pie pan on the baking sheet.

In a mixer bowl, mix the white and brown sugar with the butter, and then blend in the eggs and vanilla extract. Fold in the flour and salt, and then the chocolate chips and walnuts. Spoon into the pie shell.

Bake one hour or until just set. Serve with ice-cream.

Serves 8-10

Golden Butternut Squash Applesauce Bundt Cake

One of my favourite creations from my beginner days as a baker. Years later I still adore this recipe, which makes the most of garden squash, mellow applesauce and spice. It features an incomparable flavor and crumb. The deep-flavoured apple glaze is a final touch that ensures this moist cake stays moist for days.

2 cups sugar

½ cup unsalted butter, melted

1 teaspoon lemon zest, finely minced

1 cup canola oil

4 eggs

2 1/2 teaspoons pure vanilla extract

1 cup cooked butternut squash puree (approximately one small squash)

1 cup unsweetened applesauce

3 1/2 cups all-purpose flour

2 teaspoons baking powder

2 teaspoons baking soda

2 teaspoons cinnamon

1/4 teaspoons ginger

1/8 teaspoon salt

1/2 cup yellow raisins, plumped and dried

½ cup dark raisins, plumped and dried

1/2 cup finely chopped walnuts

APPLE SUGAR GLAZE
3/4 cup apple juice

¾ cup sugar

Preheat the oven to 350°F. Line a baking sheet with parchment paper. Spray a 12 cup Bundt or 10 inch angel food cake pan generously with non-stick cooking spray. Spray the fluted indents of the Bundt pan especially well so as to avoid baked cake sticking later and/or smear on vegetable shortening to ensure perfect cake release. Place pan on the baking sheet.

In a mixer bowl, blend sugar, butter, zest, and oil. Blend in the eggs and vanilla and then the squash puree, applesauce; blend well. Fold in the flour, baking powder, baking soda, cinnamon, ginger and salt. Blend well and fold in the raisins and nuts.

Spoon batter into pan. Bake 50-55 minutes or until cake tests done; it will spring back when gently touched with fingertips. Cool cake in the pan 15 minutes before inverting onto a cooling rack or serving platter.

For the Apple Sugar Glaze, simmer the apple juice and sugar in a small pot until it reduces to about ½ cup and is thickened, 8-12 minutes. Cool slightly. Meanwhile, fork small holes or using a paring knife, small slits on top surface of the cake. Drizzle on cake, allowing syrup to soak in.

Serves 12-16

Cream and Spice Sweet Potato Pie

A silken smooth and elegant sweet potato pie. I serve it warm with thick whipped cream or vanilla or caramel ice-cream. Use quality, fresh spices always but as this is a terrific Thanksgiving offering, make sure you go all out with the best.

1 9 inch unbaked pie shell, such as My Favorite All Butter Pie Pastry

2 cups sweet potato puree

2 eggs

¾ cup sugar

Pinch salt

¼ teaspoon ginger

¼ teaspoon nutmeg

¼ teaspoon cinnamon

1/8 teaspoon cloves

1/8 teaspoon allspice

1 cup evaporated milk

2/3 cup whipping or light cream

1 teaspoon pure vanilla extract

½ cup unsalted butter, melted

Preheat the oven to 400°F. Line a baking sheet with parchment paper. Place pie shell on the baking sheet.

In a mixer bowl, blend sweet potatoes with eggs, sugar, salt, spices, evaporated milk, cream, vanilla and melted butter.

Bake until the pie seems barely firm or set in the center, 40-50 minutes. If pie seems to be browning around edges and not cooked in the center, lower the temperature to 350°F and bake a little longer, about ten minutes. Serve with ice-cream, custard or whipping cream.

Serves 6-8

NEW HARVESTS, FRESH SPICES

New harvests deserve a fragrant batch of spices so refresh your canisters and jars. Invest in the finest spices you can find (and the choices in stores these days, as well as online, are unlimited) to make your recipes soar with flavour. Don't use cinnamon or nutmeg without first inhaling the spice and checking it out. Spices are gold! In fact, they were once legal tender and used instead of regular currency. In some ways, spices are as exotic now as they were when Columbus set on turbulent seas, on mission to finding the best spices in the world. Now all we have to do is click online or visit Costco. Baking demands so little, or rather such basic, pure ingredients. So when a recipe calls for a little bit of spice, it might as well be the best. Be a mistress of spices and you'll find yourself master of your baker's domain.

Oregon Vanilla Chai Tea Cake

This recipe calls for one cup of brewed chai tea. You may use any good spice and orange tea such as a standby like Bigelow's Constant Comment or Harney Tea Company's Chai, Teavana (Oprah's pick) or David's Tea signature Chai. A touch of vanilla is what makes this 'Oregon', but the spice and wonderful golden, moist, fragrant crumb is what pulls this together into a legendary cake.

1 cup brewed chai or spice and orange tea *

1 cup unsalted butter

1/2 cup white sugar

1 1/2 cup brown sugar, firmly packed

4 eggs

2 ½ teaspoons pure vanilla extract

1/4 teaspoon pure orange extract

1/4 teaspoon orange oil, optional

3 cups all-purpose flour

2 1/4 teaspoons baking powder

1/2 teaspoon baking soda

1/4 teaspoon ginger

1 tablespoon cinnamon

1/8 teaspoon nutmeg

1/2 teaspoon cloves

1/8 teaspoon mace

1/4 teaspoon allspice

3/8 teaspoon salt

CHAI GLAZE

1 cup confectioners' sugar

2 tablespoons brewed chai tea

½ pure vanilla extract

* For the chai tea, steep 3 to 4 chai tea bags in 1 1/2 cups of water, or brew one strong cup of chai tea made with a chai tea leaf blend. Cool.

Preheat the oven to 350°F. Line a baking sheet with parchment paper. Generously spray a 9-inch tube or angel food cake pan with non-stick cooking spray and place it on the baking sheet.

In a mixer bowl, cream the butter with the white and brown sugar. Add eggs, vanilla and orange extracts and orange oil. Then fold in the flour, baking powder, baking soda, ginger, cinnamon, nutmeg, cloves, mace, allspice and salt. Mix and slowly pour in one cup of the chai tea. Scrape bowl sides and bottom, ensuring no unblended ingredients are stuck in the well of the bowl, and blend well.

Spoon batter into pan and place pan on baking sheet. Place cake in oven and bake until cake tests done (50-55 minutes). Cool 20 minutes in the pan before removing to a cake rack to completely cool.

For the Chai Glaze, in a small bowl, mix the confectioners' sugar, (some reserved) chai tea and vanilla with a small whisk, adding more tea as required for the right consistency. Drizzle over cool cake. Re-glaze.

Serves 12-16

Country Pumpkin Bread

This is country, not bumpkin style, quick bread that is vibrant with fresh spices and has a beautiful, deep orange hue. Roasted pumpkin is perfect for this recipe but convenient canned pumpkin puree works just as well. This is the pumpkin bread recipe I use for Pumpkin Eruption Cheesecake but on its own, it's a terrific slicing loaf and as most quick breads, it makes great muffins too.

1/2 cup canola oil

1/2 cup white sugar

1/2 cup dark brown sugar, firmly packed

1/2 cup golden brown sugar, firmly packed

2 eggs

2 teaspoons pure vanilla extract

1/3 cup cola beverage or water

1 cup pumpkin puree

1 3/4 cups all-purpose flour

1 1/2 teaspoons baking powder

1/4 teaspoon baking soda

1/2 teaspoon cinnamon

1/4 teaspoon cloves

1/2 teaspoon pumpkin pie spice

Pinch salt

Preheat the oven to 350°F. Line a baking sheet with parchment paper. Spray a 9 inch layer cake pan with non-stick cooking spray and place it on the baking sheet. Alternatively, spray a 9 by 5 inch loaf pan with cooking spray and place it on the baking sheet.

In a mixer bowl or food processor, blend the oil with the white, dark and light brown sugars. Add in the eggs, vanilla, and then the cola and pumpkin puree and blend well. Fold in the flour, baking powder, baking soda, cinnamon, cloves, pumpkin pie spice and salt; blend well. Spoon into the prepared pan. Bake until cake tests done or cake springs back when gently pressed with fingertips, about 35-45 minutes. Cool well in pan for 30 minutes and then turn out onto a cake rack to finish cooling.

Serves 8-10

Zucchini Carrot Bread with Cream Cheese Glaze

A lovely way to make a garden marriage of fresh zucchini and carrots in a winsome loaf. The trick of some shredded apple heightens the flavor and moistness; the modest cream cheese glaze just adds a touch of class and sweet decadence. This recipe does double-duty as muffins.

1/2 cup canola oil

1/2 cup unsalted butter, melted

1 cup white sugar

1/3 cup brown sugar, firmly packed

Zest of one medium orange, finely minced

3 eggs

1 tablespoon pure vanilla extract

1/4 cup buttermilk or soured milk

3 cups all-purpose flour

2 teaspoons baking powder

½ teaspoon baking soda

2 teaspoons cinnamon

¼ teaspoon cloves

Pinch allspice

Pinch nutmeg

½ teaspoon salt

1/2 cup finely chopped pecans

3/4 cup yellow raisins, plumped and dried

1 small apple, shredded

1 cup washed, (not peeled) zucchini, shredded

1 cup carrots, shredded

CREAM CHEESE GLAZE

1 tablespoon unsalted butter

4 ounces cream cheese, softened

2 cups confectioners' sugar

1 tablespoon fresh lemon juice

3-6 tablespoons orange juice or as required

Preheat the oven to 350°F. Line a baking sheet with parchment paper. Spray two 8 by 4 inch loaf pans or one 10 inch spring-form pan generously with non-stick cooking spray and place pan(s) on the baking sheet.

In a mixer bowl, blend the oil, butter, white and brown sugar, orange zest, eggs, vanilla and buttermilk until smooth. Fold in the flour, baking powder, baking soda, cinnamon, cloves, allspice, nutmeg and salt and blend slightly; then fold in the pecans, raisins, apple, and lastly, the zucchini and carrots, blending well to incorporate all ingredients into a lumpy but well-mixed batter.

Spoon into pan. Bake 45-50 minutes until cake appears to be firm to the touch and then lower temperature to 325°F and allow to bake until it tests done, another 20-25 minutes. For the spring-form cake pan, allow 15-20 minutes more baking time. This cake does take long to bake and you want it to set up, but then allow it to fully bake in the middle without the sides drying out. Let cake cool in pan 15 minutes before removing to a baking rack to completely cool.

For the Cream Cheese Glaze, add butter and cream cheese to a food processor bowl and blend briefly. Add in the confectioners' sugar and lemon juice, adding in orange juice to make a soft glaze. Once the cake has cooled, drizzle or smear on glaze. Let set and re-glaze. You can also garnish with a few tablespoons of finely minced pecans. Chill 30 minutes to let glaze set further.

Makes one large loaf or two smaller ones

CORN DOLLY, A GRAINY GIRL OF GOOD LUCK

A corn dolly is a straw and wheat sheaf figurine, woven from the last harvest wheat sheaf. It harks back to European and Celtic lore that made its way over to the Colonies. The spirit of the grain was said to live in the grain itself (corn: meaning grain). The corn dolly was created by an expert weaver and then hidden or stored away all winter, keeping the wheat spirit safe. Some craftsman dressed their dollies in women's clothes, much like dressing a toy doll. The next planting season, the doll was inserted into the newly tilled soil, to bring luck in the next harvest. These days, you can order a corn dolly from an online weaver or perhaps have luck at a local farmer's craft market. Wheat and straw weavers still have guilds for sharing of information, history and skills, as well as for helping you navigate to procuring a fine example of folk art that survives today, centuries later. Corn husk dolls are yet another rendition of a spirit/ grain symbol, woven with corn husks, and are part of Native American and Native Canadian traditions, especially among the Seneca and Iroquois.

Walnut Crunch Pumpkin Pie

I love pumpkin pie but it's truly riveting when it comes with a brown crunchy topping on top of a silky filled crust. This pie made me famous when I was a new pastry chef at the very first restaurant I worked at. If you use canned pumpkin, make sure it's pure pumpkin – not pumpkin pie 'mix' which has added sugar and spice in it.

PIE DOUGH, FOR ONE 9 INCH PIE SHELL, SUCH AS MY FAVORITE ALL BUTTER PIE PASTRY

Brown Sugar Walnut Crunch Topping

3 tablespoons unsalted butter, softened

2/3 cup brown sugar, firmly packed

1/2 cup chopped walnuts, toasted

FILLING

2 cups pumpkin puree

2 eggs

1/4 cup white sugar

1/2 cup brown sugar, firmly packed

3/4 teaspoon cinnamon

1/8 teaspoon ginger

¼ teaspoon cloves

Pinch nutmeg, allspice

1 teaspoon pure vanilla extract

1 2/3 cup whipping cream

Preheat the oven to 400°F. Line a baking sheet with parchment paper. Prepare pastry in tart or quiche pan, press into crevices to fit well. Place pie pan on baking sheet.

Prepare Brown Sugar Walnut Crunch Topping by tossing all ingredients together in a small bowl. Keep chilled.

For the pie filling, in a large bowl, whisk together pumpkin puree with eggs, the white and brown sugar and spices. Stir in the vanilla and cream and blend well.

Place pie shell on a large baking sheet (preferably covered with parchment to catch spills). Pour filling into pie shell. Place pie in oven and bake until set, 45 to 50 minutes. Meanwhile, mix topping ingredients to make a crumbly mixture.

Remove pie from oven. Turn on broiler. Gently sprinkle on Walnut Topping and return pie to the oven. Broil just to caramelize the pie caramelize topping (for 3 to 5 minutes). Remove from oven. Let cool for 20 minutes, then refrigerate until serving time. Caramel topping will soften but the taste is still the same. Serve with whipped cream or vanilla custard sauce dusted with cinnamon.

Serves 6-8

Holiday Corn Bread

This is a quintessential or definitive corn bread. It has a sweet milk, sour cream and buttermilk along with stone-ground cornmeal and bakes into a buttery wonder. Bake this in a cast iron skillet or cast iron corn bread molds. Nowadays cast iron skillets come pre-seasoned, unless yours is heirloom or a flea market special (and it's definitely pre-seasoned!)

CORN BREAD

1 cup stone-ground cornmeal

1/3 cup very hot milk

1/3 cup unsalted butter, melted or canola oil

½ cup buttermilk

¼ cup sour cream

¼ cup sugar

2 eggs

1 cup all-purpose flour

1 ½ teaspoons baking powder

½ teaspoon baking soda

½ teaspoon salt

FINISHING TOUCHES
Melted butter

Preheat the oven to 400°F. Line a large baking sheet with parchment paper. Butter a 10 inch pie pan, or 10 inch cast iron skillet or a 9 by 9 inch square baking pan with melted butter or nonstick cooking spray. Place on baking sheet.

In a small bowl, place ½ cup of cornmeal. Pour the hot milk over this, stir and let stand 5 minutes. In a mixer bowl, whisk the butter (or oil), buttermilk, sour cream, sugar and eggs together. Fold in soaked cornmeal and then the flour, baking powder, baking soda, salt and remaining ½ cup cornmeal to make a smooth batter. (This is easily blended by hand with a whisk)

Pour into prepared baking dish. Place on the baking sheet and bake until cornbread springs back when lightly touched, 25-27 minutes.

Brush immediately with melted butter when it comes out of the oven.

Serves 6-8

Thanksgiving Cranberry Ripple Biscotti

The cranberry orange filling, set in a vanilla biscotti batter makes for a sensational taste and visual impact. The nuts are optional but there is something festive about the small nubs of pistachios amid a vanilla cookie, ribboned with a bit of scarlet.

CRANBERRY FILLING

3/4 cup orange juice

Zest of one small orange

Pinch cinnamon

1/3 cup sugar

1 ½ cup dried cranberries

1 cup fresh cranberries

1/3 cup yellow raisins

BISCOTTI BATTER

1 cup unsalted butter, melted

2 cups sugar

1 tablespoon pure vanilla extract

3 eggs

4 cups all-purpose flour

2 ½ teaspoons baking powder

½ teaspoon salt

½ cup finely chopped pistachios (or almonds), optional

For the filling, in a medium sized saucepan over low heat, place orange juice, zest, cinnamon, sugar, cranberries and raisins. Stir to soften fruit. If fruit sticks, add a bit more water to help it simmer along. Stir for five to ten minutes. Remove from stove and place in food processor bowl. Let cool about 5 minutes. Process, adding water only if mixture seems too thick, to make a thick paste. Refrigerate 1-2 hours before using (or make the filling in advance).

Preheat the oven to 350°F. Line a baking sheet with parchment paper. Spray a 9 by 13 inch pan with non-stick cooking spray and line it with a piece of parchment paper and place the pan on the baking sheet.

For the biscotti, in a mixer bowl, blend the butter and sugar well, adding in the vanilla and eggs. Fold in the flour, baking powder and salt to make a thick batter or dough. Fold in the pistachios. Place half the batter in the prepared pan. Spread on the cranberry filling. Spread the remaining batter on top (if it is too thick, you can also try loosening it with some orange juice or water but not too much – just to allow you to spread batter on top; it does not have to be perfect – it will bake and spread).

Bake until biscotti seem set and dry to the touch, about 45-60 minutes. Let cool well in pan and then in freezer about 1-2 hours (this makes them easier to cut)

Preheat the oven to 325°F. On a large cutting board, cut the biscotti into sticks, about ½ inch thick. Place on parchment paper lined baking sheet and bake to dry out biscotti, turning once to bake about 15 minutes per side to dry out or crisp each side.

Makes 30-40

Pumpkin Eruption Cheesecake

Chocolate Eruption Cheesecake from my cookbook, A Passion for Baking, needed competition in another festive, seasonal mode. I created a pumpkin patch triumph that's a sublime vanilla, pumpkin swirl cheesecake, pumped up with hunks of fresh pumpkin bread, brown sugar fudge, and a bit of spice to fuse the flavors. When the recipe first appeared online, at Betterbaking.com, it had 3200 downloads in one hour!

CRUST

1 cup graham crumbs

1/2 cup shortbread crumbs

1/3 cup unsalted butter, melted

1/4 cup dark brown sugar, firmly packed

1/4 teaspoon cinnamon

Pinch cloves

Pinch allspice

CHEESECAKE FILLING

2 1/2 pounds cream cheese, softened

1 cup sugar

1 14-ounce can sweetened condensed milk

1/3 cup all-purpose flour

2 1/2 teaspoons pure vanilla extract

5 eggs

1/2 cup whipping cream

1/4 cup sour cream

1/4 teaspoon cinnamon

1/2 teaspoon pumpkin pie spice

1/3 cup pumpkin puree

2 1/2 cups, loosely packed pumpkin bread cubes

1/2 cup chopped gingersnaps

1 1/4 cups diced vanilla fudge

1/4 cup butterscotch sundae topping

or 1/3 cup dulce de leche (warmed) *

WHITE CHOCOLATE DRIZZLE

1/2 cup chopped white chocolate, melted

1/4 teaspoon pure vanilla extract

1/8 teaspoon orange oil or orange extract

1/8 teaspoon cinnamon

* Dulce de leche, a caramel topping made from simmered condensed milk is usually available ready-made in most supermarkets or Latin food stores. If it is very solid, warm it a bit to use it in this and other recipes.

Have a pumpkin bread loaf ready. You will need 2 ½ cups cubed pumpkin bread for this recipe.

Preheat the oven to 350°F. Line a baking sheet with parchment paper. Generously spray a 10-inch spring form pan with non-stick cooking spray and place it the baking sheet. Cut pieces of parchment paper to make a collar for the pan, using non-stick spray as the 'glue' to hold it in place. This cake has a lot of batter in it and the parchment collar acts as a girdle to hold in the batter and allow the cake to rise and not topple over and out.

For the crust, put all the ingredients in the cheesecake pan and toss to moisten. Press crumbs into bottom of pan.

For the cheesecake filling, in a mixer bowl, blend the cream cheese with the sugar, condensed milk and flour. Then add in the vanilla and eggs. Blend in the shipping cream, sour cream, cinnamon, and pumpkin pie spice and mix well. Remove 1/3 of the mixture to a separate bowl and blend it with 1/3 cup pumpkin puree. To the remaining batter, gently blend in the pumpkin bread cubes, gingersnaps and fudge pieces. Spoon half into the cheesecake pan, drizzle on half the caramel sauce and then top with the reserved pumpkin-tinted cheesecake filling. Top with the remaining caramel sauce and then the remaining cheesecake batter. Using a knife, swirl slightly. Bake until just set, 45-55 minutes. Turn off oven and let sit in oven 2 hours and then refrigerate 8 hours or up until three days.

For the White Chocolate Drizzle, slowly melt the white chocolate over warm water and then whisk in extracts and cinnamon.

To serve the cheesecake, drizzle on the White Chocolate Glaze just before serving and offer Crème Anglaise on the side, per serving slice.

Serves 16-24

Butterscotch Bread Pudding

A gorgeous, caramel comfort dessert that is as good plain, as it is with fresh cream or a quick orange rum sauce, served warm. Another delectable option would be to serve warm, spiced, stewed apple slices on the side. This is deluxe Thanksgiving dessert choice.

BREAD PUDDING

6-7 cups leftover challah or brioche in 1-inch chunks

1 cup leftover blondies, coarsely chopped, optional

1/2 cup unsalted butter, melted

1 1/4 cup white sugar

1/4 cup light brown sugar, firmly packed

1 can evaporated milk

2 cups whipping cream

1 cup milk

8 eggs

1 tablespoon pure vanilla extract

1 teaspoon butterscotch extract, optional

2 tablespoons all-purpose flour

2 teaspoons baking powder

Pinch salt

1/3 cup butterscotch chips

1/4 cup Heath Bar or toffee chocolate bar, coarsely chopped

1/3 cup dulce de leche or caramel sundae topping

FINISHING TOUCHES

Butterscotch Orange Rum Sauce

Dulce de leche or butterscotch topping, warmed

BUTTERSCOTCH ORANGE SAUCE

¾ cup butterscotch or caramel sundae topping

¼ cup rum or orange juice

Juice of one orange

Preheat the oven to 350°F. Line a baking sheet with parchment paper. Generously spray a 9 by 13 inch baking pan with non-stick cooking spray and place on the baking sheet.

Prepare bread cubes and blondies and set aside. In a large bowl, whisk the butter, sugars, evaporated milk, whipping cream, milk, eggs extracts, flour, baking powder and salt until well blended. Gently fold in the bread and blondie cubes, then the butterscotch and toffee bar chips. Add the dulce in dollops and mix gently. Let soak 1 hour in the fridge.

Preheat the oven to 350°F. Bake 35-45 minutes until the custard is golden brown and sides are sizzling a bit (the butter will separate a bit from the edges) and the middle seems set (when lightly touched). If it is very jiggly, lower the temperature to 325°F and bake 10-15 minutes more.

For the Butterscotch Orange Sauce, warm the sundae topping in a small pot with the rum and orange juice, stirring to blend, just to meld flavors. Serve warm over bread pudding.

This freezes well or stays 3 days in the fridge – you can also prepare it, refrigerate it and bake it just before you require it). Warm, it is a dessert after a meal; cold and cut into squares, it is a moist square – you can have with coffee or tea.

Serves 8-12

Bourbon Crème Anglaise

A classic dessert sauce, that is wonderful on Pumpkin Eruption Cheesecake or drizzled warm over Butterscotch Bread Pudding.

2 cups whipping cream

1/4 teaspoon cinnamon

Pinch nutmeg

Pinch cloves

Pinch allspice

1 teaspoon pure vanilla extract

2 tablespoons bourbon

3 egg yolks

1/4 cup sugar

For the Crème Anglaise, fill a large bowl with ice and water. In a 2-3 quart saucepan, over medium heat, stir the cream with the spices until mixture is gently simmering. Remove from the heat. Stir in the vanilla extract and bourbon.

In a medium bowl, beat the egg yolks and sugar until pale and thick, about 2 minutes. Slowly drizzle in the cream, whisking all the while. Return the mixture to the saucepan and cook over medium heat until the sauce thickens, about 5-8 minutes. If mixture starts to burn, remove immediately and place in an ice bath, stirring until cool.

Cover with plastic wrap, pressing down against the surface to prevent a skin from forming. Refrigerate until well chilled, about 2 hours.

Serve warm or at room temperature. Refrigerate up to 3 days, reheat to serve.

Makes about 2 cups

FALL'S FAVORITE - A SOFT SPOT FOR BROWN SUGAR

Keeping brown sugar soft is not really a problem if you bake often. Brown sugar usually starts soft, and if you use it regularly, it has little chance to seize up. But just in case, and bearing in mind some batches of brown sugar can get hard and dry without warning, it helps to put in half an orange into the brown sugar container to help keep it soft. Alternatively, you can buy terra cotta brown sugar bears or similar, charming little figurines made for this task. Soak the terra cotta bear with water and then pop it in the brown sugar container. If you notice the brown sugar drying out, simply soak the terra cotta bear again and throw it back in to do its work. Your muffins, quick breads, squares, and donuts will thank you.

December's Kitchen

by Marcy Goldman

The winter season settles in

But not without that quiet din

Of doves and feathers for snow

That come lightly

So as not to bother Fall.

Butter and sugar dreams,

Laced with mistletoe

There is coffee on

And cinnamon coats the air

The hearth waits, keeping warm -

Impatient for that

Winter baking storm.

Winter, Small Baking

The Festive Season Sugar, Spice,
Butter, Chocolate and Spirits

Winter in the Bakery

There's a special feeling of 'winter-on-the-way'. It's a suspended moment between autumn and that first snowfall. The air is cold and dry; the streets are brittle; the trees are bare and twiggy, spindly in their leafless state. Many of the birds, except for those that brave the winter, such as sparrows, have long flown south. On the home front, the Ugg suede boots are ready to go, winter coats are retrieved from the closet and a new snow shovel, sits, at the ready, by the door. Without remarking on the weather too much, you just sense the air is oh-so-alive, poised and taut. It doesn't matter how cold it is, until the ground has been kissed by snow, it is still that pregnant pause between one seasonal shore and the other one up ahead.

Then one night or late afternoon – it could be late November or early December, the first snow comes. Softly at first, tentative about its welcome and then finally it comes down earnest. Those gentle, little feathers, tiny as angel kisses, are soon replaced by huge squalls of white flakes that no longer melt as soon as they land; instead they stay and that nondescript tableau of 'between seasons' is now a winter wonderland!

The snow provides a blanket of serenity that's especially noticeable if you're out walking and witness the snowy beauty under the moonlight. It's a timeless portrait that makes your heart sing as it makes your toes tingle. It makes me think of Frost's poem, Stopping by the Woods One Snowy Evening or the movie, It's a Wonderful Life.

Winter is the heart of that once-a-year holiday kitchen, all decked out with an added, festive glow. The hearth has been stoked for a few months now as we bakers have been getting in gear throughout fall (as if the prior months, with their own baking bustle, was but a practice run!) Perhaps the good aura is simply about the sheer delight of being cozy inside and having vistas of baking to do. This is *our* time; we tell ourselves: *I'll make bread and a crockpot of soup as I bake up fruitcakes, strudel and sugar cookies. People, family and friends will drop by and I'll be ready with great food!* No matter what one's plans are for winter holidays, the prospect of being home and warm, away from the regular routines and reconnecting with ourselves, our homes, family and friends is a tonic.

What we also seem to need more of at this time of year is connection. Winter can make you want to hibernate but the holidays bring us together. Getting together with others, as well as baking away the days, soothes what ails us, no matter how much snow there is on the ground. Celebrate the winter holiday times with family and friends; there's nothing a little piece of shortbread can't fix or healing it can't tend to.

In December, the days are both shorter and darker but there is another sort of light in the distance. This light glows gold with joy and it's the beacon of the holidays ahead. It's the light of family-and-friends times and the promise of many gatherings, of old and new traditions, be they large or small but all bright, beautiful, celebratory and joyous. That twinkling holiday light gives credence to the calendar and historical wisdom, reminding us that there is lightness in spirit (as well as the baking) to be had, even in the darkest times. To me, this is the underlying meaning of the December holidays and why they're so cherished. They arrive just as we need them and their eternal message of good will and peace the most.

Perfume of Winter

Winter's perfume is luxury, elegance, warmth and a touch of spirits or liqueurs – brandy, rum, and velvety wines. Winter's perfume is a lush decant, rivered with dark, milk and white chocolate, fresh spices, and the best of imported dried fruits.

Base Notes

White sugar, sweet butter, Madagascar pure vanilla, brandy

Heart Notes

Chocolate, marzipan, toffee

Top Notes

Nutmeg, exotic extracts, imported spirits, clementines, cranberries, preserved cherries and pistachios

Theme Mood

Joy, Celebration, Traditions, Community

Theme Colors

Gold, Silver, Red and Green

The Scent of the Holidays

As with the every other season, I create my winter house décor in tandem with the mood and times. I bring in spruce boughs in and set them in vases or on a platter with clementines; I stick a chunky candle in a bowl of fresh cranberries (alongside a ton of Hanukkah decorations). I keep a special steaming kettle on the stove that has a lattice top that allows the fragrant steam to waft and permeate the air. I fill the steamer with water, sliced oranges, cinnamon sticks and a vanilla bean or two. It simmers merrily all day, ensuring that whether I bake or not, a wonderful scent uplifts my home and my mood. It's a homecoming welcome like no other. When friends drop by or family returns, a big 'ah that smells so good' is the reward you'll get.

The Style of Winter Baking

Winter Flavor and Ingredient Palate

Sugar, spice, butter, vanilla, chocolate, spirits, nuts, and preserved fruit, heritage recipes, nostalgia.

How does a baker interpret the winter season? In buttery decadence fused with enticing chocolate and a plethora of special-occasion ingredients, including nuts, dried fruits and tempting spirits – and for sure, lots of cream and butter!

We bakers love to showcase the winter season with plenty of homey as well as elegant cookies, luxurious, sweet-yeasted pastries, majestic holiday cakes, with dried or preserved fruits, toasted nuts and a generous dose of spirits, in the way of aged liqueurs, wines and brandy. But all of it, modest or extravagant, is lovingly laced with tradition. We might add something new, indeed, that is how food evolves but no doubt about it, winter baking is about heritage and customs passed down for generations. No wonder this time of year's baking is so cherished. It packs a punch of sentimentality like no other.

At year's end, there's yet another occasion to bake: the black tie New Year's Eve baking and then sweetly, two months later, just as you think winter will never end and have forgotten the happy times of the holidays just past, there is Valentine's Day. With Cupid's cue, our baking impetus is revived as we bake for others, gifting chocolate and butter, and passing on the love. And then of course, there is mid-term break and impromptu snow-days, bake sales of winter and birthdays – always something baking up a storm in the winter kitchen.

Winter, Small Recipes

Sweet Clementine Marmalade

Scone Mix, Holiday Gift Baking

Punitions or French Butter Cookies

Pumpkin Pie Biscotti

Butter and Cream Shortbread Biscotti

Orange Hazelnut Biscotti

Winter Fruits Hanukkah Mandelbrot

Classic Pecan Pie Squares

Ice-Cream Dough Rugulah

Meyer Lemon Hamantashen

Cookies and Cream Cheesecake Truffles

Cookie Swap Sugar Cookie Dough

French Mint Cookies

Blueberry Cranberry Eccles Cakes

Fiori di Sicilia Cookies

New Zealand Gingernuts

Czechoslovakian Butter Cookie Bars

Fleur de Sel Scottish Shortbread

Dark Brown Sugar Scottish Shortbread

Bavarian Sugar Cookies

Moravian Sugar Cookies

Dark Brown Sugar Shortbread

Fleur de Sel Shortbread

Moravian Butter Thin Cookies

Apricot Kolache

Pink Heart Cream Scones with White Chocolate and Dried Strawberries

Red Velvet Chocolate Chunk Cookies

Snow Day Brownie Stuffed Tollhouse Cookies

Mexican Dark Chocolate Cupcakes

Classic Madeleines

Sweet Clementine Marmalade

This is an extraordinary marmalade that's not at all bitter and guaranteed to make a marmalade lover out of anyone. The trick is using sweet, seedless clementines which are wonderfully thin-skinned, making them perfect in marmalade. You'll love this tart, citrus, uplifting conserve. Serve with scones or English muffins, it does double duty as a holiday gift, packed with a jar of homemade scone mix.

3 pounds or one small wood crate of seedless small oranges (clementines, mandarins, tangerines)

2 large lemons

10 cups of water

7 cups sugar

Wash fruit well. Slice the clementines and lemons and slice in 1/8 inch slices. Remove any seeds.

Soak sliced fruit in the 10 cups of cold water overnight.

Next day, simmer fruit and water in an open kettle until peel is tender and mixture has reduced somewhat - about 15 minutes. Add sugar and over low heat, stir to dissolve sugar.

Cook over low to medium heat, simmer fruit until gel stage is reached (1-2 hours or less, but otherwise, 220°F on candy/jelly thermometer). When mixture thickens, it means it's at gel stage. Sometimes, depending on the natural pectin in the fruit or the particular batch clementines, this can take 90 minutes or a bit more. It will certainly take at least an hour so just give it the time it needs, relax, and put listen to music as it cooks down.

Remove pot from heat just as marmalade seems ready - maybe a bit before soft ball stage (220°F) as preserves thicken and continues to cook after removing from stove.

Allow marmalade to stand for one or two minutes, then ladle into sterilized jars. Process in boiling water bath 15 minutes.

Makes about 4-5 small (pint) jars

IS THE JAM SET? COLD SAUCER TEST FOR DONENESS FOR CLEMENTINE MARMALADE AND MORE...

This is my favourite and easiest test. I call it the cold saucer test. Place a saucer in the freezer for 20 minutes. Ladle some marmalade on the saucer. If it begins to thicken, or when the saucer is tilted, the marmalade runs in one thick stream, it is probably done. When the look of the marmalade and the temperature reading, as well as the time (45-90 minutes) as well as the saucer test all point to "done", then the marmalade is done. It will also thicken further on cooling.

Scone Mix, Holiday Gift Baking

Saco Foods makes a buttermilk powder which is a core part of this secret mix for gourmet scones, You can also see if your local bulk food store carries buttermilk powder but to me, nothing compares with Saco. Don't forget to include directions to use the dry mix in your gift card.

9 cups all-purpose flour

3/4 cup Saco Buttermilk Blend or dry buttermilk powder

2 1/4 cups sugar

1 3/4 teaspoons salt

3 tablespoons baking powder

1 1/2 teaspoons baking soda

3 cups very cold, unsalted butter, cut into chunks

TO MAKE SCONES

3 cups scone mix

1 egg

1/3 - 1/2 cup water or one of the following: orange juice, lemonade, ginger ale, seltzer

1 teaspoon vanilla

FINISHING TOUCHES

1 egg, whisked

Sugar

In a large bowl, place flour, buttermilk powder, sugar, salt, baking powder and baking soda. Using a large whisk, stir dry ingredients together very well. By hand, or using a pastry blender, cut butter into ingredients to form a grainy, uneven mixture (it doesn't have to be perfect - some larger chunks are fine). You may also do this with a food processor. Process about one-third of the mix at a time, pulsing the processor to cut the fat into the flour.

Freeze in containers or bags, using about four cups of mix per bag or pack in a decorative Mason jar.

You can also add chocolate chips or raisins (2 cups) per batch of dry mix.

Preheat the oven to 425°F. Line a baking sheet with parchment paper.

Place mix in a bowl and make a well in center. Stir together egg, water and vanilla and gently blend in with fork to make a soft mass. Turn out onto a lightly floured work surface and knead about 15 seconds. Pat into an 8-inch round and cut into wedges. Brush with whisked egg and sprinkle with sugar. Bake on upper third of oven. After 10 minutes, reduce heat to 400°F. Bake until nicely golden, 15-18 minutes.

Makes 8-12 scones, depending on size

Punitions or French Butter Cookies

Punitions are a cross between shortbread and a butter cookie and are about the size of a fifty-cent coin. Crisp and sandy, they keep as well as biscotti, making them a perfect holiday gift cookie. One of my favorite variations is to make Punitions into Pink Champagne New Year's Cookies.

1/2 cup plus 2 tablespoons unsalted butter

1/2 cup fine sugar *

1 egg

Pinch salt

2 cups all-purpose flour, or more, as required

FINISHING TOUCHES

Fine sugar

* To make fine sugar, grind or pulverize until fine in a food processor.

Stack two large baking sheets together and line the top one with parchment paper.

In a food processor, pulse the butter and sugar together to make a crumbly mixture, and then process longer, to make a creamed, pasty mixture, a couple of minutes. Add in the egg and blend well and then the salt and flour. Blend a minute or two until it clumps but does not hold together. Turn the dough out onto a lightly floured board. If it seems too soft to roll, knead in a bit more flour, up to 1/4 cup or so. Wrap and refrigerate the dough 10-20 minutes to help it roll easier (and so as not to add excess flour).

Preheat the oven to 350°F. Divide dough in half. Roll each half out about 1/8- ¼ inch thickness. Cut in little cookies or discs about 2 inches. If you don't have a cookie cutter small enough, use a shot glass.

Bake until browned around the edges and beginning to color slightly on the tops, 14-18 minutes. Cookies crisp as they cool. Dust with finely ground sugar.

Makes about 80 small cookies

NEW YEAR'S PINK CHAMPAGNE COOKIES

PINK CHAMPAGNE GLAZE

2 cups confectioners' sugar

2-5 tablespoons, or as required, pink champagne or rose sparkling wine, to make thick glaze

Prepare cookies as per recipe. For Pink Champagne Glaze, in a small bowl, whisk together confectioner's sugar and champagne to make a spreadable glaze. Spread over cookies, let set.

Pumpkin Pie Biscotti

Crisp, spicy, seasonal treats. This is a seasonal sweet at its best, and it's a great holiday gift too. This is one of my personal favorite recipes but for some reason it's never before made it into any of my cookbooks. It is a blue-ribbon hit, perfect for munching or as a gift.

3/4 cup unsalted butter, melted

1 1/2 cups light brown sugar, firmly packed

1/2 cup white sugar

2 eggs

3/4 cup pumpkin puree

1 1/2 teaspoons bought or Homemade Pumpkin Pie Spice

1/2 teaspoon cinnamon

1/4 teaspoon cloves

2 teaspoons baking powder

1/4 teaspoon baking soda

¼ teaspoon salt

4 1/2 – 5 cups all-purpose flour

FINISHING TOUCHES
1 1/2 cups chopped white chocolate, melted

Preheat the oven to 350°F. Line a large baking sheet with parchment paper.

In a mixer bowl, blend the butter, brown sugar, white sugar, eggs, and pumpkin puree together. Stir in pumpkin pie spice, cinnamon, cloves, baking powder, baking soda, salt and most of the flour. Blend to make a stiff dough. Add in a bit more flour as required to make a stiff but soft batter.

Spread out the batter in two logs on baking sheets. (For larger biscotti, use the one large sheet and spread out one large log of biscotti).

Bake until the logs are set and dry to the touch about 35-50 minutes. Remove from the oven and lower the temperature to 325°F. Cool 15-20 minutes. Using a very sharp, long knife, slice each log into about 30 pieces. (Larger biscotti will take 15-20 minutes longer and you will less pieces, but larger size)

Replace biscotti back on baking sheets and bake a second time to dry and crisp cookies, about 20-30 minutes, turning the cookies once at midway point, to ensure even baking. Cool well. Smear white chocolate on one side of each cookie. Chill in the refrigerator to set.

Makes approximately 30 biscotti

Butter and Cream Shortbread Biscotti

This cookie soars the with unrivaled, pure flavors of the butter and brown sugar making it a biscotti with a shortbread pedigree. Serve these big and impressive or cut into smaller biscotti 'blocks' or cubes.

4 cups all-purpose flour

2 teaspoons baking powder

1/4 teaspoon baking soda

3/4 teaspoon salt

2 cups brown sugar, firmly packed

1 1/2 cups unsalted (cold) butter, in small chunks

1/2 cup whipping cream

1 teaspoon pure vanilla extract

Preheat the oven to 350°F. Line a baking sheet with parchment paper. Place an 8 by 11 inch pan on it.

In a food processor, briefly blend the flour with the baking powder, baking soda, salt and brown sugar. Cut in the butter until the mixture resembles a fine meal. Stir in cream and vanilla and process (pulsing and letting the machine run a few seconds) until you have a firm dough that just barely holds together. Add a bit more cream if mixture is very crumbly. Pat dough into the pan, ensuring it is flush with the sides, and the pan is evenly covered in the cookie dough.

Bake until lightly browned on top (35 to 38 minutes). If biscotti seems too soft in the center, lower the temperature to 325°F and allow to bake another 10-20 minutes until it's just set and gently browned all over. Alternatively, if biscotti seem to be browning too fast and are still soft in the center, lower the temperature earlier on and let it bake more slowly so it bakes through but doesn't burn. Remove from oven (keep the temperature 325°F).

Allow biscotti to cool 10 minutes and then gently cut it into 14-20 large biscotti sticks. Place the cookies on the parchment-lined baking sheet.

Return to oven to crisp for 15-20 minutes, turning once mid-bake. Cool well. Wrap or store in a lightly sealed tin or glass cookie jar.

Makes 14-20, depending on size. You can also cut these into small cookie squares or blocks for smaller cookies.

HOLIDAY BISCOTTI GETS PRETTIED UP FOR GIFT GIVING

While we're on the subject of holiday cookies, to my mind, nothing beats homemade biscotti for gift giving. It's the perfect holiday cookie and trend that won't quit. For my own gift-able biscotti, I sleuth out pretty cello bags as well as professional bakery boxes or festive tins. I also purchase a glass cookie jars and wrap them in colored cello paper and pretty ribbons. Biscotti is all about gorgeous baking that's both easy and crowd pleasing. Go one extra step and make sure the outer packaging suits the most worthy baking inside.

Orange Hazelnut Biscotti

Chocolate, citrus and buttery hazelnuts; who could ask for anything more? To remove hazelnut skins, toast the nuts at 325°F until lightly golden. Remove them from the oven, and using a clean kitchen towel, briskly rub off their dry outer skins. Pistachios are another good choice of nuts.

BISCOTTI

1/2 cup unsalted butter

3/4 cup sugar

Zest of one orange, finely minced

3 eggs

2 teaspoons pure vanilla extract

2 tablespoons orange liqueur such as Cointreau

3 cups all-purpose flour

2 1/2 teaspoons baking powder

1/4 teaspoon salt

2 tablespoons freeze dried instant coffee

1/2 cup hazelnuts, toasted, skins removed, coarsely chopped

½ cup whole hazelnuts, peeled

1 cup semi-sweet chocolate chips or chopped chocolate

FINISHING TOUCHES

1 cups semi-sweet chocolate, melted

Preheat the oven to 350°F. Line a baking sheet with parchment paper.

In a mixer bowl, cream the butter, sugar and orange zest. Add eggs, blending well, then stir in vanilla and orange liqueur. In a separate bowl, blend together the flour, baking powder, salt and instant coffee. Fold dry ingredients into batter, and then fold in nuts and chocolate. On a lightly floured work surface, divide dough in two sections. Roll each into a log about 9 inches long. Place, well-spaced on baking sheet. Flatten slightly with fingers.

Bake until lightly browned about 18-24 minutes. Cool 15 minutes then transfer to work surface. Using a serrated knife, cut in to 3/4 inch slices.

Place cookies back on baking sheet. Reduce oven heat to 325°F. Bake, 15-20 minutes, turning once at midpoint, until cookies are slightly coloured and seem dry. Cool well to crisp.

To glaze the cookies, have melted chocolate at the ready. Using a flat, small icing knife, spread melted chocolate on one side of each cookie. Cool on rack 2-4 hours until thoroughly dry. You can also freeze them but the gloss of the chocolate will dull.

Makes about 25-28 cookies

Winter Fruits Hanukkah Mandelbrot

This makes a crisp, crunchy, very homey cookie, that is similar to biscotti in that it's baked once as a log and then cut in cookie slices and baked again to crisp. The Special K gives it an added sense of nuttiness and an addictive crunch. The recipe is adapted from my friend Shari Reinhart's mother's famous mandelbrot recipe.

½ cup dried cherries

1/3 cup dried cranberries

½ cup dried California apricots

2 tablespoons dried blueberries

2 tablespoons dried yellow raisins

1 cup sugar

1 cup corn or canola oil

3 eggs

2 teaspoons pure vanilla extract

3 cups all-purpose flour

2 teaspoons baking powder

1/8 teaspoon salt

3 cups Special K cereal

¾ cup slivered almonds

FINISHING TOUCHES
Oil

Cinnamon

Sugar

Preheat the oven to 350°F. Stack two baking sheets together and line the top one with parchment paper.

Prepare the fruits (plump them in hot water, drain and pat dry) and put in a medium bowl.

In a mixer bowl, blend the sugar and oil well. Blend in the eggs and vanilla and mix well. Fold in the flour, baking powder and salt. Blend until almost smooth, and then fold in the Special K, almonds and fruits. Mix well; this is a thick dough. On a lightly floured work surface, divide dough in three and roll into three logs about 2-3 inches thick. Place on baking sheet and brush lightly with oil and dust lightly with cinnamon and sugar.

Bake until firm and dry to the touch, about 30-40 minutes. Reduce temperature to 300°F.

Cool logs well and then carefully cut into ¾ inch slices. Replace on baking sheet and bake, turning once, about 20 minutes.

Makes 3-4 dozen

Classic Pecan Pie Squares

These are also welcome at Thanksgiving or anytime you need a buttery, caramel indulgence. During winter holiday time, cut these squares into tinier little bites and serve them as part of the holiday cookie platter. This makes a big batch that does double duty as hospitality treats or a lovely gift.

BROWN SUGAR SHORTBREAD CRUST

2 cups all-purpose flour

1/3 cup white sugar

3 tablespoons brown sugar

¼ teaspoon salt

¼ teaspoon baking powder

3/4 cup unsalted butter, in 1 inch cubes

3 tablespoons whipping cream

PECAN PIE TOPPING

3/4 cup unsalted butter, melted

1 1/4 cups light brown sugar, firmly packed

½ cup corn syrup

3 eggs

2 tablespoons whipping cream

Tiny pinch salt

1 1/2 cups pecans, coarsely chopped

½ cup whole pecans (shelled)

Preheat the oven to 350°F. Line a baking sheet with parchment paper. Generously spray a 9 by 9 inch or 9 by 13 inch square pan with nonstick cooking spray. Place pan on baking sheet.

In a food processor, blend flour, white sugar, brown sugar, salt and baking powder together. Add in the butter and pulse to break in the butter and cream until the mixture just barely begins to hold together. Press into prepared pan and bake 20 minutes. Remove from oven. Reduce oven temperature to 325°F.

For the Pecan Pie Topping, in a medium bowl, using a whisk, blend the butter, brown sugar, corn syrup, eggs, cream, eggs and salt. Fold in pecans. Pour onto the baked crust.

Bake 35-45 minutes or until filling is just set. Cool well or refrigerate before cutting into bars.

Makes 2-3 dozen, depending on size

Ice Cream Dough Rugulah

I like quirky things and a dairy-rich dough for rugulah is nicely quirky but also Hanukkah-appropriate. Fill this supple dough with cinnamon/sugar or chocolate chips. Just make sure you use a great vanilla ice-cream that is rich and creamy and not 'lite' or air-filled for the flakiest pastry dough.

ICE-CREAM PASTRY DOUGH

1 cup unsalted butter

4 cups all-purpose flour

¼ teaspoon salt

2 cups vanilla ice-cream, slightly softened

FILLING

½ cup white sugar

1 ½ cups brown sugar, firmly packed

1 tablespoon cinnamon

1 cup ground walnuts

1 1/2 cups raisins, plumped and dried (miniature chocolate chips)

1 cup apricot or raspberry jam

FINISHING TOUCHES

Egg wash (2 eggs, whisked)

Sugar

For the dough, in a food processor, pulse to blend butter and the flour to make a grainy mixture. Add in the salt and mix briefly and then spoon in the ice-cream and process to make a soft dough. Wrap and refrigerate 4 hours or overnight.

For the filling, in a bowl, blend the sugars, cinnamon and nuts, and raisins or chocolate chips, whatever you are using. Divide dough into 4 portions and wrap them in a large plastic Ziploc bag. Preheat the oven to 350°F.

Stack two baking sheets together and line top one with parchment paper. On a well-floured board, roll dough out to a circle about 10-12 inches. Spread on some jam and then sprinkle with ¼ of the sugar nut mixture, and then top with raisins or chocolate chips. Alternatively, spread with ¼ of the cherry pie filling. (If using cherry pie filling, use 1 cup of filling and omit sugar/cinnamon and nut mixture.)

Cut in 12 wedges and roll each into a crescent. Place on baking sheet and brush with egg wash and sprinkle with sugar. Bake until golden brown, 25-30 minutes. Cool on a rack.

Makes 48

Meyer Lemon Hamantashen

Sometimes, particularly in winter, you need something spring-like: tart and uplifting. These pastry-like cookies are just the thing. Refreshing Meyer Lemon curd is the perfect filling as the tang of the citrus is lovely against the buttery hamantashen. These are extraordinary at holiday time and of course, perfect for Purim, when the spring rolls around.

HAMANTASHEN DOUGH

1 cup unsalted butter

1 1/4 cups sugar

3 eggs

1/4 cup orange juice or milk

1 1/2 teaspoon pure vanilla extract

4 cups all-purpose flour, approximately

2 1/2 teaspoons baking powder

1/2 teaspoon salt

MEYER LEMON CURD

3/4 cup sugar

2 eggs

2 egg yolks

1/2 cup Meyer lemon juice

½ cup fresh (regular) lemon juice

Zest of one lemon, finely minced

¼ teaspoon pure lemon oil or pure lemon extract

2 tablespoons unsalted butter, melted

FINISHING TOUCHES

Egg wash (2 eggs, whisked)

Sugar

For the dough, in a mixer bowl, cream the butter with the sugar. Add eggs and blend until smooth. (If mixture is hard to blend or seems curdled, add a bit of the flour to bind it).

Stir in orange juice or milk and vanilla. Fold in flour, baking powder and salt. Mix to make a firm but soft dough. Transfer dough to a lightly floured work surface and pat into a smooth mass. Cover and let rest ten minutes. Divide dough in three and flattened into three flattened disks. Place the discs in a Ziplock bag and refrigerate for at least an hour.

For the Meyer Lemon Curd, in a two-quart saucepan, whisk together the sugar, eggs and yolks until combined. Add in the Meyer lemon juice, regular lemon juice, lemon zest and lemon oil. Over low heat, whisk until well mixed and sugar dissolves. Add in butter and continue whisking until mixture is homogeneous. Continue heating until the mixture thickens to the consistency of a custard. Remove from stove; cool to at least room temperature and then refrigerate (snugly covered, don't leave room for a vapor barrier to form or otherwise it will induce moisture into the set curd) for 1-3 hours. Whisk before using.

Preheat the oven to 350°F.

Roll the dough out on a well-floured surface. (If dough is very cold or stiff, using a rolling pin, gently pound the dough a bit to soften it; then roll) Then roll the dough to about 1/4" thick. If it's very sticky, you may want to knead in some extra flour. Using a 2 1/2" round cutter - this can vary on your preference - cut out circles as close together as possible.

Place about 3/4 of a teaspoon of lemon curd in the center of each circle. Fold up two sides of the circle, and pinch together well to seal, then repeat with the remaining side, pinching both corners. Resist the urge to overfill these, as that will lead them to open during baking. Brush with egg wash and sprinkle lightly with sugar.

Bake 15-20 minutes, until just beginning to brown at the corners. Let cool on the sheets for 5 minutes, and then remove to a wire rack to cool completely.

Makes 3-4 dozen

Cookies and Cream Cheesecake Truffles

These are cheesecake minis and are simply a symphony of creamy cool cheesecake and hot fudge. Pretty, easy and totally gourmet-store in looks, it's a stunner in taste too.

VANILLA CHEESECAKE FILLING

1 1/2 pounds cream cheese, room temperature

1 cup sugar

1 package vanilla pudding (any size, instant or regular)

4 eggs

2 teaspoons pure vanilla extract

1 1/2 cups chopped Oreos or chocolate sandwich cookies (about ¾ package)

FINISHING TOPPINGS

1 cup semi-sweet chocolate, melted

Oreo cookies, finely chopped into crumbs

Preheat the oven to 350°F.

Spray a 10 inch spring-form pan with non-stick cooking spray. Place on a parchment paper lined baking sheet.

In a food processor, cream the cream cheese and sugar until well blended. Add in the pudding mix, eggs and vanilla and blend well until smooth. Stir in the chopped cookies.

Bake until just set, 35-45 minutes. Remove from the oven and let cool at room temperature an hour. Cover lightly with wax paper and refrigerate overnight.

Scoop cheesecake, with a melon baller or ice-cream scoop into truffles or balls. For leftover edges of cheesecake, use your hands to form balls or more pops.

Put a fork in center and dip into melted chocolate. Place on parchment paper and chill briefly and then sprinkled additional cookie crumbs if desired. Place in chocolate confectioners' liners as you would for chocolate truffles. Keep refrigerated (but they keep an hour or two at room temperature before serving)

Makes about 30-45, depending on size.

Cookie Swap Sugar Cookie Dough

The perfect sugar cookie dough is the foundation to any variation of cookie you can imagine. Add in ground nuts or spices or food coloring or citrus zest. But it all begins with this one amenable dough. This is crisp but tender and rolls like a charm. You can double the recipe as you like, refrigerate dough for a few days or freeze 1-2 months.

½ cup unsalted butter

1 cup sugar

1 egg

1 teaspoon pure vanilla extract

1 tablespoon whipping cream

2 cups all-purpose flour

¾ teaspoon baking powder

¼ teaspoon salt

In a mixer bowl, cream the butter and sugar until light and well-combined. Stir in the egg, vanilla and cream and blend well. Fold in the flour, baking powder and salt and blend to make a soft dough, making sure no ingredient remain unblended in the well of the bowl. Wrap dough in two portions and refrigerate 2-3 hours. (Dough can stay refrigerated 2-3 days; frozen 1-2 months)

Preheat the oven to 350°F. Line a large baking sheet with parchment paper.

On a lightly floured surface, using one roll of the dough at a time, roll the dough to a thickness of 1/8 inch. Cut into preferred shapes. Place on cookie sheet, and bake 10-14 minutes, until edges of cookies are lightly browned.

You can decorate these before baking (milk or egg glaze, colored sugar or sprinkles) or with icing, afterwards.

Makes 2-3 dozen, depending on size

IT'S NOT "JUST" BUTTER WHEN IT COMES TO HOLIDAY COOKIES

I never take butter for granted because it's always integral to my baking and because it's never been a bargain ingredient. (Fellow baking cookbook authors agree!). Sterling of character, butter holds the baking together in flavor harmony that's never more evident than with holiday butter cookies. You can call it sweet butter or more popularly, unsalted butter, but use all butter. This is not the time to substitute with any other fat – especially as some recipes are simply butter, sugar and flour –nothing else to detract so the flavor had better be exemplary. Although if diet requirements necessitate some other choices, coconut oil (make sure it's really chilled) is another way to go but the flavor won't be the same.

French Mint Cookies

The fusion of mint and chocolate never fails to impress. These are decadent fudge cookies with crackly tops and a texture between cookie and a brownie. Served warm, they are anointed with a peppermint patty that melts into a pool of chocolate and mint heaven which is swirled for a marbleized effect.

¾ cup semi-sweet chocolate, melted

1/2 cup unsalted butter, softened

1/2 cup brown sugar, firmly packed

3/4 cup white sugar

1 egg

1 teaspoon pure vanilla extract

1 3/4 cups all-purpose flour

1/2 teaspoon baking powder

1/4 teaspoon baking soda

1/8 teaspoon salt

1/2 cup semi-sweet chocolate chips, preferably miniature

24 small peppermint patties

Preheat the oven to 350°F. Double up two sets of baking sheets and top each set with parchment paper.

Prepare the chocolate. In a mixer bowl, with the paddle attachment, cream the butter, brown sugar and white sugar. Blend in egg and vanilla and then blend in the melted chocolate. Fold in flour, baking powder, baking soda, salt and blend until almost smooth; fold in chocolate chips.

Form dough into walnut sized balls and place, evenly spaced, on baking sheet.

Bake until just set, about 12-14 minutes.

Remove from the oven and immediately place a peppermint patty on top of each cookie and press gently. In a few minutes, gently smear melting mint to ice top of cookie. Chill slightly or leave set at room temperature.

Makes 30-40 cookies, depending on size

Blueberry Cranberry Eccles Cakes

Eccles Cakes are a wonderful British classic of puff pastry filled with dried fruit – traditionally currants and dried orange peel. I love the concept of buttery pastry and a fruity filling.

ECCLES CAKE PASTRY
½ pound all-butter puff pastry (purchased or homemade)

FILLING
1/3 cup white sugar

1/3 cup light brown sugar, firmly packed

¼ cup unsalted butter

2-3 pinches fresh nutmeg

¼ teaspoon cinnamon

Zest of one small orange, finely minced

1/3 cup dried blueberries

1/3 cup currants, plumped and dried

1/3 cup dried cranberries, plumped and dried

1/3 cup raisins, plumped and dried

1/3 cup apricot or raspberry jam

FINISHING TOUCHES
Water

Sugar, coarse or regular

Unsalted butter, melted

Preheat the oven to 425°F. Stack two baking sheets together. Line the top one with parchment paper.

For the filling, in a medium saucepan, combine the white sugar, brown sugar and butter and cook over a medium heat until the butter melts. Remove from the stove and add a dusting of nutmeg, cinnamon, the orange zest, blueberries, currants, cranberries and raisins and jam.

For the pastry, on a lightly floured work surface, roll the puff pastry between ¼ and 1/8 inch. Cut into 4 1/2 inch rounds. Place a spoonful of filling into each pastry center. Brush the edges of the pastry with egg white and fold over the pastry to make a half moon. Alternatively, put fruit filling on a circle of pastry; paint perimeter of pastry with water or some egg white and then top another circle of pastry as the top or cover. Press fork tines around the edges to seal. Roll lightly with a rolling pin to flatten pastry.

On top surface of pastries, using a paring knife, make a few slits. Brush with water and sprinkle with sugar. Bake until golden brown all over, about 20-25 minutes. Cool slightly before eating (take care, filling will be hot). Recipe doubles well.

Makes 12-16

Fiori Di Sicilia Cookies

Tiny little butter cookies, that taste like an orange-vanilla Creamsicle © in a cookie. These are good plain or if you want to go an extra step, they are spectacular when filled with a good quality, store-bought lemon curd. For the orange-scented white chocolate glaze, use an imported, high-quality white chocolate such as Lindt or Callebaut.

COOKIE DOUGH

½ cup sugar

1/2 cup plus 2 tablespoons unsalted butter, softened

1 egg

1 teaspoon Fiori Di Sicilia *

2 cups all-purpose flour

1/8 teaspoon salt

GLAZE

5-6 ounces white chocolate, melted

1 teaspoon Fiori Di Sicilia

* Fiori Di Sicilia is available from King Arthur flour. If you don't have it on hand, use ½ teaspoon each almond extract, orange extract or orange oil, and 1 teaspoon pure vanilla extract to replace to Fiori Di Sicilia.

Preheat the oven to 350°F. Stack two baking sheets together and line the top one with parchment paper.

In a food processor, pulse the sugar and butter together to make a crumbly mixture, and then process longer to make a creamed, pasty mixture, about two minutes. Add in the egg and the Fiori Di Sicilia extract. Blend well and fold in the flour and salt. Blend a minute or two until it clumps but barely holds together. Turn the dough out onto a lightly floured board. Press together to make a smooth dough. Divide in half. Roll each half out about 1/8 inch thick. Cut into small discs about 1 1/2 inch. You can make them thicker or larger but this is a nice size.

Place the cookies on the baking sheet and bake until browned around the edges and beginning to color on the tops, 12-16 minutes. Cool 15 minutes.

For the glaze, gently melt the chocolate in a bowl over steaming water. Whisk in the Fiori Di Sicilia extract to blend. Smear white chocolate on each cookie and let set.

Makes about 60 small cookies

New Zealand Gingernuts

These are hard, dunking cookies with chewy centers that will make a ginger and spice cookie lover out of you (and despite their name, they are nut-free). These sweet, hard, spicy cookies beg for tea and fireside chats, especially in the holiday season. A gift of a recipe, adapted from my friend, Leone Lamb of New Zealand.

5 tablespoons unsalted butter

3 tablespoons golden syrup (such as Lyle's) or corn syrup

2 tablespoon honey or molasses

2 tablespoons water

1 egg

3/4 cup dark brown sugar, firmly packed

1 cup white sugar

2 ¾ -3 cups all-purpose flour

3/4 teaspoon baking powder

2 teaspoons baking soda

4 teaspoons (ground) ginger

1 1/2 teaspoon cinnamon

1/8 teaspoon cloves

FINISHING TOUCHES
Sugar

Preheat the oven to 350°F. Stack two baking sheets together and line the top one with parchment paper.

In a small saucepan, melt the butter and stir in the syrup and honey (or molasses). Let cool. Stir in the water. Place in a large mixer bowl. Add in the egg, brown sugar and and white sugar, stirring well. Fold in flour, baking powder, baking soda, ginger, cinnamon and cloves to make a very stiff dough, adding more flour if required. Roll into small plum-sized balls, place on baking sheet and flatten with a fork. Alternatively, roll balls in fine sugar and place on baking sheet, flattening slightly.

Bake 15-18 minutes until set and dry to touch, and starting to crackle on top.

Makes 3-3 1/2 dozen, depending on size

Czechoslovakian Butter Cookie Bars

Layered butter cookies with imported jam of any flavour (I favour plum or apricot but raspberry or cherry are popular) make a stack of cookies you simply cut and wrap or serve. A delectable, deluxe recipe that is especially handy if you're time-pressed.

1 cup unsalted butter

1 cup sugar

2 egg yolks

1/4 teaspoon salt

2 cups all-purpose flour

1/2 cup apricot, plum or cherry jam

3/4 cup finely chopped walnuts

2 tablespoons sugar

Preheat the oven to 350°F. Line a baking sheet with parchment paper. Spray an 8 by 8 inch or 9 by 9-inch pan with non-stick cooking spray and place on baking sheet.

In a mixer bowl or food processor, cream the butter and sugar until light and fluffy. Add in egg yolks, then salt and flour to make a soft dough. Divide dough in half and wrap, then freeze half of it while preparing the rest of the recipe. (Dough needs an hour to freeze)

Spread the remaining half of the dough into the pan. Top with the jam and refrigerate while waiting for the top dough to freeze. Once the frozen dough is ready, using a cheese grater, shred the dough. Sprinkle the shredded frozen dough over the jam layer. Sprinkle on the nuts and sugar.

Bake one hour. Cool and cut into very tiny bars or squares, about 1-½ inch square each.

Makes about five dozen of (very tiny) bars or squares

Fleur de Sel Scottish Shortbread

Pulverized sugar is the trick along with a smidgen of rice flour and slow baking but the real sensation here is using the crème de la crème of salts, fleur de sel. Considered too expensive for all your cooking, fleur de sel, harvested by skimming the top layer of sea salt, is perfect for baking.

¾ cup sugar

1 cup unsalted butter

1 tablespoon rice flour *

2 cups all-purpose flour

½ teaspoon (fine) fleur de sel or sea salt *

* If you don't have rice flour, use cornstarch

In a food processor, whiz the sugar to finely pulverize, about 10 seconds.

In a mixer bowl, cream the sugar and butter on slow speed until well blended and then add in the rice flour, flour and salt and blend to make a firm dough.

Knead the dough on a lightly floured work surface about 1 minute, to make dough very firm. Flatten the dough into a disc, place in a Ziplock bag; refrigerate 30 minutes.

Preheat the oven to 325°F. Stack two baking sheets together and line top one with parchment paper.

Roll the dough out gently and cut into cookies or sticks that are ½ to ¾ inch thick. Place on prepared cookie sheet. Bake, immediately reducing temperature to 300°F until lightly browned, about 40-50 minutes.

Cool well. Keep in a tin; cookies improve with age.

Makes 24-36 cookies

SHORT TALES OF SHORTBREAD MOLDS

Shortbread is one of the simplest, most beloved of all cookies. Almost every country makes their own version but the Scots, of course, are most credited with the best, most heirloom shortbread recipes to be found. There's only four elements: flour, sugar, butter and a pinch of salt. Then there's options such as brown sugar, rice or corn flour, cream the butter or cut it in, slow bake or not, and cut freeform or pack the shortbread into molds. Shortbread molds were once made of wood or ceramic but today, you can find reproduction molds of vintage designs. Nordic Ware offers one in metal cast which guarantees easy release of the baked shortbread. Long gone, Hartstone Pottery, in Ohio was famous for their shortbread molds, so try EBay or yard sells for those. A gift of a shortbread mold, along with baked fresh shortbread and the recipe is perfect for anyone on your list.

Dark Brown Sugar Shortbread

Deep butterscotch in character, this is a very fine shortbread and stunning if you use a classic Scottish thistle or Celtic heart shortbread mold.

1 cup unsalted butter

1 cup dark brown sugar, firmly packed

1 tablespoon rice flour or cornstarch

2 cups all-purpose flour

1/4 teaspoon salt

In a mixer bowl, cream the butter and sugar. Cream on slow speed until well blended and then add in the rice flour, flour, and salt and blend to make firm dough.

Knead on a lightly floured work surface about 1 minute, to make dough very firm. Flatten the dough in a disc, wrap well and refrigerate 30 minutes.

Preheat the oven to 325°F. Double up two baking sheets and line top one with parchment paper.

Roll out gently and cut into cookies or sticks that are 1/2 to 3/4 inch thick. Place on prepared cookie sheet and in oven, immediately reducing temperature to 300°F until lightly browned, about 40-50 minutes.

Cool well. Keep in a tin; cookies improve with age.

Makes 24-36 cookies

Bavarian Sugar Cookies

Sometimes, when we lose ourselves in fear and despair, in routine and constancy, in hopelessness and tragedy, we can thank God for Bavarian sugar cookies. And fortunately, when there aren't any cookies, we can still find reassurance in a familiar hand on our skin, or a kind and loving gesture, or a subtle encouragement, or a loving embrace, or an offer of comfort. **Quote from Stranger than Fiction, a film with Will Farrell, Dustin Hoffman, and Emma Thompson**

1 cup unsalted butter, softened

1 cup sugar

2 teaspoons pure vanilla extract

1 egg

2 1/2 cups all-purpose flour, approximately

3 tablespoons finely ground toasted almonds, optional

1/8 teaspoon fresh nutmeg

2 teaspoons cream of tartar

1 teaspoon baking soda

1/8 teaspoon salt

FINISHING TOUCHES
Sugar

In a mixer bowl, cream the butter and sugar well and then add the vanilla extract and egg and blend well. Fold in almost all the flour, almonds, nutmeg, cream of tartar, baking soda, and salt and mix well to make a stiff dough. If dough is very soft (it needs to be stiff enough to be rolled out) add a more flour although chilling the dough will also help firm it up.

Cover and let rest 20 minutes or chill up until 3 days (you can also freeze this dough up to a month).

Preheat the oven to 350°F. Stack two baking sheets together and line the top one with parchment paper.

Warm up dough (on the counter) if it has been refrigerated before rolling out (an hour on the counter should be fine). On a lightly floured work surface, roll dough to a thickness of 1/8 inch or a touch less. Cut into rounds or any shape you prefer, 4 1/2-inches or so. You can also roll these very thin (but make sure your board is well-floured).

Bake 16-18 minutes and cookies or until cookies are beginning to brown around the edges and are golden brown all over top.

Makes about 3-4 dozen cookies

Moravian Butter Thin Cookies

You know those Pringle tubes of Moravian sugar cookies that come in walnut, orange, chocolate, spice and plain butter? Wafer thin, mouth-watering cookies? These are the ones.

¾ cup sugar

2 tablespoons light brown sugar

½ teaspoon salt

2 cups all-purpose flour

1 cup unsalted butter

1 tablespoon whipping cream

In a food processor, whiz the white sugar, brown sugar and salt to finely pulverize and combine about 10 seconds.

Place the flour on top of the sugar and pulse to blend. Add in the chunks of butter and cream and pulse to make a grainy meal. Then process or pulse until the mixture holds together, adding in a bit more cream, if necessary. On a lightly flour-dusted work surface, knead the dough to make a stiff dough that holds together. Chill dough 20-30 minutes.

Preheat the oven to 325°F. Double up two baking sheets and line top one with parchment paper.

Divide dough in half, keeping one half chilled as you work. Roll the dough between two sheets of floured parchment paper to a thickness of 1/16th of inch (i.e. very thin). Cut with 3 inch round or fluted cutters (any shape is fine, even heart shaped). Using a metal spatula, place on the baking sheets.

Bake until lightly browned around the edges and golden on top, 18-25 minutes.

36-48 cookies

Apricot Kolache

This Czech pastry has many different names and many European bakers make a variation on this sour-cream dough, filled with a fresh and beautiful apricot filling. You can use other fruit fillings but to me, apricot is the perfect match for this tender, buttery, sour cream dough.

SOUR CREAM DOUGH

4 cups all-purpose flour

1/2 teaspoon salt

3/4 cup sugar

1 1/2 cups unsalted butter, chilled and cut into 32 chunks

1 1/2 cups sour cream

APRICOT FILLING

3/4 cup water or fresh orange juice

1/4 cup lemon juice

3 cups dried apricot halves, preferably Californian

1/3 cup sugar

1 cup yellow raisins

FINISHING TOUCHES

2-3 eggs, whisked

Confectioners' sugar

In a food processor, blend flour, salt and sugar. Add butter and pulse to create a grainy mixture. Add sour cream and process until a mass forms (1 to 2 minutes). If dough does not form, remove mixture to a lightly floured board and knead gently. (Refrigeration will help this rich dough set up). Flatten into a large disc and divide in three equal portions. Wrap and chill for 2 to 3 hours.

For the Apricot Filling, place water (or orange juice), lemon juice, apricots, sugar, and raisins in a 3 quart saucepan and combine over low heat. Toss and stir often, 8-12 minutes. Add water if mixtures appears to be drying or thickening too quickly.

Remove saucepan from stove and let mixture cool for about 5 minutes. Place mixture in a food processor and process to make a paste. Add additional water or orange juice if mixture requires thinning. Taste mixture and add additional sugar (a tablespoon at a time) if required. Wrap and chill dough 20 minutes. (Dough can be refrigerate for 2-3 days or freeze up to 3 months).

Preheat the oven to 350°F. Stack two baking sheets together and line top one with parchment paper.

Roll out dough to ¼ inch thickness. Cut in 3½-4 inch circles. Brush the edges with the whisked eggs and deposit 1-2 teaspoons of apricot filling in the center. Fold the dough by bring each of the four 'points' (north, south, east, west) of the circle towards the center – It does not have to be perfect. You can also fold this in half-moons, and using a fork, seal the edges. Place cookies on baking sheet, spaced about 2 inches apart; brush with whisked egg.

Bake 25-30 minutes or until lightly browned. Dust with confectioners' sugar.

Makes 3-4 dozen, depending on size

Pink Heart Cream Scones

Tiny scone hearts, studded with white chocolate and bits of dried strawberries, vanilla scrapings, and topped with a luscious pink glaze. Serve warm with espresso or pack in a basket with some tea. These are lovely as gifts and the finishing decorations are unlimited.

SCONE DOUGH

1/2 - 3/4 cup whipping cream *

1 tablespoon lemon juice

1/2 cup dried strawberries, coarsely minced

3 cups all-purpose flour, or a bit more

3/4 cup sugar

4 teaspoons baking powder

1/2 teaspoon baking soda

3/8 teaspoon salt

3/4 cup unsalted butter, in small chunks

2 eggs

1 tablespoon pure vanilla extract

1/2 cup finely chopped white chocolate

Scrapings of a vanilla bean, optional

GLAZE

1 1/2 cup confectioners' sugar

1-3 tablespoons cream or milk, as required

1/2 teaspoon almond extract

2 teaspoons pure vanilla extract

Pink food coloring, as required

* Put 1 tablespoon of lemon juice in a Pyrex measuring cup. Pour the whipping cream up to the 3/4 cup mark and let stand to curdle a few minutes.

In a small bowl, plump the strawberries with boiling water; drain and dry well, Mince and set aside.

Preheat the oven to 425°F. Stack two baking sheets together and line top one with parchment paper.

For the scones, in a food processor, place the flour, sugar, baking powder, baking soda and salt and whiz to blend. Add in the chunks of butter and process by pulsing, to break in the butter and the mixture is grainy. Turn out into a large bowl. Make a well in the center and add the eggs, the extract, most of the cream, white chocolate and vanilla scrapings. Mix with a fork to make a soft dough. Turn the mixture out, while still a bit shaggy, onto a floured work surface, adding in a touch more flour if dough is too wet to handle or form or more cream, if it's too dry and not holding together.

Knead about 15 seconds to make a firm dough. Pat into a round, about 3/4 inch thick. Using a very small (2 inches or so) heart cutter, cut into heart scones.

Place the scones on the baking sheet. Bake until golden brown, about 12-16 minutes.

For the glaze, in a small bowl, mix the confectioners' sugar, cream, almond, vanilla extract and food colouring to make a smooth, gloppy glaze. Dip scones into glaze, skim off excess and place on parchment paper to set.

3-4 dozen heart-shaped scones

Red Velvet Chocolate Chunk Cookies

It's still snowing but it's already February in a brand new year; the major winter holidays, just past, are now a memory. But cheer up, it's time for Valentine's Day treats! These wonderful cookies are just the thing to awaken passion and love. Rich cocoa along with Red Velvet colour and flavor agent, takes it up a notch. It's available from King Arthur Flour.

1 cup unsalted butter, room temperature

1 cup white sugar

2/3 cup golden brown sugar, firmly packed

2 teaspoons pure vanilla extract

2 eggs

1 tablespoon Red Velvet Colour/flavor *

2 1/4 cups all-purpose flour

2/3 cup cocoa, measured, then sifted

3/4 teaspoon baking soda

3/8 teaspoon salt

1 tablespoon whipping cream

1 cup semi-sweet chocolate chips or chunks

1 cup white chocolate chunks or chips

* Red Velvet Food Color and Flavor is available from King Arthur Flour. You can also use half the amount in regular red food color (paste or liquid).

Preheat the oven to 350°F. Line a doubled up baking sheet with parchment paper. Position oven rack in upper third of oven

In a mixer bowl, cream the butter with the white and brown sugar. Stir in vanilla extract, eggs and red velvet flavor. If mixture seems curdled, stir in 1/4 cup of the flour (in recipe) to bind. In another bowl, stir together the flour, cocoa, baking soda and salt. Mix into batter on low speed of mixer, scraping bowl sides often. When almost mixed, stir in cream. Fold in chocolate chips/chunks. Chill batter 10 minutes.

Place dough on prepared sheet, using about a quarter of a cup of batter per cookie. Press down slightly with wet hands. Leave two inches of space between each cookie. Bake until cookies just look barely set - middles will seem slightly wet - about 15-18 minutes.

Let cookies cool about 10 minutes on the baking sheet before removing with a metal spatula. Cool completely on a wire rack. Store in the refrigerator.

Makes about 15-20 large cookies or 30 smaller ones

Mexican Dark Chocolate and Hot Chili Cupcakes

These are wickedly dark, delicious, and moist. I don't think there is a better chocolate cupcake to be found anywhere. Dip them in melted chocolate or a chocolate glaze. Cinnamon and chili provide Latin heat and spice but you can omit the heat for a milder (but still decadent) chocolate cupcake.

1 cup or 4 ounces unsweetened chocolate, coarsely chopped

¼ cup cocoa

3/4 cup boiling water

½ cup milk

1 cup unsalted butter

1 1/3 cup sugar

3 eggs

1 ½ teaspoons pure vanilla extract

½ cup sour cream

1 ½ cups all-purpose flour

1 teaspoon baking soda

1/4 teaspoon cinnamon

1/4 teaspoon hot chili powder

1/4 teaspoon salt

FINISHING TOUCHES
1 cup white or dark chocolate chips, melted

GLAZE
¼ cup cocoa

2-3 cups confectioners' sugar

Whipping cream or water, as required

Preheat the oven to 350°F.

Line a baking sheet with parchment paper. Line two regular cupcake or muffin pans with paper muffin or cupcake liners and place on baking sheet. You will probably get 18 cupcakes but you can make 24 smaller ones. Place the cupcake pan on the baking sheet.

Place the chocolate and cocoa in a medium size bowl and cover with boiling water. Stir to melt chocolate and cool. Stir in the milk. In a mixer bowl, cream the butter and sugar until fluffy and well combined. Blend in the eggs and vanilla, and then the sour cream. Blend in the cooled, melted chocolate and then fold in the flour, baking soda, cinnamon, chili powder and salt.

Spoon into prepared pans. Bake until cupcakes spring back when gently touched with fingertips, 20-25 minutes.

To finish the cupcakes, melt the chocolate and cool to room temperature.

Dip each cooled cupcake in the chocolate and place on wax paper to set up. Alternatively, mix the glaze ingredients together in a small bowl, adding enough water to make a glaze consistency. Dip each cupcake in the glaze and let set.

Makes 18-24 depending on size

Snow Day Brownie Stuffed Tollhouse Cookies

These are enormous cookies, crisp Tollhouse cookies that surround a huge center of fudge brownie – almost like a giant cookie dumpling. The contrast of crisp cookie and dense, moist brownie is magical. It's also in my cookbook, When Bakers Cook but it deserves a second go-round.

TOLLHOUSE COOKIE DOUGH

1 cup unsalted butter

1/2 cup white sugar

1 cup brown sugar, firmly packed

2 eggs

2 ½ teaspoons pure vanilla extract

2 ¾ cup all-purpose flour

1 teaspoon baking soda

¼ teaspoon salt

2 cups semi-sweet chocolate chips

BROWNIES

1 cup unsalted butter, melted

1 cup white sugar

3/4 cup brown sugar, firmly packed

1 1/2 teaspoon pure vanilla

3 eggs

1 cup all-purpose flour

½ cup plus 3 tablespoons cocoa

1/8 teaspoon baking soda

1/4 teaspoon salt

Preheat the oven to 350°F. Line a baking sheet with parchment paper.

For the brownies, line a baking sheet with parchment paper. Generously spray a 9 by 9 inch pan or an 8 by 11 inch pan with non-stick cooking spray and place the pan on the baking sheet. For the cookies, stack two baking sheets together and line the top one with parchment paper

For the Tollhouse Cookies, in a mixer bowl, blend the butter, white sugar and brown sugar until well-mixed. Add in the eggs and vanilla and blend well. Fold in the flour, baking soda and salt blend well. Add in the chocolate chips and mix. Wrap and chill dough while preparing brownies.

For the Brownies, in a mixer bowl, blend melted butter with white and brown sugars, then add vanilla and eggs. Blend well on slow speed. In a separate bowl, stir flour, cocoa, baking soda and salt. Stop mixer and fold dry ingredients into batter and blend well, on low speed, scraping bottom of mixing bowl often to ensure ingredients are evenly combined. Spoon into prepared pan.

Bake until done, 30-35 minutes. Brownies will appear set (versus wet) and slightly firm to the touch but not dry. Cool and then place cake (in pan) in freezer for 1 hour before cutting.

To cut, unmold the brownies and peel off parchment paper. Cut brownies into 1 ½ inch squares. (Preheat oven to 350°F)

To make each cookie, break off about 3 tablespoons or more of cookie dough and press a brownie square into the center. Seal edges whatever way you can and press gently on a (doubled up) prepared cookie sheet.

Bake until done, (edges are browned, center is just set), about 16-18 minutes, depending on size.

Makes about 12-16 large cookies or 30 smaller ones

VALENTINE'S DAY BAKING IS A SWEET DEAL

Valentine's Day is a romantic holiday which makes it an ideal occasion to bake something special. Perfume and flowers may fade, but the taste of fresh, decadent baking lasts a long time. I love getting gifts and notes on Valentine's Day but I like baking and giving even more. The key is to bake with loving intentions – it doesn't have to be fancy; it just has to be heartfelt. Valentine's Day baking is the promise of love in a spoonful of sugar with a sprinkle of chocolate chips. So bake it forward and share the love. Like all holidays, this is not the time to skimp. This is all about fussy, pretty, buttery baking. It's also, which it should go without saying, not about diets. Cupid doesn't count calories; why should we, at least not on Valentine's Day.

Classic Madeleines

These are sophisticated (but easy to make) little snack cakes, French style, somewhat like a pound cake but in mini form. You do need a madeleine mold for these. These wee cakes were immortalized, according to culinary legend, by Marcel Proust who wrote of these "plump little cakes called petites madeleines". I think madeleines are just perfect for Valentine's Day.

3 eggs, room temperature

1 egg yolk

3/4 cup sugar

1 1/2 teaspoon pure vanilla extract

2 teaspoons lemon zest, finely minced

1 1/3 cup all-purpose flour

1 tablespoon cornstarch

1/2 teaspoon baking powder

¼ teaspoon salt

¾ cup unsalted butter, melted

In a mixer bowl, with whisk attachment at high speed, beat the eggs, egg yolk, and sugar, vanilla and lemon zest until pale mixture forms. In a small bowl, whisk together flour, cornstarch, baking powder and salt. Set aside.

Drizzle butter into egg/sugar mixture. Then, on slow speed, dust in a tablespoon or two at a time of dry ingredients until all are incorporated. Let batter rest 30 minutes.

Preheat the oven to 450°F. Generously spray with non-stick cooking spray: 12 small or medium muffin cups, 12 to 18 traditional madeleine molds or 24 mini-madeleine molds, or 12 mini Bundt molds. Place on a parchment covered baking sheet.

Spoon batter into prepared molds. Bake 10-12 minutes (for smaller cakes) 12-14 minutes (for larger ones) until they are puffed, set and starting to brown around the edges. Cool on a rack.

Makes 12-18

SNOW DAYS AKA THE UNOFFICIAL HOME BAKING HOLIDAY

There are official holidays in the winter season, such as Christmas and Hanukkah and New Year's Day. Then there are the unofficial holidays, such as Snow Day, an unexpected holiday that comes just when you need it most.

The snow usually starts gently the night before and by morning it starts coming down in big heaves like someone dumped out the inside of a feather quilt. You wake up to a transformed white world and hear the drone of the snow ploughs going non-stop. Everything takes a backseat to Nature's whim. The kids wake up listening to the radio, hopeful their school will be announced closed. And then bingo - this or that school board is announced closed due to the snow! It's official: it's a Snow Day! Mother Nature blankets the world with snow so thick and fast so that normal comings and goings (school bus routes, work car pools, newspaper delivery) are impossible and our usual scheduled day, as we know it, is cancelled.

What makes a snow day extra special is the gift of time and having to surrender to the things out of our control. Frankly, it's nice to know that even in this fast-paced life and time, a little bit of snow can still have the last word. Snow Day is time to make a snowman, fort or a snow angel. But what really suits a snow day best (aside from snow angels and snow forts) is baking. Cookie-and-brownie style baking with a special someone (a parent, grandparent, friend or sitter) on a slow motion, house-bound day is something no one ever forgets. The world is still, quiet and chilly outside but inside, there's baking, sweetness and a plate of warm cookies. It's an oasis that does us all a world of good.

By February or so, lots of folks complain about the weather. But then an impromptu gift of a Snow Day comes along with snowflakes and smiles. Your heart lifts as the oven preheats and you remember what the most joyous moments in life are all about.

Winter, Big Baking

Including Holiday and Special Occasions

Winter, Big Baking
Recipes

Chocolate Brownie Bread Pudding with White Chocolate Ganache

Nutcracker Suite Apple Cranberry Strudel

Eggnog Bundt Pound Cake

Clementine Cake

White Chocolate Linzertorte

Golden Almond Holiday Stollen

Salted Butter, Salted Caramel Cheesecake

Siena Fruitcake

Cayman Island Rum Cake

Carrot Spice Plum Pudding (should be after Cayman Island Rum Cake)

Terry's Sour Cream Chocolate Orange Cake

Classic Brandy Hard Sauce

Hot Chocolate Layer Cake with Marshmallow Fudge Icing

Caramel Brownie Pie

Chocolate Lover's Cake with White Chocolate Ganache

Sweetheart Chocolate Cherry Cheesecake

Chocolate Brownie Bread Pudding with White Chocolate Ganache

This is different and impressive, not quite a chocolate soufflé cake and not a cheesecake in taste, but somewhere in-between. This is good served chilled in wedges with warm white chocolate sauce or with caramel sauce, whipped cream or even a scoop of softened vanilla ice-cream.

BREAD PUDDING

4-5 cups cubes of leftover chocolate cake

1 1/2 cups leftover brownies, cut in chunks

2 cups coarsely chopped challah or brioche

1/2 cup unsalted butter, melted

1 1/3 cup sugar

¼ cup cream cheese, softened

2 cups evaporated milk

½ cup whipping cream

6 eggs

2 teaspoons pure vanilla extract

2 tablespoons flour

1 teaspoon baking powder

Pinch salt

½ cup semi-sweet chocolate chips

½ cup white chocolate chips

WHITE CHOCOLATE GANACHE

1 cup whipping cream

1 ½ cups white chocolate chips

Line a baking sheet with parchment paper. Generously spray a 10 inch cheesecake pan with non-stick cooking spray. Line interior with a parchment paper collar, cut to fit, using some softened butter to make it stick. Place pan on baking sheet.

Prepare cake cubes, brownie and bread pieces and set aside. In a large bowl, whisk the butter, sugar, cream cheese, evaporated milk, whipping cream, eggs, vanilla extract, flour, baking powder and salt until well blended. Gently fold in the cake, brownie, bread pieces and the chocolate chips. Pour into prepared pan. Refrigerate for an hour.

Preheat the oven to 350°F. Bake the bread pudding 35-45 minutes until the custard just begins to brown or seems set. For the White Chocolate Ganache, bring the cream to a gentle boil and then stir in the chocolate chips, turning off the heat, and whisking briskly to melt the chocolate and make a smooth mixture. Drizzle over slices of the dessert (this may be served warm or cold)

Serves 8-12

Nutcracker Suite Apple Cranberry Strudel

This strudel is put together in no time flat. Its interior brags a beautiful deep scarlet hue and the whole strudel log is likely to be devoured in one sitting. This is a perky dessert that makes festive use of three fruits, bringing sweetness, tartness and a rosy colour to a nippy mid-winter evening.

16 filo leaves

1/2 cup unsalted butter, melted

4 cups sliced, peeled apples (about 4-6 large), such as Golden Delicious

1/2 cup fresh cranberries, coarsely chopped

1/2 cup frozen pitted sour or sweet cherries

Juice of half a lemon

1 cup sugar

1/4 - 1/2 teaspoon cinnamon

4 tablespoons cornstarch

Preheat the oven to 375 degrees°F. Line a baking sheet with foil. Top the foil with a sheet of parchment paper. Have filo leaves nearby, as well as the melted cooled butter.

In a large bowl, toss apples, cranberries and cherries together. Add in lemon juice, sugar, cinnamon and cornstarch.

Lay out one filo leaf on a work surface. Using a pastry brush, lightly paint with melted butter. Repeat layering in this fashion with seven more leaves of filo. Spoon out half of apple filling mixture down the length of edge closest to you, leaving a margin or border of one inch. If there is a lot of juice in the filling bowl, spoon some over fruit filling sitting on the pastry. Gently and loosely roll up pastry to form a log or strudel roll. If cracks occur or bits of pastry come off, it is fine. Place on prepared cookie sheet. Repeat with remaining ingredients to make as second strudel roll. Transfer rolls to the baking sheet. Lightly paint both strudels with remaining butter and dust with sugar.

Bake until golden brown and juices are running out (this unavoidable and normal for strudel) about 35-40 minutes. As strudel cools down, the juices will congeal. Serve warm or room temperature.

Makes two 12 inch strudels

Eggnog Bundt Pound Cake

Eggnog makes for a tender, gently spiced pound cake. Topped with the addictive Buttered Egg Nog Glaze for a masterpiece of a cake.

CAKE

1 cup unsalted butter, softened

1 1/2 cups sugar

3 eggs

3 egg yolks

1 tablespoon pure vanilla extract

1/2 cup eggnog *

¼ cup rum

3 cups all-purpose flour

1 tablespoon baking powder

¼ teaspoon baking soda

1 teaspoon nutmeg

1/4 teaspoon mace

¼ teaspoon cinnamon

3/8 teaspoon salt

BUTTERED EGG NOG GLAZE

1/2 cup sugar

1/3 cup unsalted butter

1/3 cup evaporated milk

Pinch nutmeg, cinnamon, cloves

* If you don't have prepared egg nog, substitute the 1/2 cup egg nog with 1/2 cup half-and-half, 1/8 teaspoon nutmeg and 1 egg yolk.

Preheat the oven to 350°F. Line a baking sheet with parchment paper. Generously spray a 12 –cup Bundt Pan or angel food cake pan with non-stick cooking spray and place on baking sheet.

For the cake, in a food processor, blend the butter and sugar to make a pasty mixture. Add in the eggs, yolks, vanilla, eggnog and rum and process to blend. Fold in flour, baking powder, baking soda, nutmeg, mace, cinnamon and salt. Pulse, then process, to make a soft batter, about 1 minute. Spoon batter into cake pan.

Bake until cake tests done by pressing lightly with fingertips, about 55-75 minutes.

Cool in pan 20 minutes before unmolding on a cake rack to cool 15 minutes.

For the Buttered Egg Nog Glaze, put all ingredients in a 2 quart saucepan. Over low to medium heat, stir and gently bubble, 5-10 minutes until the mixture thickens. Set cake on a rack, set over a parchment line baking sheet. Pour glaze over cake while the cake is still warm. Re-scoop excess drippings from parchment paper and reglaze cake.

Serves 8-12

Clementine Cake

Clementine Cake bursts with delectable flavor of sweet clementines, buttery toasted almonds, and a luscious clementine frosting, perfect in winter when you need some extra Vitamin D. Boyajian is the source for all-natural tangerine oil.

CAKE

1 medium clementine (about 3-4 ounces), washed and stem end trimmed

1/2 cup unsalted butter, softened

1 1/3 cup sugar

2 eggs

1/2 cup warm orange juice or milk

1 teaspoon pure vanilla extract

1/2 teaspoon pure tangerine or orange oil

1/2 teaspoon pure almond extract

2 cups all-purpose flour

2 teaspoons baking powder

¼ teaspoon salt

1/4 cup ground toasted almonds

CANDIED CLEMENTINE SLICES

3-4 clementines, thinly sliced

2 cups sugar

1 cup water

CLEMENTINE ICING

2 cups confectioners' sugar

3 tablespoons unsalted butter, softened

2-3 tablespoons water

1/4 teaspoon pure orange oil

1/4 teaspoon pure tangerine oil

Line a baking sheet with parchment paper. Spray a 9 inch spring-form pan or 8 inch layer cake pan generously with non-stick cooking spray. Line the bottom with a circle of parchment paper. Place the pan on the baking sheet.

For the cake, in a small saucepan, cover the orange with water, and bring to the boil. Reduce heat and let simmer for 15-20 minutes, or until the skin is softened and tender. Remove and dry the orange and grind in a food processor and set aside.

Preheat the oven to 350°F.

In a food processor, add the butter and sugar and process, using the pulse speed, to make a pasty mixture, about 30 seconds or so. Blend in eggs until mixture is smooth. Add in the ground up orange and blend until smooth, about 8 seconds. Add in orange juice and extracts and blend briefly. Add the flour, baking powder, salt, and almonds and process to make a smooth, well-blended batter, about 30-45 seconds. Spoon batter into prepared pan. Bake until cake springs back when lightly touched, about 50-55 minutes.

Meanwhile, for the Candied Clementines, place the sliced clementines in a saucepan; stir in sugar and water. Bring to a boil and then reduce to a simmer. Let simmer 15-20 minutes. Cool well and remove clementine slices to a plate to cool fully and allow excess syrup to drain off.

For the Clementine Icing, whisk confectioners' sugar, butter, water, orange and tangerine oil to make a soft icing. Spread on cake. Chill an hour and then garnish the top with clementine slices.

Serves 10-12

White Chocolate Linzertorte

This is the quintessential European treat of a nutty shortbread, kissed with a touch of cinnamon and cloves, topped with raspberry preserves followed by a lattice-work crust and a halo of confectioners' sugar. A happy offering at Christmas that's fashionably all season appropriate.

BOTTOM CRUST

½ cup unsalted butter, softened

2/3 cup sugar

1 egg

2 egg yolks

1 teaspoon pure vanilla extract

1/2 cup finely ground almonds

1/4 cup finely ground walnuts

1/3 cup ground hazelnuts

1/3 cup ground white chocolate

2 cups all-purpose flour

¼ teaspoon baking powder

1 teaspoon cinnamon

½ teaspoon cloves

1/8 teaspoon salt

FILLING

½ cup apricot preserves

½ cup raspberry preserves

1 teaspoon lemon juice or red wine

1 tablespoon raspberry eau de vie, optional

FINISHING TOUCHES

Confectioners' sugar

Preheat the oven to 325°F. Line a small baking sheet with parchment paper. Generously butter a 9-inch tart pan, with removable bottom.

For the Bottom Crust, in a food processor, cream the butter and sugar until smooth, about 1-2 minutes. Add in the egg, egg yolks, vanilla, almonds, walnuts, hazelnuts and white chocolate. Blend, about 40 seconds. Add the flour, baking powder, cinnamon, cloves and salt. Process to make a thick, firm dough, about 20-40 seconds. Wrap the dough and chill 20 minutes.

For filling, mix apricot, raspberry preserves, lemon juice and raspberry eau de vie in a small bowl; set aside. Roll out the dough to fit bottom and sides of tart pan. If dough breaks, patch together pieces. Spoon preserve filling over bottom crust in tart pan.

Gather scraps together and on a lightly floured board, roll about 1/8 th inch thick. Cut into strips, using a knife or serrated pastry wheel. Arrange strips in a criss-cross or latticework fashion on top of tart, ending at edges, pressing slightly with fingertips to hold in place.

Place tart on baking sheet and place in oven. Bake 35-45 minutes until nicely browned and preserves are gently bubbling.

Cool to warm or room temperature. Remove from tart pan and place on a serving platter. Dust with confectioners' sugar before serving.

Serves 8

Golden Almond Holiday Stollen

This is delicious European holiday sweet bread, reminiscent of Danish. It's filled with the ambrosial goodness of almond paste, dried sour cherries and orange peel bits. Nothing is finer fresh or toasted with butter, especially on a wintery, holiday morning.

FRUIT MIXTURE

1 cup yellow raisins

1/2 cup candied orange peel, or dried cranberries or dried sour cherries

1/4 cup currants

Zest of one lemon, finely minced

2 tablespoons brandy, optional

DOUGH

1/2 cup warm water

5 teaspoons instant yeast

1/2 cup unsalted butter, softened

3/4 cup warm milk

1 teaspoon pure vanilla extract

1 teaspoon pure almond extract

2/3 cup sugar

1 1/4 teaspoon salt

1 cup slivered or chopped almonds, preferably toasted

4-5 cups bread flour

FILLING

12 ounces almond paste or marzipan

FINISHING TOUCHES

1 egg, whisked

4 tablespoons unsalted butter, melted

Sugar

1/2 cup slivered almonds

Sugar Syrup

1 cup water

1 cup sugar

FINISHING TOUCHES

Confectioners' sugar

Place the fruit mixture ingredients in a small bowl. Toss to blend and set aside. Line a large baking sheet with parchment paper and set aside.

In a mixer bowl, hand whisk the water and yeast briefly; let stand one minute. Add the butter, milk, vanilla, almond extract, sugar, salt, almonds, and about half of the flour. Stir with a wooden spoon to blend. Stir in fruit mixture. Attach the dough hook and begin kneading, adding more flour as required, to make a soft bouncy dough. Knead on slow speed, 6 - 10 minutes until smooth and elastic. Remove dough hook.

Shape dough into a mound in the bowl and insert bowl in a large plastic bag. Let rise until somewhat puffy, 45-60 minutes.

Gently turn dough onto well-floured floured board and gently deflate. Divide dough into three equal portions. Meanwhile, divide the marzipan in three portions and roll, on a lightly floured board to a 5 inch disc. Set aside.

Roll or press each portion of dough in an 8-inch round. Press a portion of marzipan in each. Using a rolling pin, roll or depress center of dough, and then fold over each side (the upper and lower parts) slightly overlapping, into the center, tucking the dough in somewhat snugly, with fingertips. Place each stolen, evenly spaced, seam-side down, on the baking sheet.

Brush each with a beaten egg and then some of the melted butter. Dust on some sugar and almonds. Cover with a large plastic bag and let rise, until somewhat puffy (it won't balloon or rise too much) 50-60 minutes. A cold rise is perfect (overnight in the fridge) is fine for this recipe if you want to divide up the preparation and baking time.

For the Sugar Syrup, simmer water and sugar 5-8 minutes on low to dissolve sugar. Cool.

Preheat the oven to 350°F. Bake until nicely browned, 35 - 45 minutes. Cool well and dust with confectioners' sugar if desired. Alternatively, as stollen comes out of the oven, glaze 2-3 times with sugar syrup.

Makes 3 medium stollens

NUTCRACKER SWEETS

You may not be a fan of the ballet but chances are, you've seen the Nutcracker Suite at least once. It's always magical, so magical in fact, that each December, as I bake and create, the very spirit of Tchaikovsky seems to permeate my kitchen with the same fairyland dust the Nutcracker Suite invokes. It's not just the Nutcracker Suite; it's the magic of the holiday TV specials, romantic comedy movie openings, choirs and school concerts - reminders at every turn that warmth, good will and a positive spirit are all around us. People remark that it's too bad this wonderful ambiance prevails only once a year. But if you bake, and enjoy quiet times in the kitchen, in service to sharing your craftsmanship and holiday cheer, that wonderful mood is not just once a year. It's holiday time and mood, each and every day, all year round.

Salted Butter Caramel Cheesecake

So easy, decadent and irresistible! I'm not sure what I like better, the salted graham crust with the creamy cheesecake filling or the sinful real salty/sweet caramel topping. Most people are chocoholics but a few of us (the baker is included), go weak at the knees for caramel.

**SALTED BUTTER
GRAHAM CRUST**

1 ¼ cup graham crumbs

¼ cup salted butter, melted

¼ cup brown sugar, firmly packed

1/8 teaspoon fleur de sel salt

CHEESECAKE

2 pounds cream cheese, softened

1 cup sugar

5 eggs

1/4 cup whipping cream

2 ½ teaspoons pure vanilla extract

Tiny pinch salt

**SALTED CARAMEL
SAUCE**

1 cup water

2 cups sugar

1 cup whipping cream, warmed

¾-1 teaspoon fleur de sel

Preheat the oven to 350°F. Line a baking sheet with parchment paper.

In a 9 inch spring-form pan, mix the graham crumbs, butter, brown sugar and salt and press into the pan. Place on the baking sheet.

For the Cheesecake, in a mixer bowl, cream the cream cheese and sugar until smooth. Add in eggs, cream, vanilla and salt and blend until smooth. Pour into prepared pan and bake until just set, 40 -45 minutes. Chill for a 6-8 hours for a few days, until serving.

For the Salted Caramel Sauce, in a small saucepan, warm the water and sugar over low heat, 20-30 minutes, allowing to slowly bubble or simmer, brushing down sides with a brush dipped in water. Once it turns medium or light amber, remove pan from burner and put it in the sink. Pour warmed cream slowly into sauce (take care, it bubbles up and is hot!) and whisk until blended in.

To serve cake, pour half of sauce over cake and serve by the slice, reserving extra sauce for those that want it or for another occasion (it makes a lot but it takes a bit of pot-watching; might as well make more and keep it – it lasts in the fridge for two months)

Serves 12-16

Siena Fruit Cake

This is more of a candied confection that it is a traditional cake. Imported versions of this heritage treat are found in Italian food stores but you can make one at a fraction of the cost and with the freshest spices and nuts available.

1 cup hazelnuts, chopped

½ cup almonds, chopped

1 ½ cups mixed candied fruits

½ cup all-purpose flour

Pinch coriander

¼ teaspoon cloves

¼ teaspoon cinnamon

Pinch salt

½ cup honey

½ cup sugar

½ cup confectioners' sugar

Preheat the oven to 300°F. Generously spray an 8-inch layer cake pan with nonstick cooking spray. Line a baking sheet with parchment paper and place the pan on it.

In a large bowl, combine the nuts, fruits, flour, coriander, cloves, cinnamon and salt. Stir to blend.

In a heavy 3 quart saucepan, heat the honey and sugar and bring to a gentle boil. Cook until mixture is between soft and hard ball stage, about 235°F on a candy thermometer. Pour the syrup into the flour/fruit/nut mixture; blend well with a wood spoon. Using wet fingertips or a wet, metal spoon, press the mixture into the prepared pan.

Bake for one hour. Cake will seem soft when done but sets up as it cools.

Turn out onto a serving plate. Dust with confectioners' sugar.

Wrap well in wax paper to store.

Serves 12-16

A SHORT HISTORY OF FRUITCAKE

Although many people balk at fruitcakes, I happen to be a fan of them – at least of good ones and I've included a fruitcake in almost each cookbook I've done. One of my favorites from A Passion for Baking, is the Black Cake, a fruitcake that harks back to Emily Dickinson.

Fruitcakes were once sticky, fruity cakes, like the Siena Cake, which is more of a confection with spices, nuts and candied fruits or fruitcakes were like Panforte, a yeasted sweet bread, much like brioche. The dried fruit used helped preserve the cakes, especially as the fruits were first marinated in brandy or port. Once baked, fruitcakes were brushed with yet more alcohol, then wrapped in cheesecloth and left to age (and brushed, throughout their aging, with more spirits). No wonder fruitcakes have an impressive shelf life. Fruit cakes should be made in fall and then served around the December holidays. They're great slicing cakes to have on hand when people drop by.

Cayman Island Rum Cake

This ultra-tender gold cake is reminiscent of famed Cayman Island Tortugas Rum Cake except this is a luxurious, buttery scratch cake, made with all natural ingredients. My rum cake uses the British method of cake blending which results in a rich, deeply golden cake. For the Rum Glaze, use the rum you are most familiar with or love for a cake you will also adore.

CAKE

1/2 cup chopped walnuts

3 cups all-purpose flour

6 tablespoons Bird's Custard powder or 6 tablespoons instant vanilla pudding

2 cups sugar

4 teaspoons baking powder

1/2 teaspoon salt

1 cup unsalted butter, slightly softened, in small chunks

¼ cup canola oil

3/4 cup milk

4 eggs

1 yolk

1/2 cup amber rum

1 ½ teaspoon pure vanilla extract

SPECIAL RUM GLAZE

1/2 cup butter

1/4 cup water

1 cup sugar

1/2 cup amber rum

Preheat the oven to 350°F. Line a baking sheet with parchment paper. Generously spray a 10 inch tube or angel food cake pan with non-stick cooking spray and place on baking sheet.

For the cake, in a large mixer bowl or food processor, blend the nuts, flour, custard powder or pudding mix, sugar, baking powder and salt. Add in the butter and mix on low speed until well combined, and the butter and flour is a grainy meal. Add in the oil, milk, eggs, egg yolk, rum and vanilla and blend for 2-3 minutes until very smooth, scraping down sides of bowl once or twice to ensure ingredients are well combined.

Spoon into prepared pan and bake for 55-65 minutes or until cake tester comes out clean. Remove from oven and cool. Don't remove from pan.

Meanwhile, for the Special Rum Glaze, bring butter, water and sugar to a boil in a small saucepan. Lower the heat and simmer gently until sugar is dissolved and syrup thickens. Remove from heat and stir in rum, taking care not to splash yourself as you mix in the alcohol to the syrup.

Gently skewer the warm cake with a fork, paring knife or long skewer to create holes (cake is still in pan). Then drizzle syrup over the cake – this takes a bit of time but allow cake to soak up syrup.

Allow cake to cool completely in the pan before very gently turning it out onto a large plate. Then gently flip a second time onto a cake serving plate). Recoup extra glaze from the pan and drizzle on cake.

Serves 10-12

THE SPIRITS OF THE FESTIVE SEASON

Although I'm a tee-totaller, it doesn't stop me from baking, and quite liberally, with spirits. Alcohol, liqueur, spirits, whether they be brandy, rum, red and white wines or liqueurs such as eau de vie frambroise, Frangelico, Bailey's Irish Cream, and Cointreau, impart a very special grace note to your holiday baking. Each year, I experiment with another liqueur, aged brandy or fine Port. It takes my baking up a notch. Each time I do, I appreciate anew, what extra dimension a wee bit of spirits adds to the mix. It certainly gives holiday baking that extra something. But take care: a little spirits go a long way, in flavor, and in warming the body and soul. I guess you can say alcohol, in reasonable measure, uplifts the mood. I guess that is why they call it 'spirits'.

Carrot Spice Plum Pudding

A beautifully spiced, dark plum pudding that is totally delectable, when served with warm Brandy Hard Sauce. Brioche, egg bread or a quality white bread is fine for the bread cubes part but fresh spices are crucial.

FRUIT MIXTURE

1 cup Thompson raisins, coarsely chopped

1 1/4 cup sultana raisins

1/2 cup currants

¼ cup chopped dates

1/2 cup very hot brandy or Cognac

Zest of a medium orange, finely minced

PLUM PUDDING

1 pound unsalted butter, melted

1 cup light brown sugar, firmly packed

¾ cup white sugar

4 eggs

2 tablespoons molasses

5 cups fresh bread crumbs (small ½ inch cubes of semi-stale bread)

1 cup all-purpose flour

¼ teaspoon baking soda

¼ teaspoon baking powder

3/4 teaspoon nutmeg

1 ½ teaspoons cinnamon

3/4 teaspoon cloves

1/2 teaspoon allspice

½ teaspoon mace

Pinch salt

¼ cup ground almonds

½ cup finely grated carrot

½ cup finely grated apple

1 lemon, juice and zest (finely minced)

1/3 cup brandy

1-2 teaspoons gravy browning, such as Kitchen Bouquet*

QUICK RUM AND BRANDY HARD SAUCE

6 tablespoons unsalted butter

3 tablespoons water

2 cups confectioners' sugar

2 tablespoons dark rum

2 tablespoons brandy

*Use if you prefer a nice dark plum pudding or omit, if you like a medium hued pudding.

Place the fruit in a large bowl and cover with boiling water. Let stand 5 minutes and then drain well. Then add in the brandy over the fruit, add the orange zest and toss. Cover and let stand overnight or 1-3 days before baking.

Prepare a large, deep roasting pan by filling halfway with water and placing in the oven. Put a trivet or two trivets in the roasting pan. Preheat oven to 250°F.

Generously spray two 1 quart (4 cup) or one 2 quart ceramic baking molds with non-stick cooking spray. Line each with a layer of cheesecloth with generous overlap of cheesecloth.

In a mixer bowl, blend the butter with the brown sugar and white sugar, and then blend in the eggs and molasses. Fold in the bread crumbs, flour, baking soda, baking powder, nutmeg, cinnamon, cloves, allspice, mace, salt, ground almonds, carrot, apple, and lemon juice and zest, stirring well with a large spoon. Add in the brandy and the marinated fruits and blend well by hand. If you want a dark plum pudding, add in gravy browning at that point and stir well.

Pack into the prepared baking dishes. Cover the top of each bowl with buttered wax paper, fold the excess cheesecloth on top, then cover with foil and tie with string to hold foil snugly.

Place a large roasting dish in the oven and fill it two-thirds with water. Place a trivet or small wire rack on the pan. Let the water warm up 15 minutes. Then place the filled baking dishes in the roasting pan, on the trivets or wire rack.

Simmer 5 hours – adding more water as you need to maintain water level. You want the water very low – to steam the puddings. The puddings are done when they are firm to the touch and seem quite solid.

Cool well, then refrigerate overnight or up until a few weeks. To reheat, rewarm by steaming in hot water (still in molds).

Serve in small slices with warmed Hard Sauce. (Plum pudding can be made and kept refrigerated a good 1-2 months ahead. To reheat, steam in a pan with simmering water, making sure your pudding is not only sealed in its bowl with a snug lid or cover)

For Rum Brandy Hard Sauce, in a 3 quart saucepan, over medium heat, stir together the butter, water, confectioners' sugar until smooth. Simmer and stir 5 minutes, remove from heat and stir in rum and brandy. Let cool a bit, and then stir and serve over plum pudding. Or cut small pieces of the pudding/cake, and spoon over some warm sauce on each serving.

Serves 10-14

PLUM PUDDING ANYONE?

Like fruit cake, plum pudding is so old, it's become new again. My own plum pudding is rather contemporary and it's an artful amalgamation of the best of vintage plum pudding recipes along with my own baker's preferences. Ironically, no plum pudding recipe I ever read about contains any sort of plum! Suet is the traditional fat for plum pudding but I prefer unsalted butter. Historically, Plum Pudding seems to pre-date fruit cakes. Most plum puddings are very dark, owing to generous use of spices, dark brown sugar and molasses. You'll find the spice in my recipe is vibrant but not too intense. Also most plum puddings called for candied citron or orange. Instead, I've used the lighter note of orange zest. In the end, this plum pudding is old-fashioned but very now - which should ensure that tradition will endure. Carry on, plum pudding!

Terry's Chocolate Pound Cake

Terry's Chocolate Orange is a whole chocolate 'orange' wrapped in silver which splits apart into milk chocolate, orange-scented wedges. I love the chocolate/citrus combo so I had to create a cake with that same theme and add some chopped up Terry's Orange chocolate to the batter. A favorite cake from Betterbaking.com, now at 'home', nested in this cookbook.

¼ cup semi-sweet chocolate

¾ cup unsalted butter

1 1/3 cup sugar

3 eggs

1 cup sour cream

2 teaspoons pure vanilla extract

1 ½ teaspoons pure orange oil

Zest of one small orange, finely minced

¼ cup milk

3 cups all-purpose flour

2 ½ teaspoons baking powder

½ teaspoon baking soda

3/8 teaspoon salt

1 175 g Terry's Chocolate Orange, minced, 1/2 cup miniature milk chocolate chips

FINISHING TOUCHES
Confectioners' sugar

½ cup white or milk chocolate, melted

Preheat the oven to 350°F. Line a baking sheet with parchment paper. Generously spray 9 inch Angel food cake pan with non-stick cooking spray and place on baking sheet.

Melt the chocolate and set aside.

In a mixer bowl, cream the butter and the sugar until fluffy. Add in the eggs, sour cream, vanilla extract, orange oil, orange and blend well. Mix in the milk, the melted chocolate, and then fold in the flour, baking soda, baking powder and salt, scraping the bottom of the bowl to make sure it is all blended. Remove ½ cup of the batter to a small bowl and stir in the melted chocolate. Spoon white batter into pan and then drop dollops of the chocolate batter on top of that and swirl briefly with a knife to marbleize.

Bake until cake springs back when lightly touched with fingertips, about 45-65 minutes (depending on pans used)

Dust with confectioners' sugar or drizzle on melted white and dark chocolate or melted milk chocolate.

Serves 10-12

Classic Brandy Butter Hard Sauce

A rich hard sauce, this holiday classic is a British stove top affair in which vanilla and brandy figure heavily. This adored concoction graces steamed puddings, chocolate tortes, pumpkin cheesecake and bread puddings.

1/4 cup sugar

Pinch salt

1 tablespoon flour

1 cup milk

1 egg yolk

1 tablespoon unsalted butter

1/2 teaspoon pure vanilla extract

1 tablespoon brandy

Combine sugar, flour and salt in a medium saucepan. Add 1/3 cup of milk and stir until mixture is smooth. Add balance of milk and bring to a boil, stirring constantly. Cook 2 minutes.

Beat egg yolk in a small bowl and add a touch of the warm mixture to it, then add this to sauce. Cook, stirring constantly, over low to medium heat for about one minute. Remove from heat. Fold in butter, vanilla and brandy. Serve over puddings, hot cakes, steamed pudding or fruit cake. (Refrigerate until serving)

Makes about 1 cup

PUDDING BOWLS

The ceramic bowls I use for steamed puddings are still made in England by Mason and Cash, as well as by Roseville Pottery in Ohio, USA. But you can use metal pudding molds or regular stainless steel mixing bowls, or a French soufflé 2-3 quart dish. Part of the fun of plum pudding is sourcing out a perfect bowl, either new or vintage. EBay (and yard sales) seems invented for just for finding things like old-pudding bowls. But use whatever you have on hand until you decide that plum pudding is your new tradition and worth investing in a specialty mold.

Hot Chocolate Layer Cake with Marshmallow Fudge Icing

Mellow and sweet, this is as old-fashioned as chocolate cake gets. Brown sugar offers a subtle caramel afterglow to this moist, dark hunk of a cake. The piece de resistance is the irresistible marshmallow fudge frosting. After the ski hill or toboggan run, this is a cake to come home to.

CAKE

4 ounces unsweetened chocolate, melted

3/4 cup unsalted butter

2 ½ cups brown sugar, firmly packed

3 eggs

2 teaspoons pure vanilla extract

2 1/3 cups all-purpose flour

3 tablespoons cocoa

2 teaspoons baking soda

3/8 teaspoon salt

1 cup sour cream

1 cup boiling water

MARSHMALLOW FUDGE FROSTING

5 cups miniature marshmallows

1/2 cup unsalted butter

1 cup semi-sweet chocolate chips

3-4 cups confectioners' sugar

1/2 cup cold butter, in small pieces

2 teaspoons pure vanilla extract

Whipping cream, as required

FINISHING TOUCHES

Marshmallow cream fluff

Miniature marshmallows

Cocoa

Chocolate syrup

Preheat the oven to 350°F. Line a large baking sheet with parchment paper. Generously spray a 9 by 13 inch rectangular pan with non-stick cooking spray and place on the baking sheet. Alternatively, generously spray two 9 inch layer cake pans with non-stick cooking spray and place on prepared baking sheet.

For the cake, have the chocolate melted and ready. In a mixer bowl, cream the butter with the brown sugar. Add in the eggs and vanilla and blend until smooth. Then fold in the flour, cocoa, baking soda and salt and mix very slightly. Then fold in the sour cream, boiling water and melted chocolate. Blend well and make sure no matter is stuck in the well of the mixer bowl. Spoon into the pan.

Bake until cake springs back when gently pressed with fingertips, 45-55 minutes. If cake appears to rise in center but is not thoroughly baked, reduce temperature to 325°F and let cake bake a little longer, but at lower temperature so that it rises more slowly but bakes all through.

For the Marshmallow Fudge Frosting, in a small saucepan, slowly melt the marshmallows with the first amount of the butter. Add in the chocolate chips. Remove from the heat, mix until smooth and let cool 5 minutes. Place mixture in a food processor and add the confectioner's sugar, butter and vanilla and drizzle in cream to make a thick, glossy frosting. (It will seem almost shiny).

For 9 by 13 inch cake, spread frosting on cooled cake. Let set 1-2 hours until quite firm.

For layer cake, place one cake on a serving platter. Spread on one-third of the fudge frosting, then a layer of marshmallow fluff and then top with the other layer. Frost cake sides and top with remaining frosting. Drizzle on additional, warm marshmallow cream and a handful of miniature marshmallows and a dusting of cocoa and drizzle of chocolate syrup.

Serves 12-14

Caramel Brownie Pie

This recipe is like a pretty girl who is popular but also happens to be a nice person. Suffice it to say this is an easy recipe that is glamorous and professional looking and tastes like a dream. No wonder it's perfect for Valentine's Day and any time where some easy decadence is called for.

PASTRY DOUGH

2 cups all-purpose flour

1 teaspoon sugar

3/8 teaspoon salt

3⁄4 cup unsalted butter, very cold, cut into 1 inch chunks

4 to 6 tablespoons ice water

FILLING

1 cup unsalted butter, melted

1 3⁄4 cups sugar

4 eggs

2 teaspoons pure vanilla extract

3⁄4 cup unsweetened cocoa powder

1 cup all-purpose flour

1/8 teaspoon baking soda

1/8 teaspoon salt

1/3 cup prepared dulce de leche

2-3 tablespoons unsalted butter, melted

FINISHING TOUCHES

1/3 cup chocolate chips

Confectioners' sugar

For the pie dough, place flour, sugar and salt in a food processor and blend briefly. Pulse in the butter to create a grainy mixture. Add in ice water and pulse to create a dough that just holds together. Transfer to a lightly floured board and knead briefly and form into a disc about 6-7 inches wide. Divide into two equal portions; refrigerate one portion and freeze the other half for another day's baking. (Makes two single crusts)

Line a baking sheet with parchment paper. Spray a 9 or 10 inch tart of quiche pan (or a 9 inch spring-form pan also works) with non-stick cooking spray and place on the baking sheet.

For the filling, combine the butter and sugar in a medium bowl. Whisk to blend. Whisk in the eggs, vanilla, cocoa, flour, baking soda, and salt, blend well. Set aside.

Preheat the oven to 375°F.

Remove one portion of the pie dough from the fridge. On a lightly floured surface, roll the dough out into a 12-inch round. Line the pan with the dough. Trim off excess dough and reserve the trimmings. (If using a spring-form pan, allow dough to go up 1 inch up sides). Keep trimmings.

Bake 10 minutes; remove from oven and cool. Spread dulce de leche on bottom. Spoon the filling into the pie pan. Take the trimmings and roll very thin into a circle that just covers the top of the brownie filling. Brush lightly with melted butter. Place the pan back on the baking sheet. Place in the oven and immediately lower the temperature to 350°F.

Bake for 35 - 40 minutes, or until pastry turns lightly golden in colour and the chocolate filling seems barely set. Remove from oven and sprinkle on chocolate chips. Let chocolate melt a few minutes and then smear with a spatula. Chill 30 minutes to allow chocolate to set.

Dust with confectioners' sugar before serving. (You can also refrigerate for about 2 hours to chill it faster). To serve, cut into thin wedges and top with ice cream, and warm chocolate fudge sauce.

Serves 8 to 12

Chocolate Lover's Cake with White Chocolate Ganache

For chocolate lovers! This wickedly dark and decadent cake is surprisingly easy, and sports a touch of bourbon and a halo of white chocolate ganache which makes it riveting. The texture of this cake is moist but light. A perfect dessert for your sweetheart chocoholic on Valentine's Day. A red rose in the center would be the capper on the visuals.

2 cups all-purpose flour

1 teaspoon baking soda

1/8 teaspoon salt

1 ¾ cup brewed coffee

¼ cup brandy or bourbon

5 ounces semi-sweet chocolate

1 cup unsalted butter

2 cups sugar

2 eggs

1 ½ teaspoons pure vanilla extract

WHITE CHOCOLATE GANACHE

1 ½ cups white chocolate, chopped

1/2 cup whipping cream

FINISHING TOUCHES

2-3 ounces semi-sweet chocolate, melted, for drizzling

Confectioners' sugar

Preheat the oven to 300°F. Line a baking sheet with parchment paper. Spray a 10 inch spring-form pan with non-stick cooking spray and then wrap pan with foil outside snugly (cake is a thin batter; you don't want leaks). Place on the baking sheet.

In a medium bowl, whisk the flour, baking soda, and salt together. In a 2-quart saucepan, heat coffee with bourbon or brandy, and stir in chocolate and butter to melt. Add in the sugar, remove from the stove, and stir until smooth. Pour the chocolate mixture into a large bowl. Let cool a few minutes. Then add the dry ingredients to chocolate, and then blend in eggs and vanilla. Spoon the batter into the pan. It is a very thin batter. That is fine.

Bake approximately 1 ½ hours or until cake tests done; it will spring back when gently pressed with fingertips. Cool very well or refrigerate.

For the White Chocolate Ganache, heat the cream to just simmering and then quickly stir, then whisk the chocolate into melt. Stir until smooth. Chill until very thick but still pourable. If ganache is too thick to start with (some white chocolate melts differently), thin it with little additions of warm half-and-half or cream.

Pour over inverted cake, let drip down sides. Garnish with a drizzle of dark chocolate. Alternatively, you can coat the cake entirely in melted, dark chocolate or put a doily on the plain cake and sift confectioners' sugar on it for a pretty, Valentine's Day pattern. Also good served with ice-cream or whipped cream.

Serves 12-14

Sweetheart Chocolate Cherry Cheesecake

Bake this in a heart-shaped cheesecake pan if you have one. Chocolate-covered cherries make this cheesecake spectacular, what with its puddle of molten chocolate and cherries that sits in the center. Each slice features this amazing flavor combination.

CRUST

1 1/2 cups shortbread cookie or chocolate wafer cookie crumbs

1/4 cup sugar

Pinch cinnamon

1/4 cup unsalted butter, melted

CHEESECAKE

1 cup semi-sweet chocolate chips, melted

2 1/2 pounds cream cheese, softened

1 cup sugar

1/4 cup all-purpose flour

1 14 ounce can condensed milk

6 eggs

2 1/2 teaspoons pure vanilla extract

1/8 teaspoon almond extract

1/2 cup whipping cream

1 1/2 cups miniature marshmallows

1/3 cup chopped white chocolate

1/2 cup chopped milk chocolate

1 cup maraschino cherries

TOPPING

1 box, or 12-20 milk chocolate-covered cherries

Melted, white and semi-sweet chocolate for drizzling

Confectioners' sugar for dusting

Preheat the oven to 325°F. Line a baking sheet with parchment paper.

Mix crust ingredients and pat into a 9 or 10 inch spring-form pan and place on the baking sheet.

For the cheesecake, have the chocolate chips melted and set aside. In a mixer bowl, cream the cream cheese with the sugar and flour on lowest speed until smooth. Add condensed milk, and then add eggs and blend until smooth. Stir in vanilla and almond extract, and then cream.

Pour half of batter into pan. Fold in half of the marshmallows, white chocolate, milk chocolate, and ½ cup of the cherries. Spoon in half the melted dark chocolate. Swirl a bit with a knife or fork and then spoon on remaining batter and top with remaining white and milk chocolate, marshmallows and cherries. Drizzle on remaining melted chocolate and swirl again, gently, with a knife. (What you are trying to achieve is somewhat even distribution of the add-in elements to the cheesecake batter. It does not have to be perfect; it will still bake up just fine)

Bake 50 -65 minutes or until cake seems barely firm to the touch. Turn oven off. Open oven door and pull out cake on the rack. Gently place chocolate cherries, for topping, on top surface of cake. As chocolate warms up (on hot cake), it will ooze and melt. Leave in oven, with door ajar for 2 hours and then refrigerate 8 hours or overnight, or up to 3 days. You can also freeze it.

Drizzle with white and dark melted chocolate before serving; let set and then dust (refrigerate briefly to set chocolate) with confectioners' sugar.

Serves 14-16

Demeter's Song or Spring Wheat

by Marcy Goldman

Spring wheat is best.

Planted early

Harvested in heat

A gift of the farmer

To the baker in the town

Earth, a casual celebrant

Makes the marriage sound.

Spring wheat is best -

It makes for flour of white gold

That suits so much

Bread to chew

Sweet things with honey

Wedding cake and spiced dreams -

The miller only imagines

What the baker lass can do

And I do.

I do !

For I married the wheat a long time ago

And now it grows in my veins and my blood

I wear it as a dress

And coil it as a crown

Use the sheaf as a sash

Upon my apron gown

Spring wheat *is* best.

And to the wheat I am bound.

Spring, Small Baking

The Fresh Season, Light and Sweet

Spring in the Bakery

Spring, whether she arrives soft and surprisingly early or fashionably late as any belle of the ball is wont to do, is as inevitable as falling in love. And just like falling in love, spring is about all things fresh and hopeful; it's the host of tender new starts. As such, Spring is a beloved season.

Characteristic as only one of the two transitional seasons can be, Spring is always a touch more precious, due to for its shortness of stay and mercurial nature (stormy rains, lilac colored new mists and tulips). If there's a season that's more feminine than the others, it's spring for it celebrates a pending fertility that is magical in a way no other season can.

And just what *is* that scent that comes in April? It's a curious cocktail of mud, new grass, rain and lilacs and it's heady stuff. This *eau de parfum* is called renewal and it calls for delicate, happy baking. For me, it means baking for Passover (for many friends, it means chocolate baking for Easter); it means rhubarb recipes and also baking for special teas I like to hold.

Although the holidays of St. Patrick's Day, and Shrove Tuesday do not officially occur in spring, I've included recipes for those holidays in this chapter because to me, they are spring-oriented in spirit. Other holidays include St. Patrick's Day, Mardi Gras, and occasions such as Maple Sugaring Off, garden parties, Mother's Day, school graduations, Mother's Day brunches baby showers, and weddings. There's also spring festivals, rites of spring occasions such as Cherry Festivals, Asparagus, Azalea, Strawberry and Maple festivals and gatherings, not to mention May Day, Spring Equinox and April Fool's Day!

The Perfume of Spring

The scent of spring is lightly fruity and sparkling; if it was a fluid decant, it would come in a multi-faceted, crystal bottle, pear-shaped and feminine. One whiff and you could enjoy a sweet effervescence of champagne, tiny forest strawberries and mellow notes of apricot with hints of maple. Everything about spring is sweet and light as an early dawn of an April morning.

Base Notes

Fraises des bois, garden fresh rhubarb, fine beet sugar, white chocolate

Heart Notes

Wild strawberries, rhubarb, California apricots, touch of pure maple syrup and sweet, tart crab apples

Top Notes

White chocolate, citrus zest and morning dew

Theme Mood

Rebirth, Yearning, Hope, Optimism, and Rejuvenation

Theme Colors

Yellow, White, Green, Pink, Lilac

The Style of Spring Baking

Spring Flavor and Ingredient Palate

New strawberries, apricots, lemons, pure maple syrup, pink rhubarb, white chocolate, dairy and butter pastries, custards, i.e. all light, feminine baking. The color tone of spring is light and pretty. To me, this translates as golden and yellow baking, enlivened with strawberries and cream, lightness of color, taste and ingredients. Spring is not above the addition of a good dash of dark chocolate, especially around Passover, Easter and Mother's Day,

In spring, suddenly strawberries on sale everywhere. Why not fresh Strawberry Shortcake or a golden Daffodil Cheesecake with berries on the side or French Apricot Tart with blushing fruit, sweetly nested in rich custard? This is the time to court fatigued winter palates with zesty, pretty, colorful desserts such as pastel-fondant covered Hot Cross Buns or a luscious Flourless Chocolate Torte that does double duty for Passover or Easter. It's a whirlwind of small touches and tastes that are at once every day and somehow, special and a little celebratory – just like spring itself.

Spring, Small Baking Recipes

Maple Cheesecake Cupcakes

Deluxe Limoncello Cupcakes

Cream Scones for Strawberry Cream Tea

Strawberry Shortcake Assembly

Pure Strawberry Preserves

White Chocolate Brioche Muffins

Bailey's Irish Cream Brownies with Warm Toffee Sauce

Sugared Apricot Scones

Strawberry Rhubarb Pie Muffins

Orchard Field Preserves

Swiss Chocolate Strawberry Oatmeal Cookies

Gourmet Shop Maple Cookies

Maple Cheesecake Cupcakes

March brings the clear tapping sound of spigots being inserted in maple trees, brimming with sap and poised to bestow their sweet and sappy bounty. What better way to celebrate the first crop of the season than with these maple cupcakes?

WALNUT CRUMB TOPPING

3/4 cup finely chopped walnuts

1/3 cup butterscotch or white chocolate chips, optional

2 tablespoons sugar

1/3 cup brown sugar, firmly packed

2 tablespoons unsalted butter

CREAM CHEESE TOPPING

6 ounces cream cheese

1 egg

1/4 cup sugar

1 teaspoon pure vanilla extract

MUFFIN BATTER

1 cup brown sugar, firmly packed

1/2 cup white sugar

3 tablespoons pure maple syrup

1/2 cup unsalted butter

1 egg

1 1/2 teaspoons pure vanilla extract

½ teaspoon pure maple extract, optional *

1 cup buttermilk

2 ½ cups all-purpose flour

2 1/4 teaspoons baking powder

1/4 teaspoon baking soda

1/4 teaspoon salt

* Boyajian offers pure maple extract

Preheat the oven to 375°F. Arrange oven rack to upper middle position. Line a baking sheet with parchment paper. Line a 12-cup muffin tin with muffin liners and generously spray it (including the top surface) with non-stick cooking spray. Place the pan on the baking sheet.

For the Walnut Crumb Topping, in a food processor, grind the nuts, butterscotch of white chocolate chips, white and brown sugars and butter together to make a fine mealy topping. Transfer mixture to a mixing bowl.

For the Cream Cheese Topping, (without cleaning the food processor bowl), blend the cream cheese, egg, sugar and vanilla until smooth and then spoon out into another bowl.

For the Muffin Batter, without cleaning the food processor bowl, cream the sugar, maple syrup and the butter until well blended and then add in egg, vanilla and maple extract and mix well. Add in the buttermilk, flour, baking powder, baking soda, and salt and blend well, making sure no unblended sugar/butter is stuck around the blade. Remove blade.

Using an ice-cream scoop, deposit the batter into each muffin well, filling almost up to the top (leaving about ½ inch room for filling). Spoon on some Cream Cheese Topping and then the Walnut Crumb Streusel on each as evenly possible.

Bake 30-35 minutes on middle rack of oven until muffins seem firm to the touch when gently touched. Remove gently (after 10 minutes) as tops might stick to muffin pan.

Makes 12-16

Deluxe Limoncello Cupcakes

Anything this good becomes an instant, new classic. It all starts with limoncello, a lemon liqueur from Sorrento, Italy. This recipe features a gorgeous lemon cupcake, filled with lemon curd and a lemon lemon mascarpone frosting.

CUPCAKE BATTER

½ cup unsalted butter

1 cup sugar

Zest of half a lemon, finely minced

3 eggs

1 teaspoon pure vanilla extract

½ teaspoon pure lemon oil or pure lemon extract

2 tablespoons fresh lemon juice

2 tablespoons Limoncello liqueur

¾ cup buttermilk

1 ½ cup all-purpose flour

1 teaspoon baking powder

½ teaspoon baking soda

1/8 teaspoon salt

LEMON FILLING

3/4 cup sugar

5 tablespoons cornstarch

1 cup water

2 egg yolks

1 tablespoon lemon zest, finely minced

1/3 cup lemon juice

1 tablespoon Limoncello

1 tablespoon unsalted butter

Limoncello Syrup

1/3 cup water

1/3 cup sugar

Zest of half a lemon, finely minced

¼- ½ teaspoon pure lemon oil or extract

2 tablespoons Limoncello

1 tablespoon fresh lemon juice

LIMONCELLO MASCARPONE FROSTING

2 tablespoons unsalted butter

6 tablespoons softened mascarpone or cream cheese

1 tablespoon limoncello

½ teaspoon lemon extract or oil

1 teaspoon pure vanilla extract

3-4 cups confectioners' sugar

FINISHING TOUCHES

Lemon zest

Raspberries

Preheat the oven to 350°F. Line a baking sheet with parchment paper. Line 12 regular cupcake wells (or 24 little ones) with cupcake or muffin liners. Place the pan on the baking sheet.

In a mixer bowl, cream the butter, sugar and lemon zest until well-blended. Blend in the eggs, vanilla, lemon oil, Limoncello and lemon juice. Add in the buttermilk and blend well; fold in the flour, baking powder, baking soda and salt. Blend to make a smooth batter, making sure nothing is stuck in the well of the mixer bowl. Using a small ice-cream scoop, deposit batter 2/3's full in each muffin well.

Bake until cupcakes spring back when gently touched with fingertips and edges are lightly browned, about 25-28 minutes. Cool on a cake rack.

For the Lemon Filling, in a small saucepan, over medium heat, stir the sugar, cornstarch and water. Cook on medium heat until the mixture comes to a gentle boil stirring often. Cook for 3 more minutes, stirring continuously until it thickens. Remove from heat.

In a small bowl, whisk the yolks and then whisk in ¼-1/2 cup of the hot mixture a little bit at a time to temper the egg yolks (otherwise they will cook like scrambled eggs versus thickening the lemon cornstarch mixture). Then briskly whisk the yolk mixture into the saucepan. Let the filling return to a gentle boil and cook for 1-3 more minutes, stirring continuously. Turn off the heat. Add the lemon zest, lemon juice, limoncello and butter. Stir until it is smooth and let cool slightly. Refrigerate until needed, allowing it to set up and become more firm. Whisk it to make smooth before using.

For the Limoncello Syrup, in a small pan, heat the water, sugar, zest, lemon extract, Limoncello and lemon juice 3-5 minutes until sugar dissolves. Cool to room temperature (refrigerate until needed).

For the Limoncello Mascarpone Frosting, place the butter, mascarpone or cream cheese, limoncello, vanilla, lemon extract and confectioners' sugar in a food processor and blend until fluffy, adding in more confectioners' sugar to thicken to a frosting consistency. Chill until needed. (When you re-whip it if you need to, drizzle in some of the Limoncello Syrup; this helps it stay soft and adds yet more flavour)

To assemble, using a paring knife, scoop out a chunk of cupcake. Drizzle some Lemon Syrup into the well and then add a teaspoon or so of Lemon Filling. Top with removed cupcake chunk, drizzle on more syrup, let soak and then frost with frosting. Garnish with lemon zest (or a raspberry).

Makes 12 regular cupcakes or 24 little ones

Cream Scones for Strawberry Cream Tea

Pioneer cooks relied on fresh buttermilk for extra light biscuits. My trick is replacing buttermilk with whipping cream to which you've added some lemon juice. This mix makes for particularly lofty scones. This is the time to take out your vintage tea-cup selection.

1 cup cake flour (or all-purpose)

3 cups all-purpose flour

5 ½ teaspoons baking powder

1/2 teaspoon baking soda

3/4 cup sugar

1/2 teaspoon salt

½ cup unsalted butter

2/3 to 3/4 cup whipping cream (or more, as required), soured *

2 eggs

FINISHING TOUCHES
Milk

Sugar

Unsalted butter, melted

* To sour the whipping cream, mix the cream with 1 tablespoon lemon juice and let stand a few minutes so that it can curdle.

Preheat the oven to 425°F. Stack two baking sheets together and line the top one with parchment paper. Place the oven rack set at the upper third position.

In a large bowl, combine the cake flour and all-purpose flour, baking powder, soda, sugar and salt. Cut in the butter until mixture is coarse and grainy. Spoon on the soured whipping cream over the mixture, then the eggs, stirring lightly with a fork to blend. Turn out onto a floured board and knead 8-10 times, until mixture is just barely rollable.

Pat or roll out 1-inch thick. Cut circles of 4 inches and then cut these circles again in half to form rounded wedges. Alternatively, you can cut 3 ½ inch round scones.

Brush tops with melted butter or milk, dust with sugar and bake until golden, about 12-15 minutes.

Makes approximately 14

Strawberry Shortcake (Assembly)

Use the Cream Scones recipe as the shortcake base. These are tiny gems of flaky shortcakes that await crushed strawberries and whipping cream. Just split, cream and berry them and enjoy. This is just the thing to serve at Mother's Day, a spring tea, convocation or for the summer patriots, Canada Day or July 4ᵗʰ.

ONE BATCH CREAM SCONES

SWEET WHIPPING CREAM
2 cups whipping cream

3-4 tablespoons confectioners' sugar

1 pint basket fresh strawberries, hulled, mashed with 3 tablespoons or more, sugar

FINISHING TOUCHES
Confectioners' sugar

Strawberry halves

Split the scones in half horizontally.

In a mixer bowl with whisk attachment, whip the whipping cream slowly with the confectioners' sugar. Increase the speed and whip until soft peaks form.

To serve, put some berries on bottom half of scone, top with whipped cream and then top half of scone. Dust with confectioners' sugar or top with more cream and a berry half.

Serves 6-8

White Chocolate Brioche Muffins

No special bakeware or expertise needed. These are wonderful fresh or toasted and my rendition of a famous bakery's delicate sweet yeast muffins that features huge chunks of white chocolate in a buttery dough.

1/2 cup warm water

5 teaspoons instant yeast

3/4 cup warm milk

2 teaspoons pure vanilla extract

1 1/4 teaspoon salt

2/3 cup sugar

3 egg yolks

3 ½ - 4 cups all-purpose flour

3/4 cup unsalted butter, softened

1 1/2 cups coarsely chopped white chocolate

FINISHING TOUCHES
Unsalted butter, melted

Line 1-2 baking sheets with parchment paper. Generously brush two muffin pans with melted butter and place muffin pans on baking sheet. Line each muffin well with a muffin liner (tulip-shaped ones are lovely but regular one are fine)

In a mixer bowl, whisk together water and yeast and let stand 1 minute. Stir in milk, vanilla, salt, sugar, egg yolks, and half of the flour. Mix, then knead, adding more flour as required to make a soft elastic dough (5 to 8 minutes). Once a soft ball forms and the dough seems resilient, cover it (leave it in mixer) and let it stand 20 minutes. Gently deflate the dough (1-2 revolutions of the mixer should do it). Attach paddle (i.e. remove dough hook) and add the butter and the white chocolate chunks until it is all combined. Dough may seem greasy but that's fine.

Remove the paddle and cover entire bowl with a large plastic bag; let rest for 15 minutes. Gently deflate the dough and deposit a mound of dough, shaping each into a ball, in each prepared muffin well (you should have 18-24). (Each muffin should be ¾ full)

Brush each brioche/muffin with melted butter.

Cover the pans with a large plastic sheet or bag and let rise until quite puffy (30-40 minutes).

Preheat the oven to 350°F. Bake until done (30 to 40 minutes) until well browned). Allow to cool in pan for 20 minutes before removing. Brush again with butter.

Makes 18-24

Pure Strawberry Preserves

Nothing beats homemade fresh strawberry preserves. My recipe produces a preserve that is jam-like but studded with chunks of whole berries. As with any sort of preserving, don't skimp on the preserving pot. Invest in a well-cladded or thick-bottomed pot so that the preserves don't scorch.

10 cups semi-crushed large or small (whole) strawberries

1 orange

7 cups sugar

Prepare pot by spraying inside bottom and sides with non-stick cooking spray. Wash and hull berries. Remove all small berries and set aside. Crush or mash remaining berries coarsely in a food processor or by hand (hand method is messier but best). Wash orange, cut, seed and grind in a food processor until it is a fine paste. Combine reserved whole berries with crushed berries and pureed orange and mix well.

Place fruit and sugar in pot and stir over low to medium heat. As sugar dissolves, increase heat to medium high and simmer jam until foam forms. Skim off any foam that forms.

Boil gently until jam tests done, about 220°F on a jam and candy thermometer. Ladle into sterilized jars and process according to manufacturer's boiling bath method instructions.

Makes 8-10 small jars

SCONE AND BISCUIT TRICKS

Do you prefer high-rising scones and biscuits or would you sacrifice height for a lighter texture? This is the age-old issue with scones and biscuits. Tidy and neat scones – the ones you roll and cut, need to be cut from a firmer dough. Softer scone doughs, such as a drop scone or drop biscuit, wherein you drop a blob of dough on the baking sheet, rise higher but you may lose that pretty little shape which in the case of shortcake, is part of their charming presentation. If you don't mind roughing it, scoop (ice-cream scoop) a wetter scone batter and make less uniform scones – they're a bit less contained in shape but a lighter scone, overall.

Bailey's Irish Cream Brownies with Warm Sticky Toffee Sauce

For this bit of decadence, use any Irish Cream liqueur, which is a blend of Irish whisky, pure cream and touches of vanilla. For gift giving, bring the sticky toffee stuff in a jar and then box up the brownie. This is a perfect St. Pat's brownie.

BROWNIE PART

1 cup unsalted butter

14 ounces semi-sweet chocolate, in chunks

4 tablespoons cocoa

2 1/3 cups sugar

2 teaspoons pure vanilla extract

1 tablespoon Irish whisky

6 eggs

2 cups all-purpose flour

Pinch salt

IRISH CREAM GANACHE

1 cup Bailey's Irish Cream (or O'Casey's)

1 ½ cups semi-sweet chocolate, finely chopped

Sticky Irish Whisky Toffee Sauce

1 1/2 cups sugar

1/3 cup water

1/3 cup whipping cream

¼ cup Bailey's Irish Cream (or O'Casey's)

3 tablespoons unsalted butter

Preheat the oven to 350°F. Generously spray a 9 by 13 pan with non-stick cooking spray and place it on a parchment paper-lined baking sheet.

For the Brownie Part, over low heat, in a heavy bottomed 2-quart saucepan, melt the butter and chocolate together, and stir to smooth. Add in cocoa. Remove from heat and spoon out into a large bowl and let cool to room temperature.

Add in the sugar, vanilla, whiskey and eggs. Blend until smooth. Fold in the flour and salt and stir to make a smooth batter. Spoon into pan.

Bake 30-40 minutes or until brownies seem just set. It is impossible to totally 'test' these for doneness since they're gooey but overall, better to underbake them, and serve them chilled, than overbake them. Cool brownies a good hour before serving, allowing them to set up a bit.

For the Irish Cream Ganache, in a small saucepan, heat the Bailey's to just simmering. Stir in the chocolate and stir or whisk to melt chocolate so it's smooth and consistent. Remove from heat. Refrigerate until firm.

While the brownies are baking, prepare the Irish Whisky Sticky Toffee Sauce. In a heavy-bottomed, 2 1/2 quart saucepan mix the sugar and water over low heat. Cook, stirring occasionally, 15-20 minutes, until it reaches a dark amber color. Throughout the cooking, brush the inner sides down with a pastry brush dipped in cold water (this prevents crystals from forming on the sides and going into the syrup). Remove from the stove and place the saucepan in a sink. Taking great care to avoid spattering and standing away as much as possible, stir in the whipping cream, Bailey's Irish Cream, and butter. This will cool the mixture but it will also foam and bubble up quite significantly so take care. You should have a thick caramel.

Soften the Irish Cream Ganache (warm up a bit or soften with wooden spoon). Spread on brownies and refrigerate until an hour before serving.

To serve, place a brownie on a plate, drizzle with the warm sauce. Garnish with a shamrock.

Makes 16-30 brownies

Sugared Apricot Scones

White whole-wheat flour is a sweet, light whole-wheat flour that is available from King Arthur Flour or Hodgson Mills and I like it for its boost of nutrition along with its lighter taste. If you don't have it on hand, just use regular whole-wheat flour for these delightful apricot-kissed, rustic, sweet scones.

1 cup white whole-wheat flour

2 – 2 1/2 cups all-purpose flour

1 tablespoon orange zest, finely minced

1 tablespoon baking powder

1 teaspoon baking soda

3/4 cup sugar

3/8 teaspoon salt

1/2 cup unsalted butter, in one-inch chunks

1 egg

1 1/2 teaspoons pure vanilla extract

1 cup whipping cream mixed with 1 tablespoon lemon juice

½ cup finely diced dried apricots, plumped and dried

FINISHING TOUCHES

1/2 cup apricot preserves

Milk

Unsalted butter, melted

Sugar

Preheat the oven to 425°F. Arrange oven rack to upper third position. Stack two baking sheets together and line the top one with parchment paper.

In a food processor bowl, add the whole-wheat flour, 2 cups of the all-purpose flour, orange zest, baking powder, baking soda, sugar and salt and blend briefly. Add in chunks of butter and pulse to make a grainy mixture. Remove to a medium bowl. Make a well in the center and stir in the egg, vanilla, and most of the cream-lemon juice, stirring to make a rough, shaggy mass, adding in more (regular) whipping cream to achieve this consistency. Fold in the dried apricots. Turn the dough out onto a lightly floured work surface and gently knead to form a smooth, firm dough. If the dough is still quite wet, dust your board generously with more flour. This will get absorbed into the dough as you knead it a bit more, firming up so it can be handled.

Pat the dough into two 1-inch thick rounds. Cut into small scones, either small wedges or circles. Place on baking sheet and brush each with milk or melted butter and dust with sugar. Make a small indent in each scone and spoon on some a generous dab of apricot preserves.

Place scones in oven, immediately reducing lowering temperature to 400°F and bake until edges are golden, about 18-24 minutes.

Makes 10-12, depending on size

Strawberry Rhubarb Pie Muffins

These hug and, exciting muffins are delectable, mini coffee-cake, brightened with rhubarb and diced ruby-red strawberries, they are further dolled up with a halo of shortbread-cookie streusel.

SHORTBREAD COOKIE STREUSEL

1 ¼ cups shortbread cookie crumbs

1/4 cup unsalted butter

¼ cup sugar

MUFFIN BATTER

2 cups white sugar

1 cup unsalted butter, melted

4 eggs

1 tablespoon pure vanilla extract

5 ¼ cups all-purpose flour

4 teaspoons baking powder

1 teaspoon baking soda

1/2 teaspoon salt

1 cup buttermilk

1/2 cup sour cream

1 ½ cups diced rhubarb

2 ½ cups diced fresh strawberries

Preheat the oven to 375°F. Arrange oven rack to upper middle position. Line a baking sheet with parchment paper. Line a 12-16 large or jumbo muffin tin with muffin liners and generously spray it (including the top surface) with non-stick cooking spray. Place the pan on the baking sheet.

For the streusel, mix the cookie crumbs, butter, and sugar to make a coarse mixture and set aside.

For the muffins, in large bowl blend the sugar with the butter; briskly whisk in the eggs and vanilla. Fold in most of the flour (hold back a cup), baking powder, baking soda and salt, adding in the buttermilk and sour cream; blend to make a thick batter. If batter seems loose, fold in the reserved flour. The batter should be quite thick; if not, add in more of the flour. Gently fold in the fruit. Using an ice-cream scoop, deposit generous amounts of batter into prepared muffin cups. Deposit a generous amount of the streusel on each muffin.

Bake, immediately lowering temperature to 350°F, 30-35 minutes or until muffins spring back when gently touched with fingertips and muffins are golden brown.

Makes 12-16 jumbo muffins or about 2 dozen smaller ones

Swiss Chocolate Strawberry Oatmeal Cookies

Fresh spring strawberries shine when plunked on top of oatmeal cookies. These are chewy-centered, crisp-edged, and have the slight tang of dried strawberries, with chocolate chips, brown-sugar-and-butter wonderfulness. This is the favorite cookie from my days of coaching baseball, spring training through to summer play-offs.

1 cup dried strawberries, plumped and dried

1 cup unsalted butter, softened

1 1/4 cups brown sugar, firmly packed

3/4 cup white sugar

1 tablespoon pure apple syrup or honey *

2 teaspoons pure vanilla extract

2 eggs

1 3/4 cups all-purpose flour

1 teaspoon baking powder

3/4 teaspoon baking soda

1/8 teaspoon cinnamon

3/8 teaspoon salt

4 cups rolled or old-fashioned oatmeal

1 cup semi-sweet chocolate chips

½ cup chopped walnuts

FINISHING TOUCHES
Strawberries, hulled and cut in half or quarters

Sugar

* Apple syrup is a sweet, tangy syrup, about the consistency of molasses. I get mine from King Arthur Flour or the local health food store. Honey is fine as a substitute.

Plump the strawberries in very hot water for a few minutes. Then drain and dry them and set aside.

In a mixer bowl cream the butter with the brown and white sugar and apple syrup. Then add in vanilla and eggs and blend well, about 3-4 minutes. Fold in flour, baking powder, baking soda, cinnamon, salt and oatmeal. When just about blended, fold in chocolate, walnuts and dried strawberries. Chill the batter 15 minutes. Preheat the oven to 350°F.

Roll two tablespoons worth of cookie dough with your hands. Arrange on prepared baking sheets, leaving about 2 inches or more, between each cookie. Press gently and garnish center of cookie with a strawberry quarter or half so that it bakes with some red fruit exposed. Sprinkle some sugar on the berry (this will help it set up versus being too watery after baking)

Bake 16-20 minutes until cookies are set, and middles are slightly dry looking and edges have begun to brown. The area around the strawberry will appear slightly moister but will set up after cookies cool.

Let the cookies cool 15 minutes before removing to a wire rack to cool completely; refrigerate to store.

Makes about 16-20 medium cookies

MASON JARS, CAPTURING FRUIT FRESHNESS IN A JAR

It's impossible to talk about summer fruits without a nod to the ubiquitous glass jars that preserve the fruity treasures we so enjoy in baking or preserving in other ways. Invented by John Mason in the early 1850's, Mason jars preceded commercial canning and were the domain of farm wives and home makers – everyone jammed! Ball Corp. was a manufacturer of these jars. Since their invention, they've continued to exist and are still available in various sizes that all feature a ring top and vacuum lid. (This is actually a 'modern touch' for originally the jars were sealed with melted wax or paraffin until the early 1900's until they segued to the more modern seal lids).

Mason jars originally came in dark shades of amber, green or blue glass but these days they are clear glass (sometimes you can find blue ones). Not surprisingly, since the jars are classically country-attractive, collectors of antique Mason and Ball jars are avid about sleuthing out back-in-the-day pantry classics. Nothing says 'summer time' or pickle time (for that matter), than a case of fresh Mason jars and a new packet of lids, sitting on a counter, awaiting kitchen duty.

Gourmet Shop Maple Cookies

These are best described these as a cross between butter cookies, shortbread and biscotti. The cookie dough is rolled in crushed nuts and sugar just as they come out of the oven for a delectable finish.

1/2 cup plus 2 tablespoons unsalted butter

1/2 cup white sugar

1/3 cup brown sugar, firmly packed

1/2 cup finely ground, toasted cashews or walnuts

1 teaspoon pure maple extract

1 ½ teaspoon pure vanilla extract

2 cups all-purpose flour

Tiny pinch salt

ROLL-IN MIXTURE

1/4 cup sugar

1/4 cup ground toasted cashews or walnuts

1/4 cup brown sugar

1/4 cup confectioners' sugar

Preheat the oven to 350°F. Stack two large baking sheets together and line the top one with parchment paper.

In a food processor, pulse the butter, white and brown sugar together to make a crumbly mixture. Then process longer, to make a creamed, pasty mixture, a couple of minutes. Blend in the nuts, and then the maple and vanilla extracts, flour and salt. Blend a minute or two until it clumps but does not quite hold together. If it does not seem to hold together, test a clump by squeezing some dough in your hand and seeing if you can form a ball. If you can, it is blended enough.

For the Roll-In Mixture, mix sugar, cashews or walnuts, brown sugar and confectioners' sugar until well blended.

Form small balls of dough, about 1/2 inch thick – they should be about the size of a small golf ball. Place the cookies on the baking sheet, about 2 inches apart. Bake until browned around the edges and begin to colour on the tops, 16 –18 minutes. Cool cookies briefly and then toss in Roll-In mixture to coat cookies.

Makes about 40 cookies

Orchard Field Preserves

This is one of my original trademark recipes, that while not baking, goes with the baking (biscuits, breads, pancakes) a good combination of flavours and yields a preserve the colour of sunset with a memorable taste. It's called "orchard/field" because it uses two fruits from the orchard, and two from the field. It makes good sense in spring - when all four fruits are easily available. My favourite baker (turned jam maker) tip? To test without a thermometer, chill a saucer in the freezer for 15 minutes. Place a spoon of jam on it and see if jam runs thickly, in a single stream when saucer is tilted.

1 medium seedless orange, washed

2 cups fresh apricots, quartered

8 cups rhubarb, chopped into one inch dice

2 cups strawberries, (large ones crushed, small ones whole)

9 cups sugar, approximately (should be 3/4 cup sugar per 1 cup fruit)

Puree or grind orange, peel, rind, and all, in food processor until smooth.

Prepare other fruit. Spray a large heavy bottom pot or preserving kettle with cooking spray.

Place fruits and sugar in pot and heat on low to medium to allow sugar to melt and fruits to become more liquid and loose. Increase heat to medium to high and boil on high until foam forms. Skim off foam. Gently boil until jam is thick and sticky looking and tests done, about soft ball to jelly stage, about 220 degrees°F.

Ladle into sterilized jars and process according to manufacturer's canning instructions.

Makes about 6-8 small jars

THE REDCOATS ARE COMING OR STRAWBERRY FIELDS FOREVER

Doubtless G-d could have made a better berry, but doubtless, He never did'.

Sweet strawberries come from their wild fraise des bois cousins, woodland berries that predate the, cultivated mammoth berries you see in the supermarket. The French were really wild about strawberries but it was the English (a hundred years or so) who cultivated them. The little plants happily took root in Virginia Colony, and soon enough, the colonialists began to enjoy them.

Strawberries grow on vines and in hot houses, and in fields but the best ones always seem to found lining a country dirt road. Farm berries, like most privately owned farm produce, are still the most flavorful. Still, big, hot house strawberries are great to decorate cheesecakes with. Mashed up with sugar, summer strawberries are a fine topping for strawberry shortcake or scones. You can also dip berries melted dark or white chocolate or float them in a pool of champagne at your a home-grown wedding. I, for one, love little strawberries berries floating in a cup of chamomile tea. Jolly, sweet and always welcome as the first robin's song of spring, that's strawberries for you.

Spring, Big Baking

Including Holiday and
Special Occasions

Spring, Big Baking Including Holiday and Special Occasions Recipes

Lemon Crumble Tart

Strawberry Rhubarb Crisp Tart

Orange Rhubarb Pan Coffee Cake

Pretty in Pink Rhubarb Compote

Greek Yogurt Lemon Bundt Cake

Apricot Cream Cheese Coffee Cake

Maple Cream Layer Cake

Golden Daffodil Cheesecake

Waffle Bottom Cheesecake

Fresh Strawberry Rhubarb Pie

Rhubarb 'n Marshmallow Cheesecake with Brown Sugar Fudge

White Chocolate Strawberry Scone Cake

Basque Cream Cake

Spring Equinox Cherry Focaccio

Irish Mist Cheesecake

Miniature Wheaten Irish Soda Bread Scones

Tulip Pastel Fondant Glazed Hot Cross Buns

Chocolate Mandarin Chestnut Torte

Lemon Crumble Tart

Light and pretty, this luscious lemon tart made with shortbread or tart 'crumble' works in any season but it's particularly spring-like with it's sunny lemon filling. In days' past, lemon curd was also called 'lemon honey'. Fresh berries on the side would make this perfect.

TART DOUGH

2 cups all-purpose flour

3/8 teaspoon salt

½ cup sugar

3/4 cup unsalted butter

1 teaspoon pure vanilla extract

1 yolk

3-5 tablespoons whipping cream

LEMON CURD FILLING

¾ cup sugar

Zest of one large lemon, finely minced

4 egg yolks

6 tablespoons fresh lemon juice

¼ teaspoon pure lemon oil

½ cup unsalted butter

Pinch salt

FINISHING TOUCHES

Confectioners' sugar

Line a baking sheet with parchment paper. Generously spray a 9 or 10 inch tart or quiche pan with non-stick cooking spray.

For the Tart Dough, in a food processor, place the flour, salt and sugar and blend briefly. Add in the butter and vanilla; pulse to create a crumbly mixture, i.e. it will all but stick together and seem like clumpy crumbs. Then add in the yolk and cream and blend until it sticks together a bit more. But don't let it mix too much and become a dough that holds together in one mass; keep it somewhat crumbly. Remove one cup of the dough, bag and put in freezer. Distribute the remaining dough into the prepared pan and press the crumbs into bottom and sides evenly. Place the pan on the baking sheet.

For the Lemon Curd Filling, in a double boiler over low heat, combine the sugar, lemon zest, and egg yolks. Whisk briskly until mixture thickens, 5-10 minutes. Add in butter and salt and then let cool; stir in lemon juice and lemon oil. Spoon the mixture into a bowl, spray the top with non-stick cooking spray or holding a cold block of butter, smear the block of butter on the top so that a little butter melts onto the curd. (This will stop a skin from forming)

Cover the curd snugly with plastic wrap (no air space, otherwise humidity will form). Refrigerate overnight or until needed (and mixture is completely cool before adding to the tart bottom).

Preheat the oven to 350°F.

To assemble the tart, spoon the Lemon Curd Filling into the tart bottom and spread evenly. Grate the reserved frozen dough over the top. Place tart on baking sheet. Bake 35-40 minutes or until the top of the tart starts to gently brown.

Dust with confectioners' sugar just before serving.

Serves 8-10

Strawberry Rhubarb Crisp Tart

Elegant and easy, this streusel-topped, tart-like cake does triple duty as a breakfast sweet, coffee-break snack, or springtime dessert for a more elaborate meal. It's best refrigerated for two hours before serving for it to set up.

Strawberry Rhubarb Puree

2 cups rhubarb, diced

1 cup strawberries, diced

1/3 - 1/2 cup sugar

2 tablespoons cornstarch

TART

2 1/4 cups all-purpose flour

3/4 cup sugar

3/4 cup unsalted butter, cold

1 teaspoon baking powder

1/2 teaspoon baking soda

1/4 teaspoon cinnamon

Zest of a medium orange, finely minced

1/8 teaspoon salt

1 beaten egg

1 teaspoon pure vanilla extract

3/4 cup buttermilk

FINISHING TOUCHES

Confectioners' sugar

For the Strawberry Rhubarb Puree, place the rhubarb and strawberries in a 1 1/2 quart, heavy-bottomed saucepan. Toss with sugar and corn starch. Cook on medium low to cook down fruit, stirring occasionally, about 10-15 minutes, until fruit has dissolved, and is smooth and thickened. Keep refrigerated until needed.

Preheat the oven to 350°F. Generously spray a 9 inch tart or quiche pan with removable bottom with cooking spray (can also use a 9 inch spring-form pan). Place on a parchment paper lined baking sheet.

For the Tart, in a food processor, combine flour, sugar and butter and pulse until mixture is crumbly. Set aside one half cup for topping. Remove the rest to a medium bowl and stir in the baking powder, baking soda, cinnamon, orange zest and salt. Blend in the egg, vanilla and buttermilk to make a soft batter.

Spread 2/3 of batter over the bottom and up the sides of the prepared pan. Spread Strawberry Rhubarb puree on top of batter. Spoon or dollop remaining batter over rhubarb layer. Sprinkle on reserved sugar/flour mixture.

Bake for 45-50 minutes until cake is set and doesn't appear mushy in the center (because of the fruit, the usual done-ness test doesn't apply). If it does seem still somewhat wet, lower the temperature to 325°F and bake 10-15 minutes longer. Refrigerate at least two hours before serving. Dust with confectioners' sugar just before serving.

Serves 8-10

Orange Rhubarb Pan Coffee Cake

Nothing is a better match up than fresh oranges and garden rhubarb. Put them together in a quick bread and you have a fine treat for drop-by friends or an after dinner cake. The combination of oil and unsalted butter ensures its flavourful and a good keeper.

STREUSEL TOPPING

1 tablespoon unsalted butter

1/3 cup golden brown sugar, firmly packed

1/2 teaspoon cinnamon

1/2 cup chopped walnuts

CAKE BATTER

1 1/2 cup brown sugar, firmly packed

Zest of one orange, finely minced

1/3 cup canola oil

1/3 cup unsalted butter, melted

1 egg

1 cup fresh orange juice

2 ½ teaspoons pure vanilla extract

2 1/2 cups all-purpose flour

2 teaspoons baking powder

½ teaspoon baking soda

½ teaspoon cinnamon

1/8 teaspoon salt

1 1/2 cup diced rhubarb, (about ½ inch dice)

Preheat the oven to 350°F. Line a baking sheet with parchment paper. Generously spray a 9 by 13 rectangular cake pan with non-stick cooking spray and place it on the baking sheet.

For the Streusel Topping, in a small bowl or food processor, rub the butter into sugar, cinnamon and walnuts to make a coarse, crumbly mixture. Set aside.

For the cake batter, in a mixer bowl, combine brown sugar and orange zest and mix a few minutes. Then add in the oil, butter, egg, orange juice, and vanilla in a large bowl and stir to blend. Fold in the flour, baking powder, baking soda, cinnamon and salt; blend to partially combine. Then fold in rhubarb and finish blending into a smooth batter. Spoon into prepared pan. Sprinkle the streusel evenly over the top of the cake.

Bake until the cake tests done when gently pressed with fingertips (cake should seem firm underneath the streusel topping). If the cake appears to be browning more on the sides but not in the center, lower the temperature to 325°F and bake until cake tests done and seems firm to the touch, 50-65 minutes in total.

Serves 8-12

SPRINGTIME AWAKENINGS – THE GLORY OF RHUBARB

At the very least, rhubarb, aka Pie Plant, doesn't have an indifferent following. But most bakers eagerly anticipate the first crop of rhubarb because of all the dessert potential. For most tastes, rhubarb must be sweetened or offered along with other ingredients such as apples, apricots, or strawberries, to name some standard and appealing combinations. Fortunately, the results of such partnerships are divine. In short, almost anything you bake with rhubarb will yield some magnificent treats.

Good-natured, plentiful rhubarb has a rather long season but it does eventually end - so freeze all the rhubarb you can for baking throughout the year. It always comes in handy. To freeze, dice up the washed rhubarb, freeze on baking sheets or trays, lined with parchment paper. Once the chopped rhubarb is frozen, bag it up in proportioned freezer bags.

Greek Yogurt Lemon Bundt Cake

Yogurt and lemons combine nicely to give this statuesque Bundt cake a tender crumb with a distinctly cheesecake taste. Dust with confectioners' sugar or drizzle a lemon glaze with chopped pistachios or almonds. In spring, when it's all about lamb and fresh lemony things, offering this light cake is pitch perfect.

1 cup light (almost flavorless) olive or vegetable oil

1/2 cup unsalted butter, melted or light olive oil

2 cups sugar

4 eggs

2 cups plain yogurt

2 teaspoons lemon zest, finely minced

2 tablespoons fresh lemon juice

2 teaspoons pure vanilla extract

4 cups all-purpose flour

1/2 teaspoon baking soda

4 teaspoons baking powder

1/2 teaspoon salt

FINISHING TOUCHES
Confectioners' sugar

Preheat the oven to 350°F. Line a baking sheet with non-stick cooking spray. Generously spray a 9 or 10 inch tube pan or angel food pan (not with a removable bottom) with non-stick cooking spray. Alternatively, use a large Bundt cake mold but in addition to spraying with non-stick cooking spray, smear it very well with softened vegetable shortening. Place cake pan on baking sheet.

In a mixer bowl, cream the oil, butter, and sugar together until well blended, about 3-5 minutes. Blend in the eggs, yogurt, lemon zest, lemon juice, and vanilla. Blend well, about 2 minutes. Fold in the flour, baking powder, baking soda, and salt; blend well, making sure no un-combined ingredients cling to bottom well of mixing bowl. Spoon into prepared pan.

Bake until cake is set and tests done with a cake skewer comes out clean, 60-80 minutes. Cake will have fine cracks on the surface. If cake is browning on top but doesn't seems quite done inside, then lower reduce temperature to 325°F and let bake until done, in increments of 5-10 minutes.

Cool in pan 15 minutes before unmolding onto a wire cake rack to cool completely.

Dust with confectioners' sugar to serve. You can also offer this with lemon sorbet.

Serves 12-16

Pretty in Pink Rhubarb Compote

Rhubarb puree, the rhubarb equivalent of apple sauce is superb on its own, or slathered over fresh baking powder biscuits, shortcake, a simple vanilla cheesecake, waffles, or pancakes. In spring, it's handy to have around.

2 cups rhubarb, cut in one inch dice

1/3 - 1/2 cup sugar

For stove top cooking, place rhubarb in a 1 1/2 quart, heavy-bottomed saucepan and mix in the sugar. Cook on low heat about 5 minutes.

Cook on medium low to cook down fruit, stirring occasionally, about 10-15 minutes, until fruit is dissolved, smooth and thickened.

To prepare this recipe in a microwave, place the rhubarb in a Pyrex or similar, oven-proof 2 quart dish. Stir in the sugar, cover and microwave on High, 5 minutes. Stir fruit. Cover and microwave on High, 5-6 minutes, until fruit is dissolved. Stir to smooth consistency. Cool well before using.

Makes about 1 1/3 cups

DEMETER, GODDESS OF GRAIN

There's a goddess of grain and her name is Demeter. Demeter (or Ceres, in Roman mythology) was a sister of Zeus and the mother of Persephone. One day, Persephone was larking about a flower-filled meadow and girl reached for one of the blooms. Instantly, Hades, lord of the Underworld, emerged. Smitten with Persephone's beauty, he snatched her away to the underworld. Distraught Demeter searched, but her daughter was nowhere to be found. As Demeter mourned, the earth kept solidarity and nothing bloomed. Demeter cared less for the fallow fields she once tended (it was work to rule, you might say) and finally Zeus relented and cut a deal with his 'mother-in-law'. Persephone was returned to earth for six months each year. While her daughter was around, Demeter's joy knew no bounds; grain and fruit all thrived. But for those months when Persephone was with her underworld husband, Zeus, the earth was barren. The cycle of the seasons is tied to this myth and the seasonal revolutions parallel the flow of birth, death, life, and resurrection.

Spring, because of its light and airy baking, reminds me of Persephone more than any other season.

Maple Cream Layer Cake

Pure maple syrup makes a statement in this gorgeous layer cake that I created for first Bon Appetit feature. It calls for pure maple syrup along with a maple walnut praline. It's a fussy but extraordinary cake.

CAKE

1/2 cup unsalted butter

1/2 cup brown sugar, firmly packed

1 cup pure maple syrup

2 eggs

2 teaspoons pure vanilla extract

2 1/3 cups all-purpose flour

2 teaspoons baking powder

1/2 teaspoon baking soda

1/4 teaspoon salt

1/2 cup light cream or half-and-half

MAPLE WALNUT PRALINE

1 cup pure maple syrup

1 cup chopped walnuts

MAPLE CHANTILLY CREAM

2 cups whipping cream

1 teaspoon pure maple or vanilla extract

6 tablespoons confectioners' sugar

Preheat the oven to 350°F. Stack two baking sheets together and line the top one with parchment paper. Generously spray two 9 or 8 inch round cake layer pans with non-stick cooking spray and line with circles of parchment paper. Place pans on baking sheet.

For the cake, in a mixer bowl, on slow speed, cream the butter with the sugar until light and fluffy. Add in the maple syrup; blend well. Add the eggs and vanilla and blend until smooth. Gently and slowly fold in the flour, baking powder, baking soda and salt and mix on slow speed, drizzling in the light cream. Occasionally, scrape the bottom of the bowl with a spatula to ensure batter is evenly combined. If mixture appears curdled, don't worry about it. Add in about 1/4 -1/2 cup of the flour called for and it will bind it.

Spoon into prepared pans. Bake until cakes tests done and gently spring back when gently pressed with fingertips, about 35-30 minutes. Cool in pan 20 minutes and then turn out onto cake cooling rack and cool to room temperature about an hour or wrap in wax paper and put in freezer to speed cooling (and make for easier handling) about an hour.

For the Maple Walnut Praline, line a cookie sheet with parchment paper. Using a 2-quart heavy saucepan, with high sides (the syrup boils up the sides) gently boil syrup over low to medium heat until it reaches 300°F on a candy thermometer (hard crack stage). This takes awhile (15-25 minutes) if you do it slowly which is recommended. Remove from heat and stir in walnuts. Pour onto prepared baking sheet and cool well, until set. Transfer to a food processor and pulse to make a fine powder.

For the Maple Chantilly Cream, in a mixer bowl, slowly mix the cream with the extract and sugar. Slowly increase speed to whip cream into stiff peaks.

To assemble the cake, trim the top crusts of cake (about 1/8 inch). Set the bottom layer on a platter and spread on half of the whipped cream. Sprinkle with some maple praline. Top with second cake layer. Ice top and sides with remaining Maple Chantilly Cream. Press maple praline on sides and dust top with any remaining (or garnish with chopped walnuts).

Serve immediately or refrigerate until serving. This cake is best made a day ahead but still terrific served hours after baking and assembling.

Serves 10-12

THE SWEETEST STUFF, MAPLE SYRUP

Maple syrup is made by boiling the water out of the sap of a sugar tree. Native peoples knew this well and put maple syrup into many dishes. In fact, it was one of the first gifts they gave the newcomers who arrived on their shores. Maple sap is roughly 98% water and 2% sugar which means that 40 gallons of sap have to be evaporated to get just one gallon of maple syrup! Even with innovations such as pipeline, vacuum pumps and reverse osmosis machines, syrup production is a labor intensive undertaking, required equipment, expertise, and the cooperation of Mother Nature.

Nothing beats pure maple syrup but in the case of maple syrup, pure is very subtle and light. But when I want a bold maple flavor, I bolster things by using pure maple extract. This intensifies the maple theme. Pure maple extract is available in stores or you can get pure maple extract online from Boyajian. Whatever you do in maple baking, don't use imitation syrup known as maple table syrup.

Apricot Cream Cheese Coffee Cake

A sunny little coffee cake with apricot halves as mini 'sunshines' of fruit peeking through a baked on cream-cheese topping. Fresh, ripe apricots work best such as the new Velvet apricots.

CAKE

1/2 cup unsalted butter, in chunks

3 tablespoons sugar

2 eggs

1 1/2 teaspoons pure vanilla extract

1 1/4 cup all-purpose flour

1 teaspoon baking powder

1/8 teaspoon salt

FILLING

10-15 small apricots, halved and pitted

1 4 ounce package cream cheese, softened

½ cup sugar

¼ cup sour cream

1/4 teaspoon pure lemon oil or extract

¼ teaspoon pure almond extract

½ teaspoon pure vanilla extract

10-15 small apricots, halved and pitted

FINISHING TOUCHES

Confectioners' sugar

Preheat the oven to 350°F. Line a baking sheet with parchment paper. Generously spray a 10-inch spring form pan or fluted, deep tart pan with non-stick cooking spray and place it on the baking sheet.

For the cake, in a food processor, cream the butter and sugar together until well blended. Add eggs and vanilla extract and blend until smooth. Fold in the flour, baking powder and salt to make a soft batter. Spread batter on bottom and sides of cake pan. If batter is hard to manage, chill it for 30 minutes before speading in pan. Prepare the apricots and place them skin-side down on cake batter.

For the filling, in the same (no need to clean it) food processor bowl, blend the cream cheese, sugar, sour cream, lemon oil, almond, vanilla extract until it's a smooth mixture. Spoon cream cheese topping over the apricots. Bake until top is browned and appears set, 40-45 minutes.

Cool well before serving and dust with confectioners' sugar

Serves 8-10

Fresh Strawberry Rhubarb Pie

Use My Favorite All Butter Pie Pastry Dough for this or any good butter pastry to make this fabulous classic. There's no words that would do this simple pie justice and transmit its many merits. One tester suggested I simply double the ingredients for a two pie yield because "one pie would never be enough'.

9 inch pie shell, such as My Favorite All Butter Pie Pastry

FILLING
2 cups sliced strawberries

3 cups rhubarb, cut in half-inch dice

1 cup sugar

2 tablespoons orange liqueur or orange juice

2 teaspoons orange or lemon zest

3 tablespoons cornstarch

1/4 teaspoon cinnamon

Pinch teaspoon nutmeg

2 tablespoons unsalted butter

FINISHING TOUCHES
Milk

Coarse or regular sugar

Preheat the oven to 400 Degrees°F. Line 9 inch pie pan with pastry, reserving sufficient dough for the top crust.

For the filling, in a large bowl, toss the strawberries, rhubarb, sugar, orange liqueur or orange juice, orange or lemon zest, cornstarch, cinnamon, and nutmeg. Spoon into pie shell. Dot with bits of the butter. Place top crust on and seal and crimp edges. Brush top with milk and sprinkle lightly with coarse or regular sugar. Cut steam vents.

Place pie on a cookie sheet to catch juices. Place in oven, reduce heat to 375 F

Bake until pie is oozing fruit juices and top crust is a golden colour, 45-50 minutes.

Let pie cool well before serving, about 15-20 minutes.

Serves 5-6

Golden Daffodil Cheesecake

Daffodil Cake is a vintage yellow cake that you find in old farm cookbook. I've brought the daffodil cake forward so in this golden but light cheesecake.

FILO CRUST

8 sheets filo pastry dough

4 tablespoons unsalted butter, melted

CHEESECAKE

1 1/2 pound cream cheese

1/2 pound ricotta, cottage or baker's pot cheese, drained *

3/4 cup sugar

3 tablespoon Bird's Custard Powder or instant vanilla pudding

Tiny pinch salt

3 eggs

3 yolks

1/3 cup whipping cream

11/2 teaspoon pure vanilla extract

1/8 teaspoon lemon oil or extract

1 tablespoon fresh lemon juice

Zest of one small lemon, finely minced

1 14 ounce can apricot halves, well-drained, drained and diced

Sour Cream Topping

1 cup sour cream

1 tablespoon sugar

1/4 teaspoon pure vanilla extract

FINISHING TOUCHES

Confectioners' sugar

*To drain ricotta, place the cheese in paper towels and into a large strainer. Let stand to let excess moisture collect and drip off. Squeeze cheese a bit (in the paper towels) before using.

Preheat the oven to 350°F. Line a baking sheet with parchment paper.

For the Filo Crust, drizzle some melted butter on bottom of a ten-inch spring form pan. Brush a sheet of filo with butter and drape onto pan. Repeat with 3 more sheets (filo and butter), allowing excess filo to hang over the pan sides.

For the cheesecake, in a mixer bowl, blend the cream cheese, ricotta, with sugar, custard powder, and salt until smooth, on slow speed. Add in eggs, yolks, whipping cream and then vanilla, lemon oil, lemon juice and lemon zest. Fold in diced apricots. Spoon batter into prepared cake pan. Fold filo overhang onto the batter gently. Butter remaining filo sheets and fold in four or scrunch up and place on top of cheesecake batter. Place on the baking sheet. Bake about 40-45 minutes until filo is golden brown and cheesecake peeking through seems firm or set to the touch.

For the Sour Cream Topping, in a small bowl, stir the sour cream, sugar and vanilla together. Gently spread the topping on the middle of baked cheesecake (it will cover some of the filo; that is fine) and let bake another 8 minutes. Turn off oven, open door and let cake cool an hour. Then chill at least six hours or overnight.

To serve, remove pan sides gently and place cake on a serving. Dust with confectioners' sugar.

Serves 12-14

Waffle Bottom Cheesecake

Buttery waffles create a tender bottom crust and is the perfect throne for this lightly maple-infused cheesecake. A wonderful spring cheesecake that would also be welcome any season.

WAFFLE CRUST

5-6 frozen waffles, toasted

1/4 cup pure maple syrup

2-3 tablespoons unsalted butter, melted

FILLING

1 3/4 pounds cream cheese, room temperature

1/3 cup brown sugar

1 14-ounce can sweetened condensed milk

2 teaspoons pure vanilla extract

4 eggs

1/4 cup sour cream

1 teaspoon pure maple extract, optional

2 cups toasted (frozen) waffles, coarsely chopped

½ cup unsalted butter, melted

FINISHING TOUCHES

Pure maple syrup, warmed

Preheat the oven to 350°F. Line a baking sheet with parchment paper. Line an 8 or 9 inch spring-form pan with parchment paper.

Toast the waffles lightly and place them in the bottom of the spring-form pan, cutting into pieces to fit any spaces. Drizzle on maple syrup and butter.

For the filling, place the cream cheese in the food processor and blend with the sugar and condensed milk, stopping to ensure there are no lumps that stick together.

Add in the vanilla, eggs and sour cream and process until smooth, scraping down once or twice, about 2-3 minutes. Remove one-third of the batter and blend the maple extract into it. Spoon the maple batter onto the crust and then top with the remaining vanilla batter. Toss chopped waffles with melted butter and scatter on top of cheesecake filling. (For the bottom crust, the waffles might move around a bit; that is fine).

Place the pan on the baking sheet. Bake until just set (barely firm to the touch and not too jiggly), 40-45 minutes. If cake appears to be baking but edges are browning before middle looks set, lower oven temperature to 325°F and bake a bit longer, allowing cake to bake through but without undue browning on edges.

Let cool in turned off oven with door ajar. Then refrigerate overnight. Before serving, drizzle top of cake with warm maple syrup.

Serves 10-12

Spring Equinox Cherry Focaccia

Focaccia can be sweet as well as savory and I created this one to put vibrant Balaton cherries to good use but any sweet cherry works well. This recipe includes a touch of mahlep powder, a Turkish seasoning made from ground cherry pit centers, available in Middle Eastern food stores or online spice shops.

DOUGH

1 1/2 cups warm water

2 tablespoons instant yeast

1/2 cup sugar

2 teaspoons salt

2 teaspoons pure vanilla extract

1/2 teaspoon mahlep powder or almond extract

2 eggs

1/2 cup unsalted butter, melted

5 - 6 cups bread flour

FINISHING TOUCHES

1/3 cup unsalted butter, melted

1/2 cup sugar

1 to 2 teaspoons cinnamon

2 cups fresh (or frozen) pitted cherries

Line a large baking sheet (one with sides or rims) with parchment paper. Alternatively you can use two smaller sheets.

For the dough, in a mixer bowl, hand whisk the water and yeast together and let stand a few minutes to dissolve the yeast. Stir in sugar, salt, vanilla, mahlep powder (or almond extract), eggs, butter and most of the flour. Stir until you have a soft mass. Knead with the dough hook on the lowest speed for 8 to 10 minutes, adding more flour as necessary to form a soft dough. Remove dough hook from the machine and spray dough with non-stick cooking spray. Cover the entire mixer and bowl with a large, clear plastic bag and allow to rise, 40-45 minutes.

Turn out onto the baking sheet and gently deflate the dough. Arrange dough on baking sheet; if it springs back, let it rest a moment then coax to fit sheet. Spray with non-stick cooking spray and then cover entire sheet with the large, clear plastic bag. Let rise 30 minutes.

Preheat the oven to 350°F. Generously brush dough with the melted butter. Generously dust with sugar and cinnamon and then scatter cherries on top.

Bake until done (bread is golden, cherries are softened and oozing) - 45 to 55 minutes. Cut into slabs to serve.

Serves 10-12

Rhubarb 'n Marshmallow Cheesecake

When stress rules, I chill out with an ice-cream sundae. I create custom sundaes by playing with the toppings; this combo is one of my favorites, featuring vanilla ice-cream, swirled with brown sugar fudge, puddles of creamy marshmallow sauce and rhubarb puree. I can't possibly describe how utterly delectable this cheesecake is.

RHUBARB PUREE

¼ cup water

3 cups diced rhubarb

½ cup sugar

1 tablespoon honey

1/4 teaspoon pure vanilla extract

Few drops red food coloring

CRUST

1 ½ cups shortbread cookie crumbs

1/3 cup unsalted butter, melted

¼ teaspoon cinnamon

1/3 cup light brown sugar, firmly packed

CHEESECAKE

1 cup vanilla fudge, in ½ inch dice *

2 ½ pounds cream cheese, softened

1 ½ cups sugar

1/3 cup flour

5 eggs

1 tablespoon pure vanilla extract

1 cup sour cream

1 cup rhubarb puree

1 cup miniature marshmallows

3/4 cup marshmallow cream topping

1/3 cup butterscotch topping

*Dollar Store or otherwise bought vanilla fudge is fine for this recipe.

To make the Rhubarb Puree, place the water, rhubarb, sugar, and honey in a medium saucepan. Simmer, over lowest temperature possible until fruit is all soft and mushy. Stir to break up fruit, cooking down to a smooth, chunk-free, puree. Cool to room temperature and stir in the vanilla and a touch of red food coloring (this is so you get a rosy puree rather than a weird green). Refrigerate until ready use.

Preheat the oven to 350°F. Meanwhile, line a baking sheet with parchment paper. Spray a 10-inch cheesecake pan with non-stick cooking spray.

For the crust put all the ingredients in the cheesecake pan and mix to make a crust you can press into pan bottom and a little up the sides.

For the cheesecake, blend the cream cheese, sugar and flour until smooth. Add in eggs, vanilla and blend well, and then sour cream. Make sure no unmixed hunks of cream cheese are stuck in mixer bowl well or are not blended.

Pour half of batter into pan and add on the marshmallows and plop small dollops of rhubarb puree around perimeter. Top with some spoonfuls of cheesecake batter and then disperse hunks of the brown sugar fudge (leaving some for the top) and half of the marshmallow cream.

Spoon on remaining cheesecake batter, then some of the brown sugar fudge hunks or dustings, and the last of the marshmallow cream. Drizzle butterscotch syrup all over top surface.

Bake 45-50 minutes until almost set and if still very jiggly, reduce temperature to 325°F and let bake until set but not cracked or dry (it should just be set and beginning to rise a touch), another 15 minutes. Cool an hour in oven, with door open and oven off.

Refrigerate overnight before serving. Dust with confectioner's sugar.

Serves 16-20

White Chocolate Strawberry Scone Cake

This scone cake is really a shortcake, but totally overhauled. Serve this anytime or part of a special occasion sweet table. Few recipes are as easy and as elegant at the same time.

SCONE CAKE

3 cups all-purpose flour

1 cup sugar

4 teaspoons baking powder

1/2 teaspoon baking soda

¼ teaspoon salt

3/4 cup unsalted butter

2 eggs

3/4 cup whipping cream, or more

2 teaspoons lemon juice

2 teaspoons pure vanilla extract, optional

1 cup finely chopped white chocolate, preferably Belgian, finely chopped

TOPPING

1 cup whipping cream

1 teaspoon pure vanilla extract

2 tablespoons confectioners' sugar

2 pint baskets fresh strawberries, washed, hulled and sliced

FINISHING TOUCHES

White chocolate shavings

½ cup white chocolate, melted

Preheat the oven to 400°F. Stack two baking sheets together and line top one with parchment paper. Line two 8 inch layer cake pans with parchment paper and spray with non-stick cooking spray. Place on baking sheet. (You can also simply make two circles in pencil on the parchment paper - using a bowl to trace the circle - and then pat the dough into the circles)

In a food processor, place the flour, sugar, baking powder, baking soda, and salt and process to blend briefly. Add in chunks of butter and pulse to break in the butter to make a mealy mixture.

Remove to a large bowl. Make a well in the center and stir in eggs and most of the cream and lemon juice. Let stand a minute. Add vanilla and then stir to make a soft dough and then remove to a lightly floured work surface. Knead gently to make a dough that just holds together. Divide dough in two and place each in prepared pans or pat into the circle outlines. Deposit half the white chocolate on top of each round of dough.

Place in oven and immediately lower temperature to 375°F. Bake until nicely browned 22-25 minutes or until nicely browned on top. Cool to room temperature.

Meanwhile, in a mixer bowl with whisk attachment, whip the cream with the vanilla and confectioners' sugar until soft and forms peaks. Crush half the berries and then toss with the diced berries in a bowl with the confectioners' sugar.

On each scone cake, spread on half of whipped cream, then berries and then dust on chocolate shavings. Alternatively, make it a two-layer shortcake by sandwiching the two shortcake circles, along with the whipped cream and berries. This makes a heavier, thicker cake of course but also nice and tall. Split them before serving - one per diner - and smear with whipped cream and berries.

Drizzle with melted white chocolate.

Serves 8-10

Basque Cream Cake

A shortbread bottom with a pastry cream topping – all baked together for a unique, European tart. This needs overnight refrigeration. It results in a rich, yet delicate torte that is light, delicate and unique.

CAKE

1 cup unsalted butter

1 cup sugar

2 egg yolks

1 egg

2 cups all-purpose flour

1 ½ teaspoons baking powder

1/8 teaspoon salt

½ cup raspberry preserves

Pastry Cream

1 cup milk

2 egg yolks

½ cup sugar

2 tablespoons flour

Pinch salt

2 teaspoons pure vanilla extract

Line a large baking sheet with parchment paper. Generously spray a 9 inch spring form pan with non-stick cooking spray and place on the baking sheet.

For the cake, in a mixer bowl, cream the butter with the sugar until fluffy. Add in the egg yolks and egg, and then fold in the flour, baking powder and salt to make a soft dough. Press into a mound and wrap in wax paper, then place in a plastic bag; refrigerate one hour or overnight.

For the Pastry Cream, in a 3 quart saucepan, heat the milk and egg yolks, over gently heat, until simmering. Mix the sugar, flour and salt together in a small bowl. Once milk is simmering (almost boiling) whisk in the dry mixture and whisk over low heat until it thickens. You want to cook this over gentle heat so as not to cook the egg yolks too fast. Remove from stove and cool to just warm, and then stir in vanilla. Refrigerate pastry cream.

Preheat the oven to 350°F.

Divide dough into two parts – with a slightly larger portion as the bottom of the cake. Press it into the cake pan, covering the bottom and partially up the sides. Spoon on raspberry jam. Then spoon the pastry cream on the bottom dough. With the remaining dough, roll out (between floured wax paper if that is easier) on a floured board. Place this dough portion over the pastry filling – arranging it as evenly as you can to cover it.

Place the cake on the prepared baking sheet. Bake until done, about 40 minutes, until golden brown on top.

Garnish with a dusting of confectioners' sugar.

Refrigerate overnight before serving.

Serves 10-12

Irish Mist Cheesecake

There is something in the mist. Is it a leprechaun, a pot of gold or a lucky shamrock? It's this lucky, decadent cheesecake featuring Bailey's Irish Cream.

CRUST

1 1/2 cups shortbread cookie crumbs

2 tablespoons white sugar

2 tablespoons brown sugar

2 tablespoons Bailey's Irish Cream liqueur

1/3 cup unsalted butter, melted

CHEESECAKE

1 1/3 cup sugar

2 tablespoons flour

2 pounds cream cheese, softened

4 eggs

2 teaspoons pure vanilla extract

1/3 cup Bailey's Irish Cream liqueur

GLAZE

½ cup semi-sweet chocolate chips, melted

1 cup white chocolate chips

¼ cup whipping cream

2 tablespoons unsalted butter

½ teaspoon pure mint extract

1 teaspoon pure vanilla extract

FINISHING TOUCHES

Chocolate cookie crumbs

Whipped cream

Preheat the oven to 350°F. Line a baking sheet with parchment paper. Generously spray a 9 inch spring form pan with non-stick cooking spray and place on the baking sheet.

For the crust, toss the cookie crumbs, white sugar, brown sugar, Bailey's Irish Cream and the butter into the bottom of the pan. Press to coat the bottom well and place pan on the baking sheet.

For the cheesecake, in a mixer bowl, cream the sugar, flour, and cream cheese until smooth. Add in the eggs, vanilla, Bailey's and blend well, making sure no lumps of unblended cream cheese remain in the well of the mixer bowl. Spoon batter into the pan.

Bake 40-45 minutes or until center is just set. Leave the cake to cool with oven door open for one hour and then refrigerate, lightly covered, 6 hours or overnight.

For the glaze, in a microwave, melt the semi-sweet chocolate and set aside. Using a double-boiler, melt the white chocolate with the whipping cream and butter, melting very slowly over low heat, until smooth. Blend in the mint and vanilla extracts. Drizzle semi-sweet chocolate over cake and then the white chocolate, allowing chocolate to drip down sides. Sprinkle chocolate cookie crumbs on top and garnish with whipped cream before serving.

Serves 16-18

Miniature Wheaten Irish Soda Bread Scones

These are oversized, rustic scones with a soda bread birthright. Crusty exteriors, with a moist scone interior, these are my favorite go-to rustic scone recipe and they go well with a pot of Assam tea.

SCONES

1 cup whole-wheat flour

3 cups all-purpose flour

1 cup brown sugar, firmly packed

4 teaspoons baking powder

1 teaspoon baking soda

1 teaspoon salt

3/4 cup very cold, unsalted butter, diced

2 eggs

1 cup buttermilk

2 tablespoons caraway seeds, optional

1 cup dark raisins, plumped and dried

FINISHING TOUCHES

Bran or fine oatmeal

Preheat the oven to 425°F. Stack two baking sheets together and line the top one with parchment paper.

In a large food processor briefly blend the flours, brown sugar, baking powder, baking soda and salt. Add in the butter and pulse until the mixture is grainy. Remove to a large mixing bowl and make a well in the center. Stir in the eggs and buttermilk, and with a fork, gather dough together, now adding in the caraway seeds and raisins to make a ragged dough.

Turn the dough out onto a lightly floured work surface and knead gently to make a firm dough, using flour on your board to help firm up if the dough is too wet. This is a rather firm scone dough – much like a soda bread. It should be easy to handle so add more flour if you think it needs it. If the scones are too soft, they will spread as they bake (instead of puff up).

Let rest 5 minutes and then divide in 6-8 portions. Shape each into a round shape (like a mini soda bread or round scone) and place on baking sheet. Make a cross with a knife, and dust with bran or fine oatmeal.

Place in oven, immediately lowering temperature to 400°F. Bake until done and soda breads are nicely browned all over, about 16-18 minutes. If scones seem not quite done but are browning, lower temperature to 375F and let them have a few minutes more. Cool well before serving. Makes 6-8

Fondant Glazed Hot Cross Buns

Pretty as multi-colored Easter eggs or sprouting tulips, these little sweet buns are classic but respun in a contemporary way, what with their pretty pastel fondant topping. See the Chocolate Chip Hot Cross Bun variation below or forgo the currants and raisins and use dried cherries and cranberries instead for a more contemporary approach to this spring classic.

SWEET SPICE DOUGH

5 teaspoons instant yeast

1/3 cup warm water

1 cup scalded milk, cooled

1/3 cup unsalted butter, melted

1 cup sugar

1 teaspoon salt

2 eggs

4 - 5 cups all-purpose flour

1/2 cup whole wheat flour

1 teaspoon cinnamon

1/2 teaspoon nutmeg

1/2 teaspoon allspice

1/4 teaspoon cloves

1/2 cup currants, plumped and dried

1/2 cup raisins, plumped and dried

1/4 cup chopped candied orange

EGG WASH

1 whisked egg

Pastel Fondant

2 1/2 cups confectioners' sugar

2-6 tablespoons water

1 teaspoon pure vanilla extract

Food coloring such as pink, blue, yellow, green

Stack two baking sheets together and line the top one with parchment paper.

For the Sweet Spice Dough, in a mixer bowl, hand whisk together the yeast and water and let stand a minute. Stir in the milk, butter, sugar and salt to dissolve and then blend in eggs. Fold in most of white flour, all the whole wheat flour, cinnamon, nutmeg, allspice and cloves and mix by hand to make a soft dough. When dough can no longer be mixed by hand, begin kneading (5 - 7 minutes by hand or using a dough hook on an electric mixer). Dust in more all-purpose flour if needed. When dough is somewhat smooth, knead in currants or raisins and orange zest or citron. The dough should be smooth and elastic. Shape dough into a ball and let rest, covered with a tea towel for about 20 minutes.

Divide into 12 pieces and shape into balls. You may also roll dough out and cut into 3 inch rounds (about 1/2 inch thick).

Place buns on the baking sheet about one inch apart. Using floured scissors snip a cross on the top of each bun (about 1/2 inch deep). Paint with egg wash and cover with a large plastic sheet. Let rise about 30-45 minutes or until buns look puffy and light and are almost doubled in size.

Preheat the oven to 375°F. Place buns in oven and immediately lower temperature to 350°F. Bake for 17-20 minutes until the tops are golden brown. Remove from the oven and transfer to a rack. When cool, apply fondant.

For the fondant, in a small bowl, whisk the confectioners' sugar and water to make a very soft icing. Divide into a few smaller bowls and whisk in food coloring to make pale or pastel blue, pink, green and yellow glaze. If fondant is too soft, add more confectioners' sugar. If too thick, add a touch more water. Using a flat, small metal spatula, spread fondant onto baked the cooled buns. Allow to set before serving.

Makes 12 buns

HOT CROSS BUNS OR A BAKER IN HOT WATER?

"Perhaps no cry - though it is only for one morning - is more familiar to the ears of a Londoner, than that of One-a-penny, two-a-penny, hot-cross buns on Good Friday"

Henry Mayhew, London Labour and the London Poor

To the Brits, a bun refers to a number of sweet, yeasted little breads including Chelsea Buns, Bath Buns, Devonshire Splits, Spice Buns, Scotch and Tea Buns. As beloved as cinnamon buns are here, Hot Cross buns are equally adored there, but they're more commonly relegated to Easter. Here in the North American, they're catching on more and more and you can find Hot Cross Buns well before Easter. Unfortunately with anything traditional now made commercially, Hot Cross buns vary in their quality. Sometimes supermarkets mishandle them and by the time you get them home, they're a sticky, squashy mess. Homemade Hot Cross buns are another matter altogether - light on the spices, generously plumped with raisins or currants and easily baked up by the panful. Thanks to the new breed of yeasts on the market, the buns can be made in under an hour. If you like sweet yeast baking and a touch of spice, then Hot Cross Buns are a must to try.

Chocolate Mandarin Chestnut Torte

Chestnuts offer a lovely subtle, sweetness to this wonderful torte, suitable for Easter or Passover (but substitute Passover margarine for the butter). When you want to impress, this is a refined bit of baking that does the trick.

1 ½ cups semi-sweet Swiss chocolate, melted

1 15-ounce can chestnut puree or chestnut cream (*)

1 cup unsalted butter

6 egg yolks

¾ cup sugar, divided usage

1 teaspoon pure vanilla

½ teaspoon pure clementine or orange oil or orange extract

Zest of one large clementine or mandarin

2 tablespoon orange juice or orange liqueur such as Cointreau

6 egg whites

Pinch salt

GLAZE

1/2 cup orange juice, coffee or whipping cream

1 ¼ cup semi-sweet chocolate, coarsely chopped

(*) Available in European grocery stores; chestnut puree and chestnut cream are usually imported from France.

Preheat the oven to 350°F. Line a 9-inch spring form pan with a circle of baking parchment. Spray the pan generously with non-stick cooking spray. Line a baking sheet with parchment paper and place the pan on it.

For the cake, prepare the melted chocolate and set aside and allow to cool to room temperature.

In a mixer bowl, using the paddle attachment, blend chestnut cream or puree with the butter and then add in the vanilla, orange oil or extract, orange liqueur, zest, egg yolks, ½ cup of the sugar, and melted chocolate, blending well. Remove to another bowl. Wash, clean and dry mixer bowl very well.

In the mixer bowl, whip the egg whites with the salt, just to break up and foam slightly. Gradually, while increasing mixer speed, dust in ¼ cup sugar to form stiff glossy (but not dry) peaks.

Fold 1/3 of egg whites into chestnut mixture and work in well to loosen. Gently fold in remaining 2/3 of egg whites in 2 instalments, blending well but taking care not to deflate the mixture.

Spoon into prepared pan and bake until done, 35-45 minutes. Cake rises somewhat and looks dry and slightly cracked on top when done. Middle should be soft but firm. Cool in pan for 20 minutes, and then remove to a wire rack.

For the Glaze, bring the orange juice, whipping cream or coffee to a gentle boil and add the chopped chocolate all at once. Remove from heat and stir briskly, using a wire whisk, until all of the chocolate melts.

Invert cake on a wire cake rack placed on a cookie sheet. Pour glaze over cake, using a metal spatula to spread. Garnish with chocolate shavings or dust with sifted confectioners' sugar.

Serves 14

Peaches Still Life

Marcy Goldman

Summer was

A basket of peaches

You couldn't resist

A farmers' market special

Golden hued, scarlet blushed

The peaches were

Ripe with promise

Certain for pie

Yet were eaten

One by one,

Each a perfect summer day

Come early autumn

The scent of peaches

Can barely be recalled.

Leaves fall,

Apples drop

The days quickly tumble

Into sharp sunsets

That awaken in frost.

The taste and time of peaches

Seems much too far off

But the basket is empty

And dusted with snow.

Summer, Small Baking

The Season of Fruit and Fun

Summer in the Bakery

Do you ever notice that summer seems to take forever to arrive? Yet, just like a summer road trip, just as you are saying 'Are we there yet?" summer is finally, suddenly here. It occurs on one of those early June morning: you awake just a bit earlier than usual, when all is still and quiet and realize that sometime, somehow, without you even noticing, it stopped being spring and subtly morphed into full-out summer. Now, instead of chilly mornings and nippy evenings, now the days are endless, beautiful, lazy days of luxurious heat. Not even the occasional quick summer rain storm can mute the mellow, golden mood.

Summertime is also a time when our schedules disappear. Even a regular workday feels the influence of 'summer hours' and is not so 'workish'. In winter we tuck in early but in summer, we head to bed a bit later, having enjoyed another balmy day and glorious sunset. To me, summer means baseball games, trips to Cape Cod, or when I was a kid, spending June and July at the family country cottage. It means picnic baskets and outdoor cafes, and strolling the Montreal city harbor at night, taking in fireworks and street musicians as well as all manner of outdoor music festivals wherever you happen to be.

By the end of June, summer is at her peak. Cue the harvest moon, the corn dogs, lemonade and cupcakes. There's baseball tryouts, garden parties and weddings to plan and host or casual, chatty lunches with friends, on a café open terrace, that last to mid-afternoon. Time flies when you're not counting the minutes and thinking of what you have to do and instead, are anticipating leisurely social occasions. Fittingly, instead of warehouse food stores and air-conditioned supermarkets, it's time to enjoy outdoor farmer markets and roadside produce stands. The pickings are lush; accordingly the baker's inspiration seems to flourish with each new crop from strawberries, raspberries, blueberries to stone fruits such as plums, pluots, peaches, nectarines, and then to pears and early apples. Meals are easy and quickly put together and more often than not, especially on the weekends, barbecues rule. Still, a great fresh dessert definitely is part of a memorable meal.

So gather your fruit while you may! Pick it, store it, freeze it but it will never be, at any other time of the year, as ripe, flavorful and plentiful as it is now; nor, and this is primordial - as lusciously local. Indulge, enjoy and as summer is short, make hay.

Perfume of Summer

The perfume of summer is heady stuff – it's an elixir, a fountain of youth.

It is infused with unyielding sunshine, ripe fruits and berries, lush and local...

Base Notes

Peaches, nectarines, raspberries, blueberries, raspberries, wild blackberries

Heart Notes: Orange citrus, pears, plums, sweet cherries, fresh churned vanilla ice cream

Top Notes

Honeydew, Cantaloupe, Watermelon, Green Grapes, Pineapple, Meringue

Theme Mood

Relaxed yet Brimming

Theme Colors

Red, Orange, Blueberry and Blackberry Blues

The Style of Summer Baking

Summer Flavor and Ingredient Palate Berries and more berries, stone fruit, cheesecakes, chilled pies, and easy squares, and eat- out-of-hand, picnic fare. Lite-style, short bakes recipes, sweet match ups with sandwiches, making the most of summer fruits.

Summertime and the baking should be easy – right? It should be so I've created many easy recipes over the years, to match this time of year. To me, summer is also a most varied style of baking for it includes everything from summer weddings, weekends at the cottage, seaside vacations, picnics, cookies and squares for kids who are off school and brown baggers to pack for their office-home commute. As you can appreciate, baking is fruity in theme and also somewhat light. The recipes in this Summer Chapter are all about using the broad spectrum of fruity offerings in spectacular ways from simple to rustic to sophisticated as well as elegant. There is something to tempt everyone's taste and also suit a plethora of occasions. There's crowd-appealing cheesecakes, refreshing ice box pies, and glamorous, European style tarts and crostatas as well as old-fashioned Americana cobblers, crisps and grunts. There's also kid-friendly cupcakes, muffins and a cookie or two for those nibble-and-strolls by the city park's duck pond, be it on a work or vacation day.

Summer, Small Baking Recipes

Iced Tea Lemon Bars

Cold Rise Pizza Dough

Sunny Lemon Pizza

Summerside Raspberry White Chocolate Blondies

Vanilla Glazed Blackberry Apple Muffins

Best Ever Vanilla Cupcakes

Country Kitchen Carrot Cake Cupcakes

Concord Grape Biscotti

Blueberry Pie Cookies

Crazy Quilt Berry Muffins

Raspberry Lemon Cake Muffins

Iced Tea Lemon Bars

A baker's rendition of this summer iced-tea classic. This bold lemon bar, infused with brewed concentrated black tea, is gorgeous with its finish of lemon-scented, melted white chocolate.

CRUST

1 1/2 cups all-purpose flour

1/4 cup confectioners' sugar

1/8 teaspoon salt

3/4 cup unsalted butter

1/2 teaspoon vanilla extract

TOPPING

2 tablespoons unsalted butter, melted

4 tablespoons (2 ounces) cream cheese, softened

2 cups sugar

6 eggs

1/2 teaspoon pure lemon extract or oil

3/4 cup fresh lemon juice

1/2 teaspoon citric acid, optional

1/4 cup very strong (cooled) black tea

1 cup all-purpose flour

FINISHING TOUCHES

Confectioners' sugar

½ cup white chocolate, finely minced, melted

¼ teaspoon lemon oil

Preheat the oven to 350 F. Line a baking sheet with parchment paper. Spray an 8 by 11 inch baking pan generously with nonstick cooking spray. Place on baking sheet.

For the crust, in a food processor, combine flour, confectioners' sugar and salt. Pulse to break in butter to make a fine, mealy mixture and blend in vanilla. Press into prepared pan and place on baking sheet. Bake 15 minutes and remove from oven.

For the Topping, in the food processor bowl (no need to clean), whiz the butter, cream cheese, sugar, eggs, lemon oil, lemon juice, citric acid, tea and flour together until smooth, 1 minute or so. Pour topping over bottom crust. Lower the temperature to 325 F.

Bake until set, about 35-40 minutes. Cool well and cut into tiny bars, and toss in confectioners' sugar. Alternatively, finish with melted white chocolate. Gently melt the white chocolate in a double boiler or microwave. Stir in the lemon oil/extract and whisk to blend well. Instead of confectioners' sugar, drizzle white chocolate over the bars.

Refrigerate (to allow chocolate to set) an hour before serving.

Makes 35-48 small bars

Cold Rise Rustic Pizza Dough

This is one of my favorite go-to easy pizza doughs. It's low yeast so it can stay in the fridge for a day or two without rising too much or turning 'yeasty'. It's perfect for so many pizza styles but it soars as the foundation for Lemon Pizza. Panko, are Japanese breadcrumbs sold everywhere these days but certainly they're available in Asian food shops. It makes for a crisp pizza crust.

½ teaspoon instant yeast

1 ½ cups spring water, room temperature

4-5 cups bread flour

1 3/4 teaspoon salt

¼ teaspoon sugar

2 tablespoons light olive oil

FINISHING TOUCHES
Olive oil

Panko

In a large mixer bowl whisk the yeast and water together. Add in most of the flour, salt, sugar and olive oil. Mix, then gently knead, adding in more flour as required to make a soft dough. Cover and let rise 8-12 hours. (After 8 hours, store in a plastic bag in the refrigerator for up to two days).

Place the dough in a plastic bag which has been lightly sprayed with non-stick cooking spray. Refrigerate overnight (or up to two days).

To make the pizzas, divide dough into three.

Roll or stretch out as you prefer for pizza (in a pizza pan or on a baking sheet that's been drizzled with olive oil and 1-2 tablespoons panko). Smear the dough with a little olive oil and then put on the toppings you like. Cover with a large plastic sheet and let rise 1-4 hours.

Preheat the oven to 475 F (at least for an hour before you bake). Bake pizzas on middle shelf of oven (about 9-14 minutes per pizza)

Makes 3 pizzas

Sunny Lemon Pizza

This is a savoury versus sweet recipe, and oh-so-gourmet pizza is justifiably trendy and makes a perfect summer pizza. It calls for rustic pizza dough, some herbs, garlic, lots of fresh lemon juice and arugula. When I have the time, I also top it with Garlic Hollandaise sauce for some extra sunshine. This is homemade, but bistro-quality awesome pizza. A combination of mozzarella and feta is superb.

1 batch Cold Rise Pizza Dough or any pizza dough (recipe follows)

Olive Oil

Panko

HOLLANDAISE SAUCE

3 egg yolks

1 tablespoon fresh lemon juice

1 tablespoon water

½ cup unsalted butter, diced

Salt, pepper, hot sauce to taste

TOPPINGS

2-4 tablespoons extra virgin olive oil

Salt, pepper

4-6 cloves garlic, crushed

6-8 ounces fresh buffalo mozzarella and/or feta

2-3 cups arugula

Juice of one large lemon

Thin slices of lemon

EXTRAS

Olive oil

Prepare the pizza dough in the morning or the day before. Place the dough in a plastic bag which has been lightly sprayed with non-stick cooking spray. Refrigerate overnight or up until two days.

When you are ready to make pizza (do this 1-3 hours ahead of serving), divide dough into three and let rest while you prepare Hollandaise Sauce (this is totally optional but totally delicious).

For the Hollandaise Sauce, in a small saucepan, whisk the egg yolks, lemon juice and water over low heat, for 5 minutes. Whisk in the butter and cook, allowing mixture to thicken to a sauce and stirring all the while and season to taste. Allow to cool, cover and let stand while preparing pizzas.

Pan out as you prefer for pizza (in a pan or on a baking sheet), i.e. line a large baking sheet with parchment paper. Smear on some olive oil and panko. Stretch out the pizzas and place them on sheet.

Smear each 9-12 inch pizza with some olive oil, dust with salt and pepper, and spoon on some Hollandaise sauce. Top with a few slices of the cheese. Top with the arugula, lemon slices, more cheese, crushed garlic, salt, pepper, juice of half a lemon and the lemon slices.

Cover lightly with a plastic sheet and let rise 1-3 hours.

Preheat the oven to 475 F (at hour before you bake; it makes for bistro styled pizza crust). Bake until cheese is bubbling, 16-18 minutes. Spritz with a bit more lemon juice and olive oil just before serving.

Makes 3 pizzas

Summerside Raspberry White Chocolate Blondies

Big and dense, golden, and buttery. This is the vanilla and brown sugar version of traditional brownies updated with fresh raspberries. Nothing beats the taste of mellow brown sugar enlivened with fresh summer berries.

¾ cup unsalted butter

2 cups light brown sugar, firmly packed

2 eggs

2 cups all-purpose flour

1 teaspoon baking powder

1/4 teaspoon baking soda

3/8 teaspoon salt

1 cup coarsely chopped pecans or walnuts

1 cup white chocolate chunks

1 1/2 cups semi-frozen raspberries

FINISHING TOUCHES
Melted white or dark chocolate

Preheat the oven to 350 F. Line a baking sheet with parchment paper. Generously spray the sides and bottom of a 9 by 13 inch pan with non-stick cooking spray; place pan on the baking sheet.

In a medium saucepan over very gentle heat, melt the butter and brown sugar and cook until the sugar dissolves somewhat (5 to 8 minutes). Allow to cool. Turn out into a large bowl.

Add eggs and blend well. Stir in flour, baking powder, baking soda, and salt. Then fold in nuts and white chocolate; gently fold in the raspberries. Using a wet metal spatula, spread batter evenly in pan.

Bake for 25-28 minutes or until just set. Be careful not to overbake. Cut into squares while warm and then cool fully in pan on a rack. Refrigerate about 20-30 minutes before cutting (for clean cut squares). Drizzle with melted chocolate, if desired.

Makes 18-24

Vanilla-Glazed Blackberry Apple Muffins

Bursts of fresh blackberries and a touch of tart apple all tucked into a vanilla batter that puffs up and is brushed, while still warm, with a fondant glaze. Semi-freeze the berries so they hold up well as you mix them in the batter.

1/2 cup unsalted butter, melted

1 cup light brown sugar, firmly packed

1/4 cup white sugar

1 egg

2 1/2 teaspoons pure vanilla extract

1/2 teaspoon butter extract, optional

1 cup buttermilk

2 3/4 cup all-purpose flour

2 1/4 teaspoons baking powder

1/2 teaspoon baking soda

1/8 teaspoon cinnamon

Pinch cloves

1/4 teaspoon salt

1 cup blackberries

1 cup diced apples

GLAZE

1 1/2 cups confectioners' sugar

2 tablespoons unsalted butter, melted

1 teaspoon pure vanilla extract

Whipping cream

Place oven rack to upper third or middle position. Preheat the oven to 400 F. Line a baking sheet with parchment paper. Line a muffin tin with muffin liners and spray with non-stick cooking spray and place muffin tin on baking sheet.

In a mixer bowl, whisk the butter, brown sugar, white sugar, egg and extracts together well. Stir in buttermilk, and then fold in flour, baking powder, baking soda, cinnamon, cloves and salt to make a soft batter. Gently fold in the blackberries and apples. Using an ice-cream scooper, scoop muffins quite generously – you should get about 9 muffins. Bake until nicely browned, firm to the touch and spring back when gently touched with fingertips, 30-35 minutes (less for smaller ones).. Cool well in pan at least 20 minutes before removing.

To make the glaze, stir confectioners' sugar with butter in a medium bowl. Add in vanilla and as much whipping cream as required to make a glaze. Remove muffins to a cake rack set over a baking sheet lined with parchment paper. Drizzle a generous amount of glaze over each one.

Makes 9-12 large muffins or 18-22 smaller ones

Country Kitchen Carrot Cake Cupcakes

Perfect for when you want a bit of carrot 'n spice but not a big cake. Yellow raisins offer a perky taste. Nothing could be easier or prettier than these cupcakes. All you do is stir the ingredients with a wood spoon in a large bowl, spoon out the batter, bake and enjoy!

CARROT CUPCAKE BATTER

1 cup sugar

1/2 cup canola oil

2 tablespoons fresh orange juice

1 teaspoon pure vanilla extract

2 eggs

1 cup all-purpose flour

1/2 teaspoon cinnamon

1 teaspoon baking powder

1/4 teaspoon baking soda

1/8 teaspoon salt

1 1/2 cups shredded carrots

1/2 cup finely chopped pecans

1/2 cup finely chopped yellow raisins or drained crushed pineapple

CREAM CHEESE FROSTING

4 ounces cream cheese, softened

2 cups approximately, confectioners' sugar

1 teaspoon pure vanilla extract

Orange juice or water, as required

FINISHING TOUCHES

Fresh shredded carrots

Cinnamon

Preheat the oven to 350 F. Line a baking sheet with parchment paper. Line 12-18 cupcakes (or more) with muffin liners. Spray top of cupcake tin with non-stick cooking spray and place muffin pan on the baking sheet.

In a large mixer bowl, using a whisk, blend the sugar, oil, orange juice, vanilla and eggs. Fold in the flour, cinnamon, baking powder, baking soda and salt. Fold in the carrots, pecans and raisins. Blend well and then spoon batter into prepared cupcake pan.

Bake until cupcakes are gently golden, and spring back when touched, 30-35 minutes. Cool well.

Meanwhile, in a mixer bowl or food processor, blend the cream cheese with confections' sugar and vanilla, adding in water or orange juice as required for the right consistency (and if too thin, add in more confectioners' sugar). It should be a thick icing to spread on cupcakes. Smear on cupcakes or pipe with a pastry bag using a star tip. Sprinkle on shredded carrots and a dusting of cinnamon.

Makes 12-18 regular cupcakes or about 24 mini cupcakes

APRON STRING BAKING

Aprons might seem feminine but ironically, the first aprons were anything but. In fact, they were quintessentially 'guy stuff'. Blacksmiths wore them, as did weapon makers, gardeners, carvers, furniture makers, leather smiths, cobblers, tailors, jewelers, metal forgers, fishmongers, clock makers, barbers, and stonemasons – and the first professional (male) chef.

Women 'officially' began wearing aprons about the turn of the 20th century, in Victorian England, But as the 1920's roared around, women no longer wanted to be solely associated with the home front and aprons, once a symbol of domestic pride, were given to those in domestic service. In short, the matrons went out to play; the maids stayed in and were bequeathed the aprons. The 40's saw gingham and cheery cotton aprons replace the white ones; after WW II, with women tucked back safely in the 'burbs, the pretty apron was again adopted by the happy housewife. By the sixties, the apron trend began to wane. Aprons have been taken on and off, depending on the social and political climate. Feminism and sensibilities of class seem to dictate if aprons are 'in' or 'out', fashion. To a baker of course, female or male, however, an apron is something to safeguard your clothes against stains and splatters. Bakers are just wise folks.

Best Ever Vanilla Cupcakes

What's a better occasion-maker than pure and simple, vanilla cupcakes? Summer is a perfect time for cupcakes and even better if you have summer birthdays. Of course, cupcakes are all-seasonal and no doubt you'll turn to this recipe in summer, fall, winter and spring. It's my go-to cupcake recipe.

CUPCAKES

1 cup unsalted butter, softened

2 cups sugar

3 eggs

1 tablespoon pure vanilla extract

1 1/3 cup warm milk

4 tablespoons sour cream

2 1/2 cups all-purpose flour

2 tablespoons cornstarch

1 tablespoon baking powder

1/4 teaspoon baking soda

1/2 teaspoon salt

CUPCAKE FROSTING

1 cup unsalted butter

6 cups confectioners' sugar, approximately

1 tablespoon pure vanilla extract

1/2 cup milk

FINISHING TOUCHES

Food coloring, if desired *

Sprinkles

Preheat the oven to 350 F. Line a large baking sheet with parchment paper. Generously spray two cupcake pans with non-stick cooking spray and line with muffin or cupcake liners. Place pans on the baking sheet.

In a mixer bowl or food processor, cream the butter with the sugar until well blended. Blend in the eggs, vanilla, milk and sour cream. Fold in the flour, cornstarch, baking powder, baking soda and salt and blend until smooth, about 3-4 minutes.

Spoon into prepared pan, filling cupcakes three-quarters full. Bake until cupcakes spring back when gently pressed with fingertips, 30-35 minutes.

Cool in pan 15 minutes before unmolding to cool completely.

For the frosting, in a mixer bowl, slowly cream the butter with 2 cups of the confectioners' sugar. Add in most of the remaining confectioners' sugar, vanilla and most of the milk. Whip to blend and fluff up. (You can add ½ cup cocoa for chocolate frosting) Tint with food coloring, as per preference.

Makes 20-22 medium or about 48 smaller cupcakes

Concord Grape Biscotti

These are satisfying and beautiful biscotti that feature big seedless Concord grapes (yes, they now come seedless!) and a sweet grape wine. The unique wine 'n grape juice sugar coating is an extra touch that makes these irresistible. If you don't have Concord grapes around, pitted sour cherries work just as well.

1/2 cup unsalted butter, melted

1/2 cup canola oil

1 1/2 cups sugar

3 eggs

1/2 teaspoon almond extract

2 teaspoons pure vanilla extract

1/2 cup sweet red wine

3 ¼ cups all-purpose flour, or more, as required

2 1/2 teaspoons baking powder

½ teaspoon salt

2 cups seedless Concord grapes

1/2 cup slivered almonds or pine nuts

Sugar Coating

1/2 cup red wine

1 cup grape juice

1 ½ cups sugar

Preheat the oven to 350 F. Stack two baking sheets together and line the top one with parchment paper.

In a mixer bowl, blend the butter, oil, and sugar. Add in the eggs, almond extract, vanilla and wine. Fold in the flour, baking powder, salt and then the grapes and nuts. Blend well, adding in additional flour to make a very thick dough/batter. It should be soft but not wet. Spread in a mass about 10-12 inches long by 5 inches wide; if it spreads, that is fine.

Bake 35 minutes, then reduce the temperature to 325 F and bake until very firm and dry, about 20-30 minutes more, or as long as it needs to bake through. Cool well and cut into sticks. Stack two baking sheets together and line top one with a fresh sheet of parchment paper.

For the Sugar Coating, mix the wine and grape juice in an oblong dish. Place the sugar on a sheet of parchment paper on a board. Then dip each biscotti stick in the juice and then press into sugar. Place sugar side down on the baking sheet and bake to crisp the bottoms, 20-40 minutes. If biscotti are still soft and wet, continue baking until they crisp up (check them every 5-8 minutes). They should seem sticky but dry. They will continue to crisp up as they cool completely after baking (and out of the oven)

Makes 2-3 dozen

Crazy Quilt Berry Muffins

There is Bumble Berry Pie and now there's Bumble Berry Muffins, topped with a fabulous vanilla streusel; a statuesque muffin that is totally irresistible.

VANILLA STREUSEL

2 tablespoons flour

2 tablespoons unsalted butter

1/2 cup brown sugar, firmly packed

3/4 cup pecans, finely chopped

1/4 teaspoon cinnamon

1 teaspoon pure vanilla extract

Muffin Batter

2 1/3 cups brown sugar, firmly packed

1/2 cup canola oil

1/2 cup unsalted butter, melted

2 1/2 teaspoons pure vanilla extract

1 teaspoon fresh lemon juice

2 eggs

4 1/2 - 5 cups all-purpose flour, approximately

4 teaspoons baking powder

1 teaspoon baking soda

Pinch cinnamon

Pinch cloves

1/2 teaspoon salt

2 cups buttermilk

3-4 cups semi-frozen berries, (any combination)

FINISHING TOUCHES

Confectioners' sugar

Preheat the oven to 375 F. Arrange oven rack to the middle position of the oven. Line a baking sheet with parchment paper.

Generously spray 12 –16 muffin cups with non-stick cooking spray and line with paper muffin liners and place on baking sheet.

For the Vanilla streusel Topping, in a medium bowl, or food processor, blend the flour, butter, sugar, pecans, cinnamon and vanilla. Pulse to make a coarse topping. Set aside.

In large bowl blend the sugar with the oil and butter. Briskly whisk in the vanilla, lemon juice and eggs. Fold in the flour, baking powder, baking soda, cinnamon, cloves and salt, holding back a cup of the flour, and blend somewhat before blending in the buttermilk. The batter should be quite thick; if not, add in more of the flour (but when you add in the frozen fruit, the batter will firm up so wait to see if you need more flour and then add in a tablespoon at a time). Gently fold in the berries, trying not to break them apart.

Using a large ice-cream scoop, deposit batter into prepared muffin cups, loading them as much as you can. If the batter does not stay put, you need to add more flour (so, add more flour to the rest of the batter before scooping). You need almost a scoop and a half of batter. Deposit a little streusel on each muffin top.

Bake 15 minutes, then lower temperature to 350 F and bake until muffins spring back when gently touched with fingertips about 12 more minutes and muffins are golden brown. Dust with confectioners' sugar, if desired.

Makes 12-16 large muffins

BAKING IN THE FIELD OF DREAMS, THE BAKING OF SUMMER

There's a saying on the baseball diamond (a place I know almost as well as the bakery) that comes from the film, Field of Dreams. The line is: "If you build it, they will come". I know baseball and I know baking for I've coached baseball for years and fed many a baseball team, from spring tryouts to play offs. What's true about Field of Dreams is also true about baking: if you bake it, they will come. Bake up some scones, cookies or muffins and it's like you issued a silent (but fragrant) invitation to the universe. People just appear at your door. Bake without knowing why or for whom and the world will make its way to you. It's a little life force that starts in your kitchen, lavishing everyone else with the same happy energy. When you bake, something good always happens.

Blueberry Pie Cookies

Blueberries and a touch of spice in the filling – all tucked away in a little pocket of a cookie. A tender/crisp cookie that showcases a taste of summer in a bold, blue note.

BLUEBERRY PIE FILLING

2 1/2 cups fresh or frozen blueberries

1/2 cup sugar

1 tablespoon fresh lemon juice

Tiny pinch cloves

3 tablespoons cornstarch dissolved in 3 tablespoons of water

COOKIE DOUGH

3/4 cup unsalted butter

1 cup sugar

2 eggs

2 tablespoons whipping cream

2 teaspoons pure vanilla extract

3 cups all-purpose flour, approximately

2 teaspoons baking powder

3/8 teaspoon salt

FINISHING TOUCHES

1 egg (whisked)

Regular or coarse sugar

For the filling, place blueberries, sugar, lemon juice and cloves in a small saucepan and heat gently. Stir in cornstarch mixture and over medium heat, stir to cook berries, letting them just burst open and until mixture becomes like pie filling, about 3-4 minutes. Remove from heat, turn out into a bowl, cover with greased wax paper and refrigerate until needed.

For the dough, in a mixer bowl, cream the butter and sugar. Add eggs and blend until smooth. (If mixture is hard to blend or seems curdled, add a bit of the flour to bind it). Stir in the cream and vanilla. Fold in flour, baking powder, salt and mix to make a firm but soft dough. Transfer dough to a lightly floured work surface and pat into a smooth mass. Cover and let rest ten minutes. Divide dough into two or three flattened disks. Work with one portion at a time. Wrapped in plastic, dough can be refrigerated for 2-3 days. If the dough is very chilled, allow dough to warm up before rolling out.

Preheat the oven to 350 F. Stack two baking sheets together and line the top one with parchment paper.

For the cookies, roll dough out on a well –floured work surface just under 1/4 inch thick and cut into 4-inch circles. Brush edges with egg wash, fill center with 2 teaspoons of filling; fold over to make a half-moon. Egg wash the edges, and crimp or seal with fork tines. (In my kitchen, I also use ravioli cutters)

Alternatively, simply pinch off pieces of dough, insert 1/2 teaspoon of blueberry filling and fold or squish the cookie over to cover the filling. Press it gently on the baking sheet (which will give you one flat, bottom; the rest of the cookie will be a rough 'bundle').

Brush the top surface of each cookie with egg wash and sprinkle with sugar. Bake until edges start to brown, about 25-30 minutes. To store, wrap each cookie in wax paper and place in a tin but don't cover the box (or wrap and refrigerate).

Makes 30-40 cookies, depending on size.

Raspberry Lemon Cake Muffins

These are lovely light and delectable muffins. You can even omit the berries and use poppy seeds for a lemon poppy seed muffins or substitute blackberries for raspberries.

2 1/4 cups sugar

1/2 cup canola oil

1/2 cup unsalted butter

Zest of one lemon, finely minced

4 eggs

1 tablespoon pure vanilla extract

1/2 teaspoon pure lemon extract

5 cups all-purpose flour, approximately

1 tablespoon baking powder

1/4 teaspoon baking soda

½ teaspoon salt

½ cup sour cream

1 cup buttermilk

1/2 cup sour cream

2 1/2 cups semi-frozen raspberries

LEMON GLAZE

½ cup water

Juice of one lemon

¾ cup sugar

¼ teaspoon pure vanilla extract

¼ teaspoon pure lemon oil or extract

FINISHING TOUCHES

Juice of one lemon

Sugar

Lemon zest

Preheat the oven to 375 F. Arrange the oven rack to middle position.

Line a baking sheet with parchment paper. Generously spray a 12-cup large or medium, or a 24-cup small muffin tin with non-stick cooking spray and line with paper muffin liners. Place the pan on the baking sheet.

For the muffins, in a mixer bowl blend the sugar with the oil, butter and lemon zest. Briskly whisk in the eggs, vanilla and lemon extract or lemon oil. Fold in the flour, baking powder, baking soda and salt, (holding back a cup of the flour) and blend a little before blending in the sour cream and buttermilk. Batter should be quite thick; if not, add in the additional flour a bit at a time. Gently fold in the raspberries, taking care not to break them apart.

Using a large ice-cream scoop, deposit a very large amount of batter into prepared muffin cups, loading them as much as you can. If the batter does not stay put, you need to add more flour (so, add more flour to the rest of the batter before scooping). You need almost a scoop and a half of batter. Drizzle some lemon juice on each muffin and about a teaspoon of sugar and garnish with shreds of lemon zest.

Bake 15 minutes at 375 F; then reduce temperature to 350 F and bake until muffins spring back when gently touched with fingertips about 12 more minutes and muffins are golden brown.

For the Lemon Glaze, bring the water, lemon juice, sugar, vanilla and lemon extracts to a gentle boil and simmer 5 minutes. Cool. As muffins cool, drizzle on lemon syrup, let set, re-glaze.

Makes 2 dozen small, 14 large muffins or two small quick breads

Summer, Big Baking

Including Holiday and
Special Occasions

Summer, Big Baking
Including Holiday and Special Occasions Recipe

Key West Lime Pie

Boston Cream Pie

Old Fashioned Chocolate Cream Pie

Shredded Dough Blackberry Pie

Lemon Ice-Box Pie

Mom's Blueberry Torte

Fresh French Raspberry Tart

Picnic Basket Dark Fudge Cake

Summer Bazaar Caramel Cake

Carrot Cheesecake Swirl Cake

Greek Yogurt Cheesecake

Orange Olive Oil Bundt Cake

Upside Down Peach Cake

Blueberry Raspberry Buckle

Summer Fruit Crisp with Amaretti Topping

Fruits of the Forest Summer Tart

Peach Apricot Crostata

Plum Cream Tart

Chocolate Hazelnut Cheesecake

Japanese Cotton Cheesecake

S'Mores Cheesecake

Old-Fashioned Chocolate Cream Pie

Shredded Dough Blackberry Pie

Strawberry Layer Cake with Strawberry Streak Frosting

Summer Wedding White Chocolate Coconut Cake

Red Velvet Groom's Cake

Last Tango Chocolate Cake

Key West Lime Pie

Classic Key Lime pie can go two ways –graham crust or pie dough crust. I like both because I love Key Lime Pie no matter what. The key to great key lime pie is zestiness of flavour. What makes this Key Lime is the Key Lime juice (if you have it) and condensed milk which adds sweetness and smoothness.

GRAHAM CRUST

4 cups graham cracker crumbs

3 tablespoons white sugar

2 tablespoons light brown sugar

Pinch salt

1 cup unsalted butter, melted

KEY LIME FILLING

6 egg yolks

1 14 ounce can sweetened condensed milk

6 ounces cream cheese, softened

1 large lime, finely grated

1/4 teaspoon pure lime oil *

2/3 cup fresh Key Lime juice **

FINISHING TOUCHES

1 ½ cups whipping cream

2 tablespoons confectioners' sugar

½ teaspoon pure vanilla extract

Shavings of white chocolate

Graham crumbs

Lime zest

* Any lime juice is fine; fresh Key Lime juice is best. ** Lime Oil is available from Boyajian

Preheat the oven to 325 F. Line a baking sheet with parchment paper.

For the crust, in a large bowl, stir the graham crumbs with the white and brown sugar, salt and butter. Press snugly into a 10 inch spring-form pan, covering the bottom and half-way up the sides. Bake until slight dry to the touch, about 10 minutes. Cool while preparing the filling.

For the filling, in a mixer bowl with the wire whip attachment, blend the egg yolks, condensed milk, cream cheese, lime zest and lime oil for 5 minutes. Slowly drizzle in the lime juice.

Spoon into the crust and bake for 20-25 minutes or until the filling has just set. Cool on a wire rack, and then refrigerate for 3 hours or overnight.

For the topping, whip the cream, confectioners' sugar and vanilla until nearly stiff.

Spread the topping (spread with an icing knife but a pastry bag makes for a prettier final look) and dust on white chocolate shavings, graham crumbs, and lime zest.

Refrigerate an hour before serving.

Serves 6-8

Old-Fashioned Chocolate Cream Pie

Smooth as silk and real (versus instant pie filling) this is old-fashioned, diner-style delicious. This cream pie is served with whipped cream. But you can also recoup the egg whites and whip them into a meringue and offer a meringue-topped chocolate pie instead. I hesitate to say this serves 4-6 because so far, anyone who has one taste has eaten the entire pie.

1 8 or 9 inch pie shell, such as All Butter Favourite Pie Pastry Dough

FILLING
4 ounces semi-sweet chocolate, melted and cooled

1 ½ cups whipping cream

3 egg yolks

1/2 cup sugar

2 tablespoons all-purpose flour

2 tablespoons cornstarch

Tiniest pinch salt

1 tablespoon unsalted butter

1 1/2 teaspoons pure vanilla extract

Preheat the oven to 400 F. Line a baking sheet with parchment paper and place pie shell on it. Place another empty pie plate on it to weigh it down. Bake pie shell 15-20 minutes. Cool.

Melt the chocolate (in a double boiler or microwave) and set aside.

In a double-boiler over medium heat, mix the whipping cream, egg yolks, sugar, flour, cornstarch and salt. Cook, whisking all the while, until mixture thickens, 7-10 minutes. Cool slightly and blend in the butter, vanilla and melted chocolate.

Let cool to just warm and pour filling through a strainer into the baked pie shell. Chill until serving and garnish with freshly whipped cream.

Serves 6

YE OLD ICE BOX-YESTERYEAR'S REFRIGERATION

It's hard to imagine but there once was a time when there was neither central air conditioning nor reliable, modern refrigeration. Instead, there were giant oak chests, (later they were metal) that housed a gargantuan block of ice, delivered by an ice-man. These wood chests, now sought-after antiques, were the forerunners to the modern fridge. Cold air circulated from the air and the melting ice was drained off. A good block of ice would last 2 days or so before it had to be replaced. (Before that, ice was chopped off from winter-frigid rivers or caves, and the hunks were stored under straw or in pits in a barn, to be used in summer) Ice-box pies, developed around the 1930's-1850's are a nod to that era when homemakers, thrilled with the 'ease' of their modern day ice-box, could put the chilled pies inside the fridge, secure that the pies would hold until serving time.

Boston Cream Pie

Boston Cream pie is of course, a cake with filling and not a pie at all. Purportedly invented in 1855 by the then chef at the famed Boston Parker House Hotel, the cake, as with Parker House Rolls, became an instant classic, replicated over a century later. A chilled, custard-filled gold cake, topped with deep chocolate icing, suits summer appetites to a T.

CAKE

1 1/4 cups sugar

3/4 cup unsalted butter, softened

2 eggs

2 teaspoons pure vanilla extract

2 ½ cups all-purpose flour

2 ½ teaspoons baking powder

3/8 teaspoon salt

¾ cup warm milk

PASTRY CREAM FILLING

3 tablespoons flour

1/3 cup sugar

2 tablespoons cornstarch

1/8 teaspoon salt

5 egg yolks

1 3/4 cups milk

2 tablespoons unsalted butter

2 teaspoons pure vanilla extract

2 tablespoons unsalted butter

CHOCOLATE GLAZE

¾ cup semi-sweet chocolate chips, melted

1/2 cup unsalted butter, softened

2-3 cups confectioners' sugar

1 teaspoon pure vanilla extract

4-6 tablespoon warm milk or water, as required

WHIPPED CREAM

1 cup whipping cream

1 tablespoon confectioners' sugar

Preheat the oven to 350 F. Line a large baking sheet with parchment paper. Generously spray a 10 inch spring-form pan with non-stick cooking spray and place a circle of parchment paper on the pan bottom. Alternatively, you can use two 8 inch layer cake pans. Place pan (s) on baking sheet.

For the cake, in a food processor, add the sugar and process for 20 or 30 seconds to make sugar finer. Add butter and process until blended. Add eggs and vanilla and blend. Fold in the flour, baking powder and salt and drizzle in milk, blending to make a smooth batter, 1-2 minutes.

For the Pastry Cream, in a medium bowl, whisk together the flour, sugar, cornstarch, salt, egg yolks and ¼ cup of the milk. In a small saucepan, bring remaining milk to a gentle boil. Add a little of the warm milk to the egg yolk mixture. Then whisk in egg yolk mixture, stirring all the while until mixture thickens and begins to boil gently. Remove from heat. Stir in butter and vanilla. Cool and refrigerate until needed. Spray the custard with non-stick cooking spray and cover with plastic wrap to avoid skin from forming on top of custard.

For the Chocolate Glaze, melt the chocolate and butter in a small pot. Cool to warm and then place in a small bowl and hand whisk the mixture with confectioners' sugar and vanilla, adding in enough confectioners' sugar or milk, either one, as required, for a very thick glaze/icing consistency.

To assemble, whip the cream with the confectioners' sugar until soft peaks form. Fold it into the pastry cream. Place cake on a servicing platter, top side down (so that flatter bottom of cake is not the 'top'). With a large serrated knife, split the cake horizontally in half. Spread on the pastry cream and gently press top layer down slightly on custard layer. Spread chocolate icing over top layer. Chill 45-60 minutes at least, before serving.

Serves 8-10

Shredded Dough Blackberry Pie

A gorgeous, summery pie with the deep flavor of fresh blackberries and the buttery sophistication of an easy pastry top.

PREPARED PIE SUCH AS MY FAVORITE ALL BUTTER PIE PASTRY DOUGH

STREUSEL TOPPING

1/4 cup all-purpose flour

1/4 cup sugar

¼ teaspoon cinnamon

Pinch cloves

3 tablespoons unsalted butter

1/2 teaspoon pure vanilla extract

PIE FILLING

4 cups fresh blackberries

1 cup frozen blueberries

3/4 cup sugar

1 tablespoon lemon juice

2 tablespoons fresh orange juice

2 tablespoons flour

2 tablespoons cornstarch

1 tablespoon unsalted butter, in small bits

Preheat the oven to 400 F. Line a baking sheet with parchment paper. Line a 9 or 10 inch pie pan or deep quiche or tart pan with pie dough and place on baking sheet. Freeze remaining half of the dough.

For the Streusel Topping, in a small bowl or food processor, cut or rub the flour, sugar and butter together to make a grainy mixture. Stir in cinnamon, cloves and vanilla.

For the filling, in a large bowl, toss blackberries, blueberries, sugar, lemon juice, orange juice, flour, corn starch, and butter together, tossing gently with a large spoon. Spoon into prepared pie shell.

Remove frozen dough from the freezer and shred it on a cheese grater. Arrange shredded dough to cover fruit filling. Sprinkle streusel topping over and around the shredded dough, filling in gaps but mostly covering the dough.

Bake 15 minutes at 400 F, then lower temperature to 375 F. and continue baking until golden brown (an additional 20 to 30 minutes) and filling juices are bubbling gently through the topping.

Cool well before serving.

Serves 6-8

Lemon Ice Box Pie

No need to worry about meringues; instead, this is a lemon Creamsicle in a pie. Ice box pies, which have been around when refrigerators were in fact, ice-boxes, are no sweat. Unlike meringue pies, which take a bit more care, a whipped cream topped chilled pie is a breeze to make.

1 PRE-BAKED PIECRUST OR A GRAHAM CRACKER CRUST, 9-INCH SIZE

FILLING

1 cup sugar

6 tablespoons cornstarch

Pinch salt

2 cups water

5 egg yolks

3 tablespoons unsalted butter

1/2 cup fresh lemon juice

1/4 teaspoon citric acid

1/8 teaspoon pure lemon oil

1/2 teaspoon pure lemon extract

Zest of one lemon, finely minced

TOPPING

1 package instant lemon pudding, (any size) prepared and chilled

1 1/2 cups whipping cream

1/4 cup confectioners' sugar

FINISHING TOUCHES

Lemon zest shreds

Prepare the pie crust (bake and cool) and set aside.

For the filling, in a heavy 3-quart saucepan, combine the sugar, cornstarch, salt and water over very low heat. Add in the egg yolks and increase the temperature just a little, whisking all the while. Bring to a gentle bubble, and let thicken, about 4-5 minutes. Remove the pan from the heat and add in the butter and lemon juice, citric acid, lemon oil and lemon extract. Pour the filling through a strainer (for an extra smooth filling) and into a bowl. Stir in the lemon zest and then spoon the filling into the piecrust. Chill 20 minutes.

Meanwhile, prepare the pudding and chill 15 minutes. Then whip the whipping cream with confectioners' sugar until stiff peaks form. Fold pudding into whipped cream and then mound it on the lemon pie filling. Chill at least an hour before serving. Dust with lemon zest.

Serves 6-8

Fresh French Raspberry Tart

Nothing beats raspberries and cream in a thin, golden tart shell. You can make one big tart or several smaller ones. Make the custard a day before if you have time otherwise, earlier in the day. For a lighter filling, you have the option of folding in whipped cream to the pastry cream for a variation that is no less rich and inviting.

FRENCH PASTRY CREAM FILLING

5 egg yolks

1/2 cup sugar

1 teaspoon pure vanilla extract

1/4 teaspoon almond extract

2 cups milk

6 tablespoons all-purpose flour

SWEET TART CRUST

2 1/2 cups all-purpose flour

1 tablespoon sugar

1/2 teaspoon salt

3/4 cup unsalted butter

4-6 tablespoons whipping cream

RASPBERRY TOPPING

Fresh raspberries, as required

1 cup apple jelly or sieved apricot preserves

Mint leaves

For the French Pastry Cream, in a medium bowl, whisk the egg yolks and half of the sugar until pale in color, about 3 minutes. Stir in vanilla and almond extract and 1/2 cup of the milk. Sift in the flour and blend well.

In a medium saucepan, over low heat, heat the remaining 1 1/2 cups of milk and the rest of the sugar to a boil. Remove from heat and gradually pour hot milk mixture into yolk mixture, whisking well all the while. Return entire mixture to saucepan and simmer for 1 1/2 to 2 minutes until mixture thickens, whisking briskly all the while. Remove from heat and pour into a bowl to cool.

Brush the top of the pastry cream with melted butter (this prevents a skin from forming) and cover with a piece of plastic wrap or wax paper directly onto surface of pastry cream. Refrigerate until thoroughly cool (up to three days).

For the Sweet Tart Crust, place the flour, sugar and salt in a food processor and pulse to blend dry ingredients. Add in the chunks of butter and pulse to make a grainy mixture. Add in the cream, a few tablespoons at a time and pulse until you have a mixture that hold together, adding in additional cream if required. Turn the mixture out onto a lightly floured work surface and knead gently to form a dough. Pat into a disc, wrap and refrigerate 1-4 hours.

Preheat the oven to 375 F. Line a baking sheet with parchment paper.

Roll out the tart dough on a floured work surface. Fold it in four and transfer to a 9 or 10 inch tart or quiche pan, pressing the dough snugly onto the pan and into the fluted edges. Trim pastry so it is flush with the pan edges. Place an empty pie dish on top to hold pastry down.

(For tart molds, line with parchment paper and use pie weights or dried beans to hold down the pastry).

Bake for 20 to 25 minutes (about half that time for tartlets), and remove top pie pan and parchment paper for the last 10 to 12 minutes to dry out inner crust. Cool well before filling and assembling. (You can bake these earlier in the day and fill a few hours before serving)

To assemble the tart, whisk pastry cream to loosen and lighten. Spread pastry cream into pie or tart shell. Top with raspberries and then brush with warmed red currant jelly. Garnish center with mint leaf.

Serves 8-10

A TISKET, A TASKET AND GREEN AND YELLOW PICNIC BASKET

Ah, picnic baskets – how romantic they are and how quintessentially summer. No matter how rushed and modern our lives, a picnic (and the very vision of a picnic basket) means fun, good, simple, wholesome food. The word picnic can be traced back in Old English dictionaries to 1748 since Europeans shared a flair for outdoor feasts, which were often tied to harvest events, marriages, and cultural celebrations. North Americans adopted picnics in pioneer days. When new communities settled, picnics (and barn raising suppers and harvest parties, all held outdoors) were a social occasion that brought neighbors together in a moment that was all about fun for a change. Nantucket picnic baskets, named for the island those craftsmen made some of the most functional, beautiful baskets, are still available. Nantucket whalers, seeing examples of woven cane on their voyages, returned home, eager to use this cane, along with the artistry of Native Americans and their knowledge of basket weaving. The cane and Yankee industriousness, created an American basket tradition.

Mom's Blueberry Torte

I always intended to make this recipe, found in my mom's recipe box because it seemed easy, unique and delicious but it was upstaged by a similar recipe that called for apples instead. Then one day, I made it and wow! This is a keeper.

CRUST

½ cup unsalted butter, melted

1 cup sugar

2 eggs

1 1/2 teaspoons pure vanilla extract

2 cups all-purpose flour

2 teaspoons baking powder

¼ teaspoon salt

FILLING

4-6 cups (enough to fill up pastry flush to top) blueberries

1/3 cup sugar

2 tablespoons cornstarch

1 tablespoons flour

1 tablespoon fresh lemon juice

1/8 teaspoon cinnamon

SAUCE

¼ cup unsalted butter, melted

1 cup sugar

2 eggs

2 tablespoons whipping cream

1 teaspoon pure vanilla extract

Preheat the oven to 350 F. Line a baking sheet with parchment paper.

For the crust, in a mixer bowl, hand-mix the (cooled) melted butter, sugar, eggs, vanilla, flour, baking powder and salt. Pat crust into a 10 inch spring form pan or a deep 9 inch quiche pan. Dough should go up the sides and make sure corners are not too thick with dough, i.e. even it out as best you can.

For the filling, in a large bowl, toss the blueberries gently with the sugar, cornstarch, flour, lemon juice and cinnamon. Spoon into crust. Place pan on baking sheet. Bake one hour or until crust is browned around edges and berries begin to bubble.

Meanwhile, for sauce, mix butter, sugar, eggs, cream and vanilla in a small bowl. Pour or drizzle over the blueberries. Bake another 20 minutes. Refrigerate overnight.

Serves 10-14

Picnic Basket Dark Fudge Cake

A moist, tall, slicing cake, when you want deep, dark chocolate that is fuss-free and doesn't even require icing, or glaze, just a dusting of confectioners' sugar. I prefer a tube or angel food cake pan for tall cakes like this. If you're at the cottage, you can mix this batter by hand.

2 cups white sugar

3/4 cup brown sugar, firmly packed

1 cup unsalted butter, melted

4 eggs

1 tablespoon pure vanilla extract

3 1/4 cups all-purpose flour

2/3 cup cocoa

2 ¼ teaspoons baking powder

2 teaspoons baking soda

½ teaspoon salt

1 cup warm coffee or flat cola beverage

¾ cup buttermilk

½ cup sour cream

½ cup miniature chocolate chips

FINISHING TOUCHES

3/4 cup chocolate chips, melted

Confectioners' sugar

Preheat the oven to 350. Line a baking sheet with parchment paper. Very generously spray a 9 or 10 inch tube pan with non-stick cooking spray and place on the baking sheet.

In a mixer bowl or in a food processor, combine the white sugar, brown sugar and the butter. Blend in the eggs and vanilla beat for one minute until smooth. Add in the flour, cocoa, baking powder, baking soda and salt. Stir briefly, and then drizzle in coffee or cola, buttermilk and sour cream, stirring at the same time, to make a smooth batter. Fold in the chocolate chips.

Spoon batter into pan. Bake for 60-72 minutes or until cake tests done. Bundt cakes take longer to bake than tube pans. Top should spring back when touched when cake is done.

While cake is still warm, sprinkle on chocolate chips on top of cake and allow to sit on cake to melt. Use a butter knife to swirl melted chocolate in a decorative fashion. As cake comes to room temperature, give it a gentle shake to loosen it from its bottom - but do not remove it from pan. Place cake in fridge to firm up chocolate. Once chocolate is well set, place a plate on top of pan and invert cake onto plate. When chocolate is cooled and set, dust with confectioners' sugar.

Serves 10-12

Carrot Cheesecake Swirl Cake

Something in my rogue spirit stops me from leaving even a classic carrot cake alone. This is a moist carrot cake with a tunnel of cheesecake filling running through it. Because carrots are the main event, choose sweet and flavorful organic carrots.

CHEESECAKE FILLING

8 ounces cream cheese, softened

1/3 cup sugar

1 teaspoon pure vanilla extract

1 egg

1 tablespoon flour

CAKE

2 cups sugar

1 1/4 cup canola oil

4 eggs

2 tablespoons fresh lemon juice

1/4 cup fresh orange juice

1 tablespoon pure vanilla extract

3 cups all-purpose flour

2 teaspoons baking powder

½ teaspoon baking soda

2 ½ teaspoons cinnamon

½ teaspoon salt

3 cups finely shredded carrots

1 cup yellow raisins, plumped and dried

½ cup finely chopped walnuts or pecans, optional

CREAM CHEESE ICING

4 ounces cream cheese

3-4 cups confectioners' sugar

1 teaspoon pure vanilla extract

1-2 tablespoons fresh lemon juice

FINISHING TOUCHES

Cinnamon

Grated carrots

Preheat the oven to 350 F. Line a large baking sheet with parchment paper. Generously spray a 10 inch non-stick angel food cake pan with non-stick cooking spray and place on baking sheet.

For the Cheesecake Filling, in a food processor, blend cream cheese, sugar, vanilla, egg and flour in a food processor until smooth and set aside.

For the cake, in a mixer bowl or by hand, blend the sugar, oil, eggs, lemon juice, orange juice and vanilla extract. Fold in flour, baking powder, baking soda, cinnamon and salt and blend well, adding in the carrots, raisins, and nuts.

Spoon one-third of batter into pan. Top with cream cheese filling and smooth slightly and then top with the remaining batter. Bake until cake is set, about 60-70 minutes or more (it may take longer for center to set). Lower temperature to 325 F and allow baking as required so as not to burn edges or bottom but ensuring the middle is baked. Cool well on a rack and refrigerate about 1-2 hours before icing.

For Cream Cheese Icing, blend the cream cheese with the confectioners' sugar, vanilla and lemon juice until smooth. Turn cake upside down on a serving platter (to make flat bottom the top of the cake) and smear on frosting. Dust with cinnamon and place carrots in center. Chill well.

Serves 16-24

Summer Bazaar Caramel Cake

Caramel Cake is inspired by the book, The Help (Kathryn Stockett). The world needs both great works of fiction and great caramel cakes and this one is my definitive version of the Southern classic. I simply have no resistance when it comes to this cake (just warning you) and tested it far more times than it needed – just to have one lying around, for 'extra taste testing'.

CAKE

¾ cup unsalted butter, softened

2 1/4 cup sugar

4 eggs

1 tablespoon pure vanilla extract

3 cups all-purpose flour

3 ½ teaspoons baking powder

1/4 teaspoon baking soda

1/2 teaspoon salt

1 1/2 cups warm buttermilk

CARAMEL

1/2 cup water

1 cup sugar

1 cup whipping cream, warmed up (30 seconds in microwave)

Pinch fleur des sel (or any other gourmet flaked salt)

CARAMEL FROSTING *

1 cup unsalted butter

1 1/2 cups light brown sugar, firmly packed

2 teaspoons corn syrup

Pinch salt

1 teaspoon pure vanilla extract

3-4 tablespoons whipping cream or evaporated milk

3-4 cups confectioners' sugar

* I prefer this with a fondant-based buttercream. If you can find soft fondant, use ½ pound each fondant and unsalted butter and 1 tablespoon vanilla. Whip it all together with a wire whisk, using a stand mixer until light and fluffy.

Preheat the oven to 350 F. Generously spray two 9-inch layer cake pans with non-stick cooking spray. Line a large baking sheet with parchment paper. Place pans on it.

For the cake, in a mixer bowl, cream the butter and sugar until light and fluffy. Blend in the eggs and vanilla. Blend until smooth, scraping the bottom of the bowl occasionally to ensure no ingredients get stuck or remain unblended in the well of the bowl. Fold in the flour, baking powder, baking soda and salt and drizzle in the buttermilk while blending the ingredients to make a smooth batter, scraping the sides and bottom of the bowl occasionally to ensure the batter is evenly blended.

Spoon into prepared pans. Bake until cakes test done when gently pressed with fingertips, about 35-38 minutes.

Cool in pans 10 minutes before unmolding on a wire rack to cool completely or wrap cakes lightly in plastic wrap. (They can also be wrapped up and frosted up to two days later).

For the Caramel, in a small saucepan, heat the water and sugar over low heat. For 20-30 minutes, slowly bubble or simmer, brushing down sides with a brush dipped in water. Once it turns medium or light amber, remove from burner and put it in the sink. Pour warmed cream slowly into sauce (take care, it bubbles up and is hot!) and whisk until blended in.

For the Caramel Frosting, place butter, brown sugar, corn syrup, salt and vanilla in a 3-quart saucepan. Cook over low heat until the mixture thickens and reaches a little under softball stage (234 F or less). If you don't have a thermometer, cook the mixture until a bit of the mixture on a cold plate, seems to hold together like soft taffy, 15-20 minutes. Remove from stove and add the evaporated milk and stir. Cool to almost room temperature. Place in a mixer bowl and add 2 cups of the confectioners' sugar and whip to thicken, slowing machine and adding more confectioners' sugar to make a thick but somewhat fluffy icing.

To assemble the cake, cut each layer in two, horizontally (you will have 4 layers)

Drizzle on some of the caramel on the first layer and then top with Penuche Frosting. Place another layer on top and repeat. Repeat with layers of cake, caramel and frosting. Reserve some caramel and frosting to finish outside of assembled cake. Frost top and sides of cake decoratively. Drizzle top with any extra caramel.

Serves 14-20

Greek Yogurt Cheesecake

A sumptuous little cheesecake you can whip up in no time at all. This is ideal when you want a smaller cheesecake, the nutritious and smoothness of a great Greek yogurt and the luxury of a decadent cheesecake. I suggested canned cherry pie topping or fresh fruit and apricot glaze but this cake is so good, it really doesn't need anything but a fork.

BOTTOM CRUST

1 ¼ cup graham cracker crumbs

3 tablespoons brown sugar

¼ cup unsalted butter, melted

Pinch cinnamon

FILLING AND TOPPING

2 ½ 8 ounce packages cream cheese, softened

½ cup plus 2 tablespoons sugar

3 eggs

1 1/2 teaspoon pure vanilla extract

1 tablespoon fresh lemon juice

1 cup plain, thick style Greek yogurt

1 21 ounce can cherry pie filling, chilled or fresh fruit

Preheat the oven to 350 F. Line a baking sheet with parchment paper.

For the Bottom Crust, mix the graham cracker crumbs, brown sugar, butter and cinnamon together well and pat into a 9 inch layer cake or spring-form pan. Place pan on the baking sheet.

For the Filling, in a food processor, cream the cream cheese with the sugar until smooth. Add in the eggs, vanilla, lemon juice and Greek yogurt. Process until smooth about 1-2 minutes. Pour into prepared cake pan.

Bake until just set, about 35-40 minutes.

Chill 6 hours or overnight. Spread on cherry pie filling before serving.

Serves 8-10

Orange Olive Oil Bundt Cake

Olive oil cakes are intriguing and feature the healthy attributes of unsaturated olive oil. Opt for light (almost flavorless) olive oil or even corn oil (but never extra virgin olive oil; it's too dominant a taste for this cake. You'll be rewarded with a tall, refreshing cake that's especially moist and flavourful.

CAKE

4 small clementines or mandarins, washed and quartered (or one large orange)

1 cup hot water

1 cup fine, stoneground cornmeal

3 cups sugar

1 1/2 cups mild or extra light olive oil *

5 eggs

½ teaspoon pure orange oil or orange extract

2 teaspoons pure vanilla extract

3 ½ cups all-purpose flour

2 ½ teaspoons baking powder

½ teaspoon baking soda

3/8 teaspoon salt

FINISHING TOUCHES

Orange zest

Confectioners' sugar

* Use mild, flavorless olive oil, not extra virgin. You can also use corn or canola oil.

Preheat the oven to 350 F. Line a baking sheet with parchment paper. Generously spray a 9 inch Angel food cake pan with non-stick cooking spray. Place on baking sheet. Spray pieces of parchment paper, cut to fit, with non-stick cooking spray and line pan bottom and sides with it, allowing a 'collar' to extend 2 inches over rim of pan (this will hold the cake in should it rise a bit over the cake pan edge)

In a food processor, grind the clementines to a paste. Set aside. In a small bowl, stir hot water with cornmeal and let stand.

In a mixer bowl, blend the sugar, olive oil, eggs, orange oil and vanilla. Fold in flour, baking powder, baking soda and salt. Blend in the cornmeal mixture and ground oranges to make a soft but well-blended batter. Pour or spoon into cake pan.

Bake 55 minutes at 350F and then lower temperature to 300 F and bake another 20 minutes more until cake is set and firm to the touch. Let cool 20 minutes before unmolding. Dust with confectioners' sugar and orange zest before serving.

Serves 12-16

On Cabbages and Kings and... Cobblers, Crisps, Crumbles, Brown Betty, Buckles, Grunts, Slumps, Sonkers, Puddings and Pandowdy

There are very basic things in the above desserts anyone will agree on. For one, they are all fruity (stone fruits, apples, pears, peaches, berries, etc.); two, they have a starch element (flour, breadcrumbs, biscuit topping), three: they are family style (versus individual servings) desserts most often made in a deep dish casserole and oven baked, four: they are economical and use what is in season, and five: they are as old as time, homey, simple, almost folkloric desserts, made in minutes and usually served warm. One person's Apple Crisp and another's Apple Brown Betty. Adding a topping or batter/crumb/pastry element to fruit has been around since Colonialist days and before – as newcomers to these shores brought their European recipes with them. As the Old Country bakers knew, desserts that used what was on-hand, seasonal or plentiful had special appeal.

The variations in toppings were as due to regional, cultural preferences as they likely were to what a baker had on hand. Extra pastry for a cobbler or extra biscuit dough might do double duty, appearing in a pie, biscuits and/or a pandowdy or grunt or a slump.

Crisps

These are usually fruits, often apples, baked with streusel toppings of flour, butter, sugar or oatmeal, butter, sugar, or sweetened and spiced breadcrumbs.

Crumbles

These are like crisps and turn up in British cookbooks under that name. Like a crisp, crumbles feature fruit on the bottom and something crisp or crumbly and sweet on top.

Brown Betty

Like crisps and crumbles, Brown Bettys are deep dish desserts. Often it's Apple Brown Betty that rules the BB reign. The Brits might call this a pudding; the French might do their own spin and call it a 'Charlotte' and I've seen other recipes called Dutch Apple Cake or Apple Pudding that features layers of softened apples alternating with breadcrumb, zwieback or graham crumb layers.

Cobblers

Cobblers are as varied as summer sunsets, but all feature, again, deep dish fruit, covered with pastry or biscuit crust. You can roll the pastry or biscuit dough or plop wetter blobs of biscuit dough, allowing the fruit filling to bake and simmer up between the crusty, golden biscuit sprawls that form.

Buckles

These are more oven true cake batters to which berries (most often) are added in copious amounts. Sometimes a buckle features a streusel topping but the final effect is a densely fruity cake – somewhere between a muffin and butter cake taste and texture. Buckles are the precursors of coffee cakes wherein a soft batter is folded with fruit or the batter is put on top of fruit and bakes up into cake. Deep Dish Apple Cake for instance, is a cake but its roots might be in fact, very buckle-y.

Grunts and Slumps

These seem to be English puddings respun in American terms but the distinct element in a grunt or slump is that it is top-of-the-range baked/cooked or actually steamed, versus oven baked.

Kuchen

Like crisps, cobblers and grunts, kutchens, meaning coffee cake, covers a broad spectrum of cozy cakes, sometimes yeasted, sometimes not, often with fruit, nuts, dairy goodness like sour cream or buttermilk, and quite often with a touch of spice. Kuchens can be simple or a bit fussier but are always welcome.

Sonker

These don't appear in modern day cookbooks but seem, according to some historical sources, to be North Carolinian in heritage.

Pandowdy

The recipes for these seem to be mostly made with apples, sometimes sweetened with molasses and features a biscuit topping that sinks a bit during baking, allowing the toffee apple filling to peak through. Sometimes this dessert is inverted before serving so that the fruit sits on top of the crust. There is in this particular dessert, a closer relationship to Tarte Tatin, especially if it is served inverted.

Upside Down Peach Cake

Nothing beats fresh, in-season peaches for this spin on Pineapple Upside Down Cake. It features brown-sugar infused peaches as the foundation of a dewy, buttery cake. When you invert the cake on a serving plate, it becomes a peach Tart Tatin; the brown sugar/butter bottom turns into an amber halo atop a gorgeous cake (apricots are a good swop here).

PEACH BROWN SUGAR LAYER

4-5 cups peaches, in ½ inch wedges

½ cup brown sugar, firmly packed

¼ cup fresh orange juice

½ cup unsalted butter

2 tablespoons cornstarch

CAKE

½ cup unsalted butter

1 cup sugar

2 teaspoons pure vanilla extract

2 eggs

3/4 cup buttermilk

2 cups all-purpose flour

2 teaspoons baking powder

¼ teaspoon baking soda

¼ teaspoon salt

Preheat the oven to 350 F. Line a baking sheet with parchment paper. Line a 9 inch spring-form pan with a circle of parchment paper and spray bottom and sides of pan with non-stick cooking spray. Place pan on baking sheet.

For the Peach Brown Sugar Layer, prepare the peaches and place in a bowl. To see if you have enough, spread peaches on the spring-form pan bottom and see that they fully cover the pan. If they do, you have enough fruit. If not, slice up another peach or two.

In a medium saucepan, heat the brown sugar, orange juice, and butter over medium heat, stirring to make a smooth mixture. Let cook 5-8 minutes until slightly thickened. Remove from stove and stir in cornstarch. Pour over the peaches and toss to coat. Spoon fruit/brown sugar mixture into the spring-form pan.

For the cake, in a food processor or mixer bowl, cream the butter and sugar until fluffy. Blend in the vanilla, then eggs, buttermilk; fold in the flour, baking powder, baking soda and salt, blending well to make a thick but smooth mixture. Spoon the batter onto the fruit in the pan.

Bake until cake puffs up and tests done (it will spring back when gently touched with fingertips), about 55-65 minutes and cake is evenly browned. Let stand 30 minutes and then invert onto a cake serving platter and gently remove sides of spring-form pan. Remove parchment paper liner from the cake.

Serve warm or at room temperature with whipped cream or ice cream.

Serves 8-10

Blueberry Raspberry Buckle

This is a golden, fruity buckle with an addictive streusel topping. Dense with deep berry freshness and flavor, it slices easily, making it oh-so-easy to serve. This is summery country elegance in its finest hour.

STREUSEL

½ cup all-purpose flour

2 tablespoons white sugar

½ cup brown sugar, firmly packed

¼ teaspoon cinnamon

Pinch salt

4 tablespoons unsalted butter

CAKE

1/2 cup plus 2 tablespoons unsalted butter

2/3 cup sugar

2 eggs

1 ½ teaspoons pure vanilla extract

1 ½ cups all-purpose flour

1 ½ teaspoons baking powder

1/8 teaspoon salt

3 cups blueberries

1 cup raspberries

Preheat the oven to 350 F. Line a baking sheet with parchment paper. Generously spray a 9 0r 10 inch spring-form pan with non-stick cooking spray and place on baking sheet.

In a food processor or small bowl, combine flour, white and brown sugar, cinnamon and salt. Cut in the butter (with fingers if, by hand, or pulse, if in a processor) to make a course mixture. Chill while preparing the cake.

For the cake, in a mixer bowl, cream the butter with the sugar until smooth and slightly fluffy. Blend in the eggs and vanilla. Then fold in the flour, baking powder and salt, blending well to make a smooth batter. Fold in the fruit.

Spoon batter into the pan and then top with the streusel, taking care not to congregate the streusel on any one part of the cake, especially the center.

Bake until cake seems firm to the touch, about 55 minutes. If cake is browning but does not seem 'set up', lower oven temperature to 325 F and bake 5-10 minutes longer or as required.

Cool 15 minutes in pan before removing.

Serves 8-10

FLASHPOINT! FRESH OR FROZEN, IT'S ALL IN THE WAY YOU TREAT FRUIT

Fresh fruit is plentiful in summer and fresh fruit, all things being optimal, is the ideal fruit for summery, fruit-based baking. That said, frozen and semi-frozen berries actually handle a bit easier in baking. That's because berries, tender as they are, stay intact and 'bleed' less into a batter if they are a bit more solid, i.e. frozen or semi-frozen. In summer, stock up on berries on sale and chuck them in the freezer. But, and this is so important when baking with berries, don't defrost the fruit before using it. Frozen fruit should be used frozen and popped right into the recipe (unless otherwise stated). Otherwise, semi-defrosted or defrosted frozen fruit leaches a ton of water into the baking and challenges the entire recipe balance.

Summer Fruit Crisp with Amaretti Topping

Is there a nicer way to dress up a trio of ambrosial stone fruits? The flavors are incomparable and the perfect pectin in each fruit makes things just saucy and sassy enough. Peaches can be used instead of the nectarines or apricots. With tender nectarines and apricots, there's no need to remove the skins (nor lose some vitamins)

AMARETTI TOPPING

1 1/2 cup finely minced amaretti cookies

½ cup chopped almonds

½ cup sweetened coconut shreds

2 tablespoons brown sugar

Pinch ginger

Pinch salt

½ cup all-purpose flour

½ cup unsalted butter, in small cubes

FRUIT FILLING

2 cups berries (diced strawberries, whole raspberries)

2 cups diced apricots

2 cups diced nectarines

½ cup sugar

2 tablespoons fresh orange juice

2 tablespoons all-purpose flour or cornstarch

Preheat the oven to 350 F. Line a baking sheet with parchment paper. Spray a 4-5 quart oven-proof casserole or baking dish with non-stick cooking spray and place on the baking sheet.

For the Topping, place the amaretti cookies, almonds, coconut, brown sugar, ginger, salt and flour in a bowl to combine. Then place the mixture in a food processor and add in the butter, pulsing to make a crumbly topping. This can also be done by hand in a medium bowl. Set aside.

For the filling, prepare the fruit and place in a large bowl. Add the sugar, orange juice and flour and toss. Spoon into prepared baking dish. Add the topping as evenly as possible.

Bake until juices start to bubble through the topping, and the topping browns, 40-50 minutes. Serve warm or room temperature, as is, or with ice-cream or whipped cream.

Serves 6-8

Fruits-of-the-Forest Summer Tart

They sell yogurt flavors called Fruits-of-the-Forest so why not a tart with the same appealing name and concept? This totally works – it's bright, sweet, cheery and sophisticated.

SWEET TART DOUGH

3 cups all-purpose flour

1/3 cup sugar

1/2 teaspoon salt

1 cup unsalted butter, cut in small chunks

1 egg yolk

1/2 cup whipping cream, approximately

FILLING

1/2 cup ground fresh or frozen cranberries

2 pears, coarsely grated (skin on)

1 cup raspberries

2 cups blueberries

1 cup blackberries

1 cup chopped strawberries

1 cup sugar

2 tablespoons flour

1 tablespoon cornstarch

Finishing Touches

Milk, sugar

Preheat the oven to 425 F. Line a baking sheet with parchment paper. Generously spray a 10 inch tart pan with non-stick cooking spray and place on baking sheet.

For the Sweet Tart Pastry, place the flour, sugar and salt in the bowl of a food processor. Process for a few seconds to combine ingredients. Add in butter and process to form a crumbly mixture. Stop the machine, add the egg yolk and whipping cream. Process until mixture comes together in a mass (20-40 seconds). Add more half-and-half if required to make dough come together. Wrap and refrigerate 20 minutes. On a well-floured work surface, roll out the dough to fit the tart or quiche pan. Place pan on baking sheet.

In a large bowl, gently toss the fruit with the sugar, flour and cornstarch. Mound fruit into the tart shell. Roll out remaining dough and place on top of fruit, pressing slightly, and crimp or press edges together. Make air vents with a paring knife and then brush the pastry dough with milk and dust with some sugar.

Place on baking sheet. Bake 20 minutes before reducing the temperature to 350 F for another 20-25 minutes or until you can see fruit juices coming out of the pie vents.

Serves 8

Plum Cream Tart

A bouquet of tart-sweet plums, held in place by a vanilla and lightly spiced creamy custard. This tart is best served chilled and it's even better a day after baking.

TART CRUST

2 1/2 cups all-purpose flour

1 tablespoon sugar

½ teaspoon salt

¾ cup unsalted butter

1 egg yolk

4-6 tablespoons whipping cream

FILLING

4-5 cups medium diced plums or drained canned plum halves (pitted) *

1-2 tablespoons unsalted butter

2 eggs

2 yolks

1/2 cup sugar

2 tablespoons flour

½ cup whipping cream

½ cup milk

1 ½ teaspoon pure vanilla extract

Good pinch each cinnamon and cloves

FINISHING TOUCHES

Apricot jam, warmed

* You need enough plums to completely line the bottom of the pie or tart shell.

Line a baking sheet with parchment paper.

For the Tart Crust, place the flour, sugar and salt in a food processor and pulse to blend dry ingredients. Add in the chunks of butter and pulse to make a grainy mixture. Add in the egg yolk, then the cream, a few tablespoons at a time and pulse until you have a mixture that hold together, adding in additional cream if required. Turn the mixture out onto a lightly floured work surface and knead gently to form a dough. Pat into a disc, wrap and refrigerate 1-4 hours.

Preheat the oven to 375 F.

Prepare the plums by sautéing them in the butter, 5-10 minutes over low heat, to soften a bit, cooking until juices are reduced by half. Let cool while preparing the pastry.

Roll out the tart dough on a lightly floured work surface to 2 inches larger than the tart pan. Transfer it to a 9 or 10 inch cheesecake pan, pressing the dough snugly onto the pan. Trim the pastry so it is flush with the pan edges. Place on the baking sheet.

Place the softened plums in the tart shell. In a medium bowl, whisk together the eggs, yolk, sugar, flour, cream, milk, vanilla, cinnamon and cloves. Pour over plums.

Bake until set, 60-75 minutes or until custard seems set and plums are oozing juices a bit. Cool 10-15 minutes before brushing with warmed apricot jam.

Serves 6-8

IN PRAISE OF STONE FRUIT

I love the term 'stone fruit' – which is the umbrella term for peaches, nectarines, plums and pluots (a beautiful marriage of plums and apricots). Stone fruits taste quintessentially of summer, all sunshine and sweetness, and all at once exotic but also farmhouse-accessible. Few things are as old-fashioned as stone fruit desserts and you can interchange the choice of stone fruits recipes as you wish. I love stone fruit in summery pastries and cobblers that make the most of their juiciness, flavor as well as their gorgeous hues of orange, yellow and red. Peaches, in particular, are a pastry chef's delight. You'll find many new varieties at farmer markets and at the supermarket. Peaches also combine nicely with other fruits such as nectarines and apricots, which both seem similar but have their own companionable dimensions to add to the mix.

Chocolate Hazelnut Cheesecake

Every cheesecake maker needs one incredible chocolate hazelnut cheesecake in their repertoire. This is a beautiful, gently decadent cheesecake that's perfect during the holidays – when you want something glamorous. Make sure the milk chocolate you use is of excellent quality, such as Lindt which melts well and is luxurious tasting.

CHOCOLATE SNAP CRUST

1-1/2 cups chocolate wafer cookie crumbs

1/4 cup unsalted butter, melted

2 tablespoons brown sugar

FILLING

1 cup milk chocolate, chopped, melted

2 ½ pounds cream cheese, softened

1 14 ounce can sweetened condensed milk

1 cup sugar

¼ cup all-purpose flour

6 eggs

1 tablespoon pure vanilla extract

1 cup Nutella hazelnut spread

Fudge Glaze

2/3 cup whipping cream

3/4 cup semi-sweet chocolate chips

1/2 teaspoon pure vanilla extract, optional

FINISHING TOUCHES

Semi-sweet chocolate curls

Confectioners' sugar

Preheat the oven to 325 F. Line a baking sheet with parchment paper.

For the Chocolate Snap Crust, in the bottom of a 10-inch spring-form pan, mix the cookie crumbs, butter and sugar until evenly moistened. Press into the pan bottom. Place the pan on the baking sheet.

For the filling, in a mixer bowl, cream the cheese with condensed milk, sugar and flour. Add the eggs until thoroughly incorporated and stir in the vanilla. Pour half the batter into the prepared pan. Top with dollops of Nutella. To the remaining batter, whisk in the cooled, melted milk chocolate. Pour this chocolate batter into spring-form pan. Create marble effect by dipping knife into cake batter and gently swirling it through cake.

Bake until cake is set, when gently touched in the middle, with fingertips about 50-55 minutes. Turn off oven, open oven door and let cake stay for an hour to cool down. Then refrigerate cake several hours or overnight.

For the Fudge Glaze, heat the whipping cream to just bubbling. Stir in chopped chocolate all at once and stir to blend cream and chocolate. Remove from heat and stir with a whisk until all chocolate is melted. Stir in vanilla. Cool to room temperature before using. Before serving cake, pour chocolate glaze over surface, spreading glaze evenly over cake and down cake sides with a small spatula. Let glaze set 15 minutes before serving.

Garnish this cake with chocolate curls and a dusting of confectioners' sugar.

14-18 servings

Japanese Cotton Cheesecake

I'm not sure why this crust-less cheesecake has this name (some say it's from Malaysia) but it's perfect when you prefer a modest cheesecake that takes well to fresh fruit toppings or just a dusting of confectioners' sugar (p.s. it's also really low on carbs).

CHEESECAKE

6 egg whites (reserve yolks)

Pinch sugar

Pinch salt

2 8 ounces packages cream cheese, room temperature

½ cup sugar

2 teaspoons pure vanilla extract

2 tablespoons fresh lemon juice

4 tablespoons all-purpose flour

1 tablespoon cornstarch

Tiny pinch salt

6 egg yolks

½ cup whipping cream

FINISHING TOUCHES

Confectioners' sugar or fresh fruit

Apricot preserves, warmed

Preheat the oven to 325 F. Generously spray a 9 or 10-inch springform pan with non-stick cooking spray. Line bottom and sides with pieces of parchment paper. Wrap outside of cheesecake pan very snugly with two layers of aluminum foil. In the oven, place a large roasting pan filled halfway with water (the cheesecake pan will bake, set in this water bath).

In a mixer bowl, with the whisk attachment, on slow speed, whisk the egg whites with the sugar and salt. Increase speed to high and whip until the whites are lightly and glossy (but not dried out or falling apart. Spoon whites out into another bowl. In the same mixer bowl, with paddle attachment, on slow speed, cream the cream cheese, sugar, vanilla, lemon juice, flour, cornstarch and salt until extremely smooth, 5 minutes. Blend in the egg yolks well and then the whipping cream, making an extremely smooth mixture without any lumps.

Fold one-third of the egg whites into the cheesecake batter to lighten it. Then fold in three additions, the egg whites into the cheesecake batter. Spoon into prepared pan and place in water bath. Bake 25 minutes and then lower temperature to 300F; bake, until cake is just set in the center, about 25-35 minutes. Remove from the water bath and remove aluminum foil.

Refrigerate several hours or overnight. Unmold, remove parchment paper sides and brush top with apricot glaze or decorate with fruit or simply dust with confectioners' sugar.

Serves 10-14

S'Mores Cheesecake

A graham crust is the foundation of this popular flavor cheesecake that takes the S'Mores concept into a more elegant, more enduring dessert. Perfect for a summer BBQ finale. Chunks of milk chocolate, coarse slabs of more graham cookie and a few handfuls of tender, miniature marshmallows stud the creamy cheesecake and then it's topped in a milk-chocolate ganache and swirl of warm marshmallow.

S'MORES CRUST

1 1/3 cup graham cracker crumbs

1/4 cup unsalted butter, melted

1/4 cup ground milk chocolate

1/4 cup sugar

S'MORES CHEESECAKE FILLING

1 1/4 cup sugar

2 pounds cream cheese, room temperature

3 tablespoons all-purpose flour

5 eggs

1 tablespoon pure vanilla extract

1 14 ounce can condensed milk

1/2 cup whipping cream

1 cup coarsely chopped milk chocolate bar

2 cups miniature marshmallows

2 cups graham cookies, coarsely chopped

3/4 cup coarsely chopped milk chocolate, melted and cooled

MILK CHOCOLATE GANACHE TOPPING

3/4 cup milk chocolate, melted

1/2 cup whipping cream

1/2 cup, approximately, marshmallow fluff, warmed

FINISHING TOUCHES

Graham crackers, finely crumbs

Preheat the oven to 325 F. Line a baking sheet with parchment paper. For the crust, toss the graham crumbs, butter, milk chocolate and sugar together in the bottom of a 10-inch spring form pan and press to fit the pan bottom. Place the pan on the baking sheet.

For the filling, in a mixer bowl, blend the sugar, cream cheese and flour until smooth. Add the eggs and vanilla and blend well. Blend in the condensed milk and cream and blend well, making sure no uncombined lumps of cream cheese remain. By hand, fold in the chopped chocolate, marshmallows and cookie pieces. Pour into cake pan and with a knife, swirl in melted milk chocolate.

Bake 65 -70 minutes or until center is just set. If marshmallow appear to be browning but cake is not yet set, lower temperature to 300F and let bake a bit longer so that cake will set but to prevent the marshmallows from browning too much. Cool cake on counter an hour before refrigerating. Chill at least 8 hours, preferably overnight.

Meanwhile, make the Milk Chocolate Ganache. Heat cream in a small saucepan until just simmering. Whisk in the chocolate, turn off the heat, and whisk to blend into a saucy chocolate topping. Cool well (to about room temperature)

To serve the cake, use some milk chocolate ganache to coat sides to adhere graham crumbs. Pour the rest on top, smearing to coat the top of the cake. Warm the marshmallow fluff and drizzle puddles of marshmallow over chocolate surface.

Chill slightly and serve. (This cake freezes well)

Serves 14-18

HARVEST OF ART, FRUIT CRATE ART

Back in the day, before there were supermarkets and warehouse food stores, people (if they didn't grow their own) shopped for produce at open air markets. The produce, fresh and abundant, wasn't displayed in cello-wrapped packages but in the original shipping, i.e. fruit crates that were plucked straight off the trains that brought in the produce. Between 1880 to 1950, 'fruit crate art' was characteristically vibrant, colorful graphics that identified the orchards or growers. Talk about branding! The better the art, the better the perception that the fruit was outstanding The names were also so riveting - Golden Girl, Jazz Fruit, Talisman, and Shamrock. Fruit crate art captures a feeling of more than one summer's harvest gone by – it captures an era gone by, that of private farms and non-industrial, non GMO crops, replete with migrant agricultural laborers, who toiled to keep the nation (and their own families) fed. It was a time of hardship (just read Grapes of Wrath) but also, a time of plenty. It reminds us of the pride of the growers too, and how a seasonal peach, pear or cherry was the foundation of incredible summer desserts we still savor. If it wasn't seasonal, you didn't bake with it because it simply wasn't available. And if you have a hankering for the past, fruit crate art reproductions (and originals) are still to be found.

Strawberry Layer Cake with Cream Cheese Strawberry Streak Frosting

A tall, glamour girl, layer cake, sweet with ripe strawberries and a luscious cream-cheese frosting. The secret here is the strawberry flavored syrup that soaks into the cake before it's frosted. This is a true celebration cake..

CAKE

1/2 cup strawberries, finely diced and semi-frozen

1 cup unsalted butter

2 cups sugar

3 eggs

2 teaspoons pure vanilla extract

1 cup buttermilk

3 cups all-purpose flour

1 tablespoon baking powder

3/8 teaspoon salt

SIMPLE STRAWBERRY SYRUP

1/2 cup water

1/2 cup sugar

2 tablespoons fresh lemon juice

3 tablespoons strawberry liqueur, optional

FROSTING

1 8 ounce package cream cheese, softened

¼ cup unsalted butter

2 teaspoons pure vanilla extract

¼ teaspoon orange oil or 1 tablespoon orange liqueur

1 tablespoon Chambord or strawberry liqueur, optional

½ teaspoon strawberry extract, optional

5-7 cups confectioners' sugar

¼ cup strawberry jam

1 pint basket strawberries, hulled and pureed

FINISHING TOUCHES

Fresh strawberry halves

Preheat the oven to 350 F. Line a large baking sheet with parchment paper. Generously spray two 9-inch layer cake pans with non-stick cooking spray and line each with a circle of parchment paper. Place pans on baking sheet.

For the cake, in a mixer bowl, cream the butter and sugar until light and fluffy. Blend in the eggs, and then vanilla and buttermilk and blend well. Fold in the flour, baking powder, and salt and blend to make a smooth batter, scraping down the sides and middle of bowl to ensure the batter is evenly blended. Fold in the diced strawberries gently and spoon batter into pans.

Bake 40-45 minutes, or until cake spring back when gently touched with fingertips. If cakes appear to be browning but not baked in the center, lower temperature to 325 F and finish baking as required. Cool cakes in pan 15 minutes and then remove to a cooling rack to finish cooling. Freeze 30 minutes or while preparing other elements of the cake (it will be easier to slice later)

For the Simple Strawberry Syrup, simmer the water, sugar, lemon juice until sugar dissolves about 5-8 minutes. Cool and stir in strawberry liqueur and extract.

To make the frosting, combine all ingredients in a mixer bowl or a food processor and blend well, adding in a touch of water or confectioners' sugar to achieve the right frosting consistency. By hand, fold in the strawberry jam to streak the frosting. Chill frosting while cake cools.

Place bottom cake layer (bottom side up, as it is flatter) on a serving platter and brush top generously with the Simple Syrup. Frost the cake layer thinly with frosting and then spread on the crushed strawberries. Press the top layer on this (again, making the 'top' the bottom and leaving a flat top to ice). Generously brush with syrup and let stand 10 minutes. Then frost top and sides of cake with icing. Garnish the cake with fresh strawberry halves on the bottom border of cake. Refrigerate cake until serving.

Serves 12-16

Summer Wedding White Chocolate Coconut Cake

This is not a cake; this is a Vera Wang dress. This cake is delectably moist and rich with a coconut and white rum-spiked butter cream icing. Inside is a golden crumbed cake, rampant with vanilla and coconut overtones and kissed with imported white chocolate.

CAKE

1 cup chopped white chocolate, melted and cooled

2 1/2 cups all-purpose flour

1 1/4 cup sugar

4 teaspoons baking powder

3/8 teaspoon salt

3/4 cup unsalted butter

3 eggs

2 egg yolks

1 1/4 cup warm milk or warm coconut milk

1 1/4 teaspoon coconut extract, optional

1 1/2 teaspoons pure vanilla extract

1/4 teaspoon pure almond extract

¼ cup macadamia nuts, toasted and ground

1/2 cup shredded sweetened coconut

RUM COCONUT SOAKING SYRUP

½ cup water

1/2 cup sugar

1/2 teaspoon coconut extract

2 tablespoons white rum

1 tablespoon lime juice

COCONUT BUTTERCREAM

1 cup unsalted butter, softened

1 cup chopped white chocolate, melted and cooled

3-6 tablespoons water or coconut milk, as required, or rum

1 1/2 teaspoon coconut extract

½ teaspoon pure almond extract

2 teaspoons pure vanilla extract

3-5 cups confectioners' sugar

FINISHING TOUCHES

Shredded sweetened coconut

Toasted shredded coconut

White chocolate curls

Preheat the oven to 350 F. Line a large baking sheet with parchment paper. Generously spray two 9-inch layer cake pans with non-stick cooking spray or 1 9 by 13 inch rectangular pan and set baking pan(s) on it.

In a mixer bowl, blend the flour, sugar, baking powder and salt just to combine ingredients. Blend in the butter to make a gravelly mixture. Add the melted white chocolate, eggs, egg yolks, milk, and extracts and blend well, stopping the mixer to scrape batter from sides and well of mixer bowl to ensure the batter is evenly combined. Fold in nuts and coconut.

Spoon into prepared cake pans. Bake until cake springs back when gently touched with fingertips and edges are slightly browned, 35-40 minutes. Cool in the pan and then unmold and cool completely.

Meanwhile make the Rum Coconut Soaking Syrup. In a small saucepan, combine the water and sugar and simmer 5 minutes. Cool slightly and stir in coconut extract, rum and lime juice.

For the Coconut Buttercream, cream the butter until softened and then add in the white chocolate, a little water, coconut extract, almond extract, vanilla and half of the confectioners' sugar. Blend on high speed, slowing mixer down to add more confectioners' sugar, as required, to get a frosting consistency or add liquid, if required, either coconut milk or rum.

To assemble a layer cake, place the bottom layer, bottom side facing up on a serving platter. Brush well with the Rum Coconut Syrup. Apply some frosting and place the other cake layer, also bottom side facing up, on top of the icing and gently press. Brush top layer with Rum Coconut Syrup and let soak in a few minutes. Then frost the rest of the cake, sides and top. Garnish sides with toasted coconut and sprinkle untoasted coconut and/or curls of white chocolate on top.

Serves 14-18

Red Velvet Groom's Cake

For once, a Red Velvet Cake with flavor! This classic cake is the perfect summer wedding cake as it has the twin lusciousness of sour cream and the richness of pure cocoa. These days, Red Velvet Cakes are made with too much red food coloring which accounts for their devilish hue. This recipe is also perfect for Red Velvet Cupcakes.

CAKE

3/4 cup unsalted butter, softened

2 cups sugar

3 eggs

2 teaspoons pure vanilla extract

1 cup sour cream

2/3 cup boiling water

1 tablespoon red food coloring paste or Red Velvet Food and Flavor *

2/3 cup cocoa powder

2 cups all-purpose flour

1/2 teaspoon baking powder

1 teaspoon baking soda

1/4 teaspoon salt

CREAM CHEESE WHITE FROSTING

1 cup unsalted butter

12 ounces cream cheese

8 cups of confectioners' sugar

2 teaspoons pure vanilla extract

2 teaspoons butter extract or flavour, optional

FINISHING TOUCHES

Cake crumbs or chocolate cookie crumbs

* King Arthur Flour Baker's catalogue has Red Velvet Food Flavor, otherwise use 2 additional teaspoons pure vanilla extract and 1 tablespoon red food coloring paste)

Preheat the oven to 350 F. Line a baking sheet with parchment paper. Generously spray three 8-inch layer cake pans with non-stick cooking spray and set on baking sheet.

In a mixer bowl, cream the butter with the sugar until fluffy. Add in eggs and vanilla and blend well, making sure no sugar remains unblended in the well of the mixer bowl. Mix in sour cream. In a small bowl, stir hot water, food coloring and cocoa together; set aside.

In another small bowl, mix flour, baking powder, baking soda and salt. Fold into the creamed mixture, while drizzling in the cocoa/water mixture, to make a smooth batter, blending 1-2 minutes on slow speed. Spoon into prepared cake pans and bake until done, and spring back when lightly touched, 30-35 minutes. Cool cake well.

For the frosting, blend everything together on slow speed until ingredients are combined a bit and then whip on high speed, with whip attachment, drizzling in a bit of water if necessary for the right consistency.

Trim the cakes to create a flat surface. Keep the trimmings which you can grind into cake crumbs to coast the side of the cake.

Frost cake layers and chill cake. Garnish with ground chocolate cookie crumbs or ground cake crumbs

Serves 12-14 (or makes 24 standard cupcakes, 22 minutes baking time)

Last Tango Chocolate Cake

Like tango, this cake takes a few steps but also like tango it's totally seductive. I think of this cake whenever I attend outdoor tango in summer since I created this cake for a tango festival years ago. As the last recipe in the book of baking by the seasons, this cake is a masterful goodbye-to-summer in a cake that will make you a baking legend for all seasons.

CAKE

2 cups sugar

1 ¼ cups unsalted butter, melted

4 eggs

2 teaspoons pure vanilla extract

2 3/4 cups all-purpose flour

1 1/2 teaspoons baking powder

1 1/2 teaspoons baking soda

½ teaspoon salt

1 cup cocoa, measured then sifted

1 1/2 cups warm coffee

CHOCOLATE BUTTERCREAM

1 cup unsalted butter, softened

2 teaspoons pure vanilla extract

3/4 cup cocoa

4-6 cups confectioners' sugar

1/4 - 1/2 cup whipping cream

SIMPLE SYRUP

1/2 cup sugar

½ cup water

½ teaspoon pure vanilla extract

GANACHE GLAZE

1 cup whipping cream

1 ¼ cup chopped, semi-sweet (preferably Swiss) chocolate

WHIPPED CREAM FILLING

1 ¼ cups whipping cream

1 teaspoon pure vanilla extract

2 tablespoons confectioners' sugar

NUTELLA RASPBERRY

1 cup Nutella or hazelnut spread, softened

1/2 cup raspberry preserves

1 cup fresh raspberries

FINISHING TOUCHES

Red rose

White chocolate, melted

Raspberries

Red sugar

Preheat the oven to 350 F. Line a baking sheet with parchment paper. Generously spray two 9-inch layer pans with non-stick cooking spray and line with parchment paper circles. Place the pans on the baking sheet.

In a mixer bowl, cream the butter and sugar. Add eggs, vanilla and mix until thick. In a separate bowl, stir together flour, baking powder, baking powder, salt and cocoa. Fold dry ingredients into wet and mix, drizzling in the coffee as mixture blends. If using an electric mixer, use slow speed for about 3 minutes, scraping sides and bottom once to incorporate all ingredients evenly. (This is a thin batter). Spoon into the pans. Bake 40-45 minutes, or until cakes spring back when lightly touched with fingertips.

For the Chocolate Buttercream, in a mixer bowl, cream the butter and vanilla with cocoa and one cup of the confectioners' sugar. Add remaining confectioner's sugar and whip on high speed, adding in cream to achieve a light, fluffy consistency. Drizzle in additional warm water to get correct consistency. (Refrigerate if not using immediately; re-whip before using).

For the Simple Syrup, in a small saucepan, bring the water and sugar to a gentle boil and let simmer 5 minutes. Remove from heat and stir in vanilla extract.

For the Whipped Cream Filling, in a mixer bowl, whip the cream with vanilla and confectioners' sugar until soft but firm peaks form.

For the Ganache Glaze, heat cream to just scalding and add in the chocolate. Remove from heat and whisk to blend/melt chocolate to make a thick glaze. Set aside (Refrigerate if not using right away and warm up slightly when needed).

Semi-freeze the cake before decorating for an hour. This makes handling the cake easier. To decorate, slice each cake layer in two layers, using cardboard circles to remove two layers and set aside. Place one layer on a cake stand that turns. Brush it with Simple Syrup and then spread on half the raspberry jam, Nutella, and then the whipped cream. Dot on some raspberries on the whipped cream filling. Top with the second layer of cake, drizzle with syrup then about 1/2 inch of frosting. Repeat filling and layering with remaining two layers. Once cake is assembled, ice cake, frosting the sides first.

Ice cake with a thin layer of chocolate buttercream. Freeze 30 minutes and then pour Ganache Glaze over cake and let it set 10-20 minutes. Then make a border on the bottom and top with more chocolate butter cream. Garnish with touches of melted white chocolate, fresh raspberries, and a dusting of red crystal sugar (like sugar for holiday cookies).

Refrigerate until serving.

Serves 14-20

Teas, Coffees and Potables

Looking for something nice to drink to go with all that baking? You've come to the right place. In this special tea chapter, I've included many of the my best, original recipes I've first created in my own kitchen when I've hosted family, friends and other guests. Many of those recipes have appeared on my website, www.BetterBaking.com. There's over 25 unique tea recipes to suit the time and occasion or your taste. Like the baking recipes, they're all arranged by season.

I also pride myself in being a tea and coffee 'intuitive', that is, I can usually tell at a glance what someone will be partial to – who is a coffee drinker or tea drinker, or both. At any rate, this baking book is also an occasion to offer my best concoctions in teas, as well as a cocoa or two, white sangria and fresh, old-fashioned lemonade to go with summer recipes.

There's also some informative bits in my *Tea and Coffee Notes* and in the *Source Guide*, you'll find some of my favorite tea purveyors including Harney's Tea, David's, Teavana and Upton Tea, among others.

Happy brewing!

Complete Tea, Coffee and Potables Recipe Listing

FALL

Pumpkin Pie Latte

Sticky Toffee Tea

Thanksgiving Cranberry Orange Spice Tea

Hot Mulled Cranberry Apple Cider

Persian Cardamom Tea

Buckwheat Tea with Fresh Mint and Greek Honey

WINTER

Winter Wonderland White Hot Chocolate

Lovers' Spiced Ibarra Hot Chocolate

Yerba Mate

Chocolate Mandarin Tea Holiday

Clementine Tangerine Tea

SPRING

Village Baker Chamomile Apple Tea

White Detox Tea

Cream Earl Grey Tea

Miss Austen's Tea Blend

Strawberry Chamomile Tea

Green Tea with Ginger and Dried Sweet Cherries

Red Robin Rooiboos Tea

SUMMER

Iced Peach Green Tea

Home Blend Chai Tea

Iced Chai Latte

Thai Iced Coffee

Back Porch Lemonade

Sun Tea

Hong Kong Tea with Coffee or Yuangyang

Wedding White Sangria

Pumpkin Pie Latte

What's more inviting that spice and autumnal warmth in a cup? This is a seasonal perk that will make your espresso pot beam. If you have a steamer for the milk, that's super. If not, simmer the milk and half and half to simmering, so that is shivers with foam. For a less rich drink, use all milk, instead of cream. Pumpkin Pie spice is available in the spice section of most supermarkets or make your own which guarantees a pungent, fresh spice mixture to enhance all your baking. I love this brew with a drizzle of caramel on top with fresh whipped cream.

PER SERVING :

2 shots espresso (1/4 cup) or ½ cup strong coffee

1/2 cup half-and-half or light cream, steamed

½ cup milk, steamed or heated to simmering

½ teaspoon pure vanilla extract

¼ teaspoon homemade or bought pumpkin pie spice

In a medium saucepan, heat coffee, half-and-half and milk to almost boiling, and stir in vanilla and pumpkin pie spice. Whisk well and pour into a heated latte cup (ceramic or glass). Double recipe as required.

Serves one

Sticky Toffee Tea

Black tea, touched up with minced Skor or Heath Bars is tea decadence. This is sweet, toffee-ish and a heart-warming brew for a nippy fall day. Perfect with a slice of banana bread.

1 cup leaf tea such as Assam

¾ cup minced Skor Bar or Heath Bar toffee chocolate bars

Toss tea and minced candy together. Use 2 teaspoons or so, per 10 ounces boiling water.

Thanksgiving Cranberry Orange Spice Tea

This is a heavenly tea bouquet in a fine. 'cuppa'. Hint of orange and cranberry in a black tea that is a strong cup, tempered by the elegance of some spice and citrus. Blend it yourself and you have gourmet tea at a fraction of the cost. A great holiday gift (dollar store jars or a Mason jar and a bow would be fine) or hostess present. Ah shucks, just make it for yourself! The spice is very subtle, by the way.

1 cup Orange Pekoe or Ceylon tea leaves

1/4 cup Irish Breakfast tea leaves

3/4 cup English Breakfast tea leaves

Zest of two large oranges, finely minced

1/2 teaspoon, Boyajian orange oil or 1 teaspoon Nielsen Massey orange extract

1/2 cup dried cranberries, very finely minced

1/4 teaspoon cloves, allspice

1/4 teaspoon cinnamon

Toss tea, zest, orange oil and cranberries together in a large bowl.

Store in a tea canister. Makes about two cups

To brew, use 1 1/2 teaspoons per 10-12 ounce cup of tea or 4-6 teaspoons per 6 cup pot of tea.

Hot Mulled Cranberry Apple Cider

This will sure take the chill out of the air and warm up your spirits! This is a wonderful hostess potable to serve throughout the fall into winter. Some things, like the tradition of cranberry and apples in fall, are best left classic, as this recipe is. Part of the fun of cider is sussing out great mugs, at a potter's table at an autumn flea market or strolling a kitchen store for a heat-proof glass mug which really shows off the pretty hue of this lovely drink.

1/4 cup sugar

3 cinnamon sticks, cracked into pieces

1 teaspoon whole cloves

8 cups cranberry juice

6 cups apple juice

Finishing Touches

Orange slices

In a large stock pot, simmer the sugar, cinnamon, cloves, apple and cranberry juice over lowest heat, until sugar dissolves.

Serve warm with orange slices in glass mugs.

Serves 6-8

Persian Cardamom Tea

A friend of mine once introduced me to this delicate and refined tea of Darjeeling or Ceylon tea mixed with crushed cardamom seeds. Find some little glass tea cups (they look like shot glasses) to serve this amazing blend. Serve this with classic shortbread or scones.

6 cups prepared, fresh Darjeeling or Ceylon Tea, hot and steaming

2-3 pods cardamom slightly cracked

Prepare the tea and place the cardamom pods in the teapot. Allow tea to seep a few minutes. Serve with sugar or honey in the most gorgeous, preferably demitasse teacups or glass teacups.

Serves 4

Buckwheat Tea with Mint Leaves and Greek Honey

Buckwheat Tea or Soba Cha (much like the word Chai which also means tea) buckwheat tea is one of those things only a minority of people outside Japan, where it comes from, seem to know much about. If you know kasha, then you are also acquainted with buckwheat grouts.

Although buckwheat is often thought of as a cereal, and the word wheat is in its name, buckwheat is related to sorrel, knotweed and rhubarb.

Roasted, buckwheat it has a wonderful, full-bodied flavor. It's often served as a pulse like chickpeas or as a starch side dish such as quinoa or rice, although it is more protein packed than it is a starch. Many crepe recipes are call for buckwheat flour. You can find buckwheat tea at specialty tea suppliers, or Japanese stores, online or those in your neighbourhood, as well as health food stores (whose buckwheat is more likely to be organic).

This is a soothing, mellow drink, caffeine free (unlike green tea) and offers no limit of healthy benefits from aiding in digestion, lowering blood pressure, managing diabetes, weigh gain or helping with weight loss and is overall, a calming brew.

Because buckwheat tea is earthy and nutty, I 'soothe' it down with either a slice of orange or tangerine or alternatively, with mint and Greek honey. It's sublime.

If you find raw buckwheat, pan roast it (toss it in a non-stick pan over low heat until it roasts and turns a medium brown), otherwise just follow my recipe. The best buckwheat tea I've discovered so far is from www.Harney.com. Once the tea is brewed, you can also 'eat the tea leaves' in this case since it becomes softened buckwheat, offering you a little substance and protein once you've had your tea.

BUCKWHEAT TEA

4 teaspoons roasted buckwheat

12 ounces water

Fresh mint leaves, as required

Greek honey, as desired

Place the buckwheat in a micro-wave proof large mug and pour water over it. Bring to a boil in the microwave (3-4 minutes). Remove and stir and let tea sit a minute. Stir in a little Greek honey and garnish with a few mint leaves. (Double recipe or as required. You can also make a larger amount in a saucepan and then pour it out into a teapot for serving). You can strain out the cooked buckwheat grains and discard it or enjoy it as an after-tea 'chaser'.

Serves one, recipe can be doubled or tripled, as required

Winter Wonderland White Hot Chocolate

This is a gentle, foamy, hot chocolate - subtly flavoured with white chocolate (for a change). You must use imported, high quality white chocolate for this recipe. Anything less will not melt and mix properly. Use a quality semi-sweet dark chocolate such as Lindt or Callebut for traditional, but upscale and satisfyingly deeply-flavored hot cocoa.

4 ounces white chocolate

2 cups very hot milk

2 marshmallows

1/2 teaspoon pure vanilla extract

FINISHING TOUCHES
Chocolate syrup

Melted white chocolate

Cocoa

Place the white chocolate in a large Pyrex measuring cup. Microwave on lowest setting until just melted. Whisk in the milk, marshmallows and vanilla until marshmallows are semi-melted and chocolate is combined with the milk.

Pour into two small mugs. Drizzle on chocolate syrup, white hot chocolate and/or dust with cocoa.

Makes 2 servings

YERBA MATE

I first found out about the herbal tea, Yerba Mate in tango class. Teachers and students from Argentina or those who had been to Argentina seemed to sport special cups, in either hollowed out gourds or more often, stainless steel, that in turn, sported stainless steel straws (called bombillas) one sipped the tea from.

Yerba mate is a species of holly, native to South America. A small shrub, its leaves are like evergreen needles and feature small, greenish-white flowers. Dried, the yerba mate dry leaves and twigs are infused in very hot (versus boiling) water, much like black tea. You can enjoy yerba mate in any sort of cup or mug but traditionally, it is served in a hollowed out gourd and sipped with a metal straw called a bombilla (which allows you to enjoy the tea and not the leaves and twig pieces). The flavor of yerba mate is reminiscent of green tea although toasted yerba mate is a touch less 'green' and more mellow. There are many reputed health benefits to yerba mate and like coffee, it is somewhat of a stimulant, containing similar components as caffeine. Yerba Mate is available in Latin food stores and bombillas and the guampa or yerba mate drinking cups are found in the same stores or online from South American or particularly Argentinean supply retailers.

Lovers Spiced Ibarra Hot Chocolate

Perfect for a chilly night. Inspired by the movie Chocolat. Use 2 % milk with extra calcium if you want to be extra caring. Use a quality semi-sweet chocolate here or velvety Mexican Ibarra chocolate blocks, available at Latin food shops or online at many gourmet food places. Vanilla syrup can be found at places such as Starbucks.

2 cups whole milk

1 ounce semi-sweet chocolate, melted

4 tablespoons unsweetened cocoa powder

2 tablespoons warm water, approximately

1/4 cup sugar

1/4 teaspoon cinnamon

1/2 teaspoon pulverized instant coffee or espresso powder

1/2 teaspoon pure vanilla extract

1 teaspoon cornstarch

2 good pinches ground dried red chilli pepper

FINISHING TOUCHES
Vanilla syrup

Marshmallows

In a 2-quart saucepan, heat the milk over medium or low heat.

Meanwhile, melt the chocolate, and then mix it with the cocoa powder, warm water, sugar, cinnamon, instant coffee, vanilla, and corn starch. Whisk or stir chocolate mixture into warming milk. Stir in chilli peppers. Heat until frothy. Add a marshmallow or two if you want it frothier (it will sweeten the mixture). You may also add 1/2 teaspoon pure vanilla bean paste.

Pour mixture into warmed glass cups or fancy tea cups.

Serves two

Chocolate Mandarin Tea

You won't believe how good a strong black tea is when coupled with chocolate notes and a dash of orange! This is dessert-in-a-cup, an extravagant cup of tea to sit back with. You could vary this by using white chocolate instead of the milk chocolate. This is a great tea to bring in a vintage tea canister or pretty cello bag and a colored tie as a gift or for serving to guests with spice cake, butter cookies, or a delicate pastry.

Zest of small orange, finely minced and left to dry one hour

1/4 cup Assam tea leaves

1 cup Orange Pekoe tea leaves

1/4 cup English Breakfast tea leaves

2 tablespoons finely ground milk chocolate

1/3 cup finely ground semi-sweet chocolate

3/4 teaspoon orange oil or tangerine oil

1 teaspoon pure orange extract

Prepare the orange zest and let dry out on a counter one hour.

In a large bowl, toss the tea leaves, chocolate, orange zest and extracts.

Store in a tea tin.

To brew, use 1 1/2 teaspoon per cup or 3 tablespoons per 5-6 cup teapot

Clementine Tangerine Tea

What's more refreshing than a citrus laced tea with a bit of spice? What could be more festive?

3 cups cold water

1 ½ cup fresh clementine, tangerine or orange juice

1 tablespoon sugar

¼ teaspoon cinnamon

Pinch cloves

Zest of one orange, finely minced

¼ teaspoon pure orange or tangerine oil

2 Assam or other strong tea bags

FINISHING TOUCHES
Honey

Heat water in a medium saucepan to simmering. Add in citrus juice, sugar, spices, zest, and orange or tangerine oil. Add in tea bags and let brew five minutes. Mix, serve hot with a slice of clementine.

Village Baker's Chamomile Apple Tea

I like chamomile tea but it sometimes tastes like someone brewed wildflowers (which is essentially what chamomile is), grass and hay. Depending on your palate and where you purchase your chamomile tea it can taste smooth and gentle or a bit gamey. It varies from brew to brew. But just add cinnamon and apples, you have a soother tea with mellowness, style and autumn flair. Chamomile tea, done my way, is almost celestial.

6 cups brewed chamomile tea, from bags or dried chamomile flowers/tea

½ cup dried apples, diced or chopped

3-4 sticks cinnamon (or ½ teaspoon ground)

1 vanilla bean, diced (or 1 teaspoon pure vanilla extract)

FINISHING TOUCHES
1 large apple, such as Red Delicious, thinly sliced

Honey

Brew the tea and as soon as it is brewing, stir in the dried apples, cinnamon and vanilla. Let stand 5 minutes. Strain into tea cups to serve.

Garnish each with a thin slice of apple.

Serves 4

White Detox Tea

I love the idea of a mellow detox tea – something palate cleaning and mild to go with my meditations and more mindful way of living. It's easy to make something organic, earthy and gourmet at home. It's also a help in weight loss (it seems!). Start with filtered or spring water since it's pure and clean tasting – just what a detox tea brew needs.

2 quarts of filtered spring water

2 cups white tea, brewed

Juice of one small lemon

1 washed (organic lemon)

1 washed (organic) lime

1 washed (organic) small cucumber

1 tablespoon fresh ginger, in thin slices

Fresh mint (15-18 small leaves)

Place the water in a pouring container that will fit the water and add-ins. Add the white tea. Add in the lemon juice and then slice the lemon, lime, cucumber, and ginger. Stir these things into the water. Stir in the mint. Keep chilled.

Serves 8-10

Cream Earl Grey Tea

This is one of my personal favorites. Is this a tea or a potion, a beverage or an oasis? Whatever it is, it is magic. A local coffee and tea bistro serves up "Cream Earl Grey". I had it and it was the type of elegant elixir that makes you float away to an English Country garden reverie. It is Earl Grey, but subtly so and a hint of sweet dairy goodness that comes from a secret ingredient. This tea concoction is heavenly and makes a beautiful gift if you've a mind to share it.

¾ cup Earl Grey tea leaves

¼ cup Orange Pekoe Ceylon tea leaves

1/3 cup finely minced white chocolate or white chocolate chips

1 teaspoon pure vanilla extract

Toss ingredients together and store in a tin or tea canister.

Use 1 ½ teaspoons for a medium brew cup of tea (10 ounces of just barely boiling water); 2 teaspoons for a strong cup.

Miss Austen's Tea Blend

A hearty, spirited tea blend especially created in honor of one of my heroines, Jane Austen. This is a heady mix of English Breakfast, Assam, Orange Pekoe, a touch of Darjeeling to smooth things over and a secret ingredient or two extra to make it more memorable. Isn't this the perfect blend for Elizabeth or "Lizzie' Bennet of Pride and Prejudice? One sip both soothes and inspires and might even manifest Mr. Darcy. This is a perfect tea for spring, especially scones and wonderful with muffin or just the thing to serve with a platter of holiday cookies.

Zest of half a lemon, finely minced, and left to dry one hour

Zest of half an orange, finely minced and left to dry one hour

1/4 Assam tea leaves

1/2 cup Orange Pekoe tea leaves

3/4 cup English Breakfast tea leaves

3 tablespoons Darjeeling tea leaves

1 tablespoon Earl Grey tea leaves

Tiny pinch cinnamon and ginger, optional

Prepare the citrus zest and let dry out on a counter one hour.

In a large bowl, toss the tea leaves, spice and citrus zest. Store in a tea tin.

To brew, use 1 1/2 teaspoon per cup or 3 tablespoons per 5-6 cup pot of tea.

Strawberry Chamomile Tea

A particularly soothing tea with feminine notes which makes it wonderful for the Gaia spirited among us or as a Mother's Day tonic. It is truly ambrosial with hints of berries, honey and orange, teaming up with wild chamomile leaf tea. If you don't have chamomile leaves, use chamomile tea bags instead. I like this served in glass tea cups or fine bone China. I like this tea with strawberry and scones.

3-4 cups brewed chamomile tea

3 large strawberries, mashed fine

2 teaspoons honey

1 teaspoon fresh orange zest

Place the chamomile leaves or tea sachets in a small, pre-warmed tea pot. Place the mashed berries in a strainer over the tea pot. Pour the tea through the strainer, allowing some berry juice to combine with the tea.

Stir in some honey and the orange zest.

Serves 2-3

Green Tea with Ginger and Dried Cherries

Green tea needs but a brief stay-over in simmering water to yield a fine, delicate cup of restorative. The best way to do this is bring water to 160-170 F (gentle boil) and let stand 2-3 minutes to cool to 145-150 F; then use it to brew the green tea. Choose a pretty and delicate teapot for this brew such as a blown glass one. Japanese green tea (which I find milder) takes less time to seep than Chinese green tea. At any rate, almost everything you read on green suggests it's wonderful for body and soul; it's touted in everything from achieving serenity to shedding extra weight. You can omit the ginger if you're not a fan but the cherries offer a sweet fruitiness that is so appealing.

4 cups simmering water (150 F)

4 teaspoons green tea leaves

½ teaspoon finely minced ginger or some fresh ginger shavings

¼ cup finely minced dried cherries

Bring water to correct temperature. Scald a 4 cup teapot with boiling water. Place tea in pot, add ginger and cherries and stir in the prepared water. Let seep 1-3 minutes.

Serves 2-3

Red Robin Rooiboos Tea

First robin in spring? Make a wish. And then go brew a cup of mineral-rich, caffeine-free, anti-oxidant infused, rooiboos tea, also known as Red Tea or Red Bush tea. Rooibos is a plant, native to South Africa, and the tea that is derived from it is a stomach and headache soother. I just find it tastes lovely. It comes in a variety of flavors, depending on your tea supplier and brews into a mellow potion, as good unsweetened or with honey or agave.

¼ cup rooibos or red bush tea

3-4 cups lightly boiled water

Cinnamon, some broken pieces

A few raspberries or strawberries

Simmer the tea with the hot water in a 6 cup teapot. Stir in cinnamon and berries.

Serves 2-3

Iced Peach Green Tea

This smacks of a very gourmet, small brew, gourmet company ice -tea mix, with its magical flavors of summery peach shining through the oh-so-healthy, anti-oxidant green tea. Just make sure you don't brew the green tea too long; you don't want it bitter. Serve this over crushed iced in wine glasses with a sprig of mint of shaving of fresh ginger or go country style, and offer in half-pint Mason (or preserving) jars. Make the tea; cue the hammock.

2 cups brewed green tea *

3-4 cups peach nectar or peach juice

1 large ripe peach, ground up (optional)

* You can use green tea bags for this recipe (1-2 bags per 12-14 ounces water, or 1 teaspoon green tea leaves for 8-10 ounces of steaming kettle water). I don't mind a trace of peach pulp in my Iced Peach Green Tea and so I add one ground up ripe peach. But if you like clear tea, leave it out.

Brew the tea and cool. Mix the tea with the peach juice in a juice container and chill a few hours.

Serves 4-6

Home Blend Chai

This spice tea, renowned from the Indian kitchen, is usually served with hot milk and honey. You can vary the spices and tea but the gist is spice and black tea. Keep this dry mix and brew with boiled water and hot milk, adding in some fresh ginger at time of tea brewing.

3/4 cup Darjeeling tea leaves

¼ cup Orange pekoe tea leaves

30 cardamom pods, or more, as per taste

2 tablespoons black pepper corns

3 cinnamon sticks, broken up

6 star anise pods

3 tablespoons fennel seeds

4 teaspoons cloves

1-2 vanilla beans, cut in pieces, optional

FINISHING TOUCHES

Hot milk

Honey

Fresh minced ginger, optional

In a medium bowl, toss tea leaves with spices. Use 2 teaspoons tea blend per 1 cup boiling water and ½ teaspoon fresh ginger slivers.

Brew tea as required, stir in hot milk, honey and ginger.

Makes 1 cup Chai tea blend

Iced Chai Latte

A chilly approach to spice which makes this the perfect summer refreshment, great with a slice blueberry cobbler or a slice of cinnamon coffee cake, a scone or a summery muffin. Quality chai makes all the difference here and I suggest Harney and Sons or Upton Tea. Some chai blends are too cinnamon; these are perfect for my taste. You can also make your own.

4 cups strongly brewed chai tea bags, chilled

½ cup cold evaporated milk

½ cup cold milk

½ teaspoon cardamom

Pinch each, cloves, cinnamon

14 cup warm honey

Brew the tea in 6-7 cups of boiling water and cool. Stir in the evaporated milk, milk, cardamom and vanilla. Taste, adjust milk or honey. Chill well and serve over crushed ice.

Serves 3-4

Thai Iced Coffee

Add the cardamom and it is Thai iced coffee (versus Chai Tea); leave out the cardamom, and it's Classic Iced Coffee. Either way, this is a pretty cool coffee, brewed to creamy perfection and served with biscotti, transforms your back deck into an outdoor café. Starbucks chez vous? I use a blend of 30% black coffee beans to 70% brown for this potable.

6 cups strongly brewed coffee, cooled

1 cup, or to taste, evaporated milk

½ teaspoon ground cardamom

1 tablespoon pure vanilla extract

FINISHING TOUCHES
Crushed ice

Brew the coffee and cool. Stir in the evaporated milk, cardamom and vanilla.

Chill well.

Serve over crushed ice. (Sugar or honey is optional).

Serves 3-4 servings

Back Porch Lemonade

With this zesty, refreshing real old-fashioned lemonade, you have it made in the shade. You could make this with extra icy spring water but it ventures into "spritzdom" when you add Perrier or another bubbly water.

1 1/2 cups fresh lemon juice

1 cup sugar

1/4 teaspoon (optional) Boyajian Lemon Oil

1/8 teaspoon citric acid, optional

FIXINGS
Ice cubes, lightly crushed

Lemons (washed), sliced thinly

Mint leaves

In a small saucepan, simmer lemon juice and sugar to dissolve sugar. Cool well and stir in lemon oil and citric acid.

Prepare each tumbler with some ice cubes - pour in about 2-4 tablespoons of lemon mixture. Fill tumbler with chilled Perrier or spring water.

Garnish with lemon slices and mint leaves. Don Panama hat.

6-8 servings

Sun Tea

Sun Tea is the old reliable of iced teas. Allow the tea bags to slowly seep in a bottle of water and let the sun do its work. A few hours later, you have a mellow tea that you sweeten with sugar or honey, add a few lemons, pour over ice and you'll all set. All you need is a tall glass and a hammock. This doesn't keep as well as boiling-water brewed tea but it's also always gone in a day or two – such is the nature of a good quencher. I love this tea with a slice of summer fruit pie.

4-6 black tea bags, (such as Orange Pekoe or English Breakfast)

2 quarts spring or filtered water

Place tea bags in a clean 2 quart pitcher. Cover with the water and stir.

Cover the pitcher and place in the sun for a few hours, moving as required, to keep the pitcher in the sun. Remove tea bags and refrigerate. Flavor with sugar and lemon.

Serves 4-6

Hong Kong Tea with Coffee or Yuangyang

Hong Kong Tea with Coffee or Yuangyang is also known as "pantyhose tea" or "silk stocking tea" because it is often brewed in a large tea sock that resembles pantyhose. It is a smooth, comforting concoction that is sweet and somehow manages to marry both coffee and tea into a riveting elixir. It's most often served over ice, like an iced coffee but I prefer it warm. If you prefer, you can make this exclusively with condensed milk (sweeter) or evaporated milk (less sweet) or even regular milk.

3 tablespoons black tea leaves, such as English Breakfast, Ceylon or Orange Pekoe

3 cups water

1 14 ounce can sweetened condensed milk

1 12 ounce can evaporated milk

3 cups strong brewed coffee or espresso

In a 2 quart saucepan, simmer the tea leaves in the water for 3 minutes. Using a tea strainer, strain into a 2 cup measuring cup.

Meanwhile, in the same saucepan, heat the condensed milk and evaporated milk, blending and stirring until simmering and hot. Add tea and coffee to the sauce pan and stir well.

To serve iced, chill mixture first and then pour over ice, in glass coffee mugs. Alternatively, serve when ready, as a warm beverage.

Serves 2-4

Wedding White Sangria

This is an exception to the tea-totaller tea potions in this book for its alcoholic, containing fruit, sparkling water and wine. White Sangria is the right perk for summer weddings. You can vary the fruits but the pretty colours of pale peach and light green offer a summery lightness. If you prefer this non-alcoholic, leave out the spirits and use peach and apple juice instead. Toss in some frozen green grapes before serving; they keep things cooler and offer a sweet bite once they defrost.

1/4 cup peach schnapps

1/4 apple liqueur such as Calvados

1/4 cup white sugar

2 oranges, sliced thin

2 green apples, sliced thin

1 lime, sliced thin

1 pint raspberries

1 bottle medium white wine, chilled

4-5 cups ginger ale, chilled

EXTRAS
Crushed Ice

Chilled Sparkling Water, such as Perrier or Pellegrino

Place all ingredients (except the ice and sparkling water) in a large pitch and stir. Chill. Serve over crushed ice and top off with a bit of sparkling waters. Serve in long-stemmed wine glasses.

Serves 6-8

Tea Notes

Tea - One Leaf, Many Brews, A Temptress in a Teacup

Like coffee, tea is one of the world's oldest, most revered beverages. It's also an umbrella term referring to almost any sort of tea 'leaf' infusion (be it herbs, black tea leaves, floral as dried chamomile leaves) that makes for a soothing, warm drink. Herbal teas themselves can cover a lot of ground, but most people think black tea when they think 'real tea' or 'regular' tea.

Similar to spices, which were also once first medicinal and secondarily used in cooking and baking, tea began its journey as tonics and curatives. Just think how comforting a good cup of tea can be! I'm not surprised how it evolved from medicine to sheer enjoyment. Of tea, Lu T'ung, a T'ang poet wrote, 'The first cup moistens my lips and throat, the second breaks my loneliness'. That is powerful writing and tea, by association, is an equally potent potable.

What's significant about tea is that all black tea and its derivatives (white tea, yellow tea, green tea, oolong and finally, black tea, i.e. fully dried to black) are the same. That is, regardless of the different flavors or blends of brew, growing region, or the way it is handled and cured, fermented or dried, all tea comes from the same biological plant, the tea plant or Camellia Sinensis. This modest little plant is the root, so to speak, behind all tea; the variations come from where and how the tea is cultivated, harvested, and dried and whether the tea in question is the full leaf or unfurled bud, or tips. On tea plants, only the top 1-2 inches of the mature plant are picked. These buds and leaves are called flushes. Black teas can include whole leaf, broken and small leaf, which also accounts for the type of brew you will get. Size and appearance are criteria for tea leaf grading. Whole-leaf teas are called flowery orange pekoe, orange pekoe, or pekoe. Broken leaf tea is graded yet again into a nomenclature of size including broken leaf, then fannings, orange fannings and dust (which alas, is what is recouped into commercial tea bags). India, Ceylon, and China grow a huge portion of the world's finest black teas and Japan has a reputation for green teas of renown

Tea Types

White Tea is unwilted and unoxidized tea.

Yellow Tea is unwilted and unoxidized but allowed to yellow

Green Tea is wilted and unoxidized

Oolong Tea is wilted, bruised, and partially oxidized

Red Tea or Rooiboos is from the Rooiboos plant (and is not really 'tea' per se).

Tencha Tea is a blend of both green and yellow tea leaf bits

Black Tea is wilted, sometimes crushed and fully oxidized and is a dark, almost black color

Herbal tea means an infusion or what we might also call a tisane; this might be of a varied leaves, flowers, fruits and herbs and other botanicals but it does not contain traditional tea, aka camellia sinensis.

White Teas

White tea is the purest and least processed of all teas. This loose leaf tea brews a light color and flavor, and has a light floral note. Said to have a higher percentage of anti-oxidants than Green Tea, White Tea takes well to blending (I add dried peaches and a slice of fresh ginger) and is a slightly easier-digesting tea, some say, than it's counterpoint, Green Tea.

Green Teas

Green tea is the most popular type of tea, mainly because it is the beverage of choice in Asia. Some loose green teas are scented with flowers or mixed with fruits to create scented or flavored teas. There are varying types of Green Tea and one of my favorites is the Japanese one, called Sencha, because I find it milder. Most green teas are said to be good anti-oxidants, good for the digestion and help with weight loss. Green Tea, despite the organic, earthy sound of it, are not caffeine free (unless you purchase decaffeinated green tea).

Oolong Tea

Oolong tea, also known as Wu Long tea, is full-bodied with a flavorful fragrance and sweet aroma. Most people commonly recognize oolong tea as the Chinese tea served in Chinese restaurants. It's mild and uplifting, slightly floral, and a good tea to drink without milk or sugar.

Black Tea

Black tea is the tea most people know since they likely grew up with tea-bagged black tea as the go-to house tea and the one that made both hot tea, and ice-tea with lemon. Black teas vary from the most bland ('tea dust' versus quality tea leaves) and come plain or flavored and are said to have two-thirds as much caffeine as coffee (along with tannic acid, found in tea). Famed black teas (and blends) include English Breakfast, Assam, Irish Breakfast (predominantly made of Assam tea), Darjeeling, Earl Grey and many others, given names by their blenders.

Herbal Tea

Herbal tea does not contain any leaves from the Camellia plant family, so it is sometimes referred to as a tisane. Herbal teas can be broken into three categories: rooibos teas, mate teas, and herbal infusions. Herbal infusions are the most varied and can consist of pure herbs, flowers, and fruits. They can be delicious hot or iced. Chamomile, thought to be a natural soothing or 'sleepytime' tea is the first herbal tea people seem to learn about, followed by Mint and popular Passion Fruit. The selections in herbal teas is endless, the quality can vary, as can the benefits but in general, the better the quality of the tea, the more impactful the said benefits.

Pu'erh Tea

Ou'erh Tea is a variety of fermented dark tea that comes from the Yunnan province, China. This tea is fermented, oxidized and rolled and is a specialty of Chinese teas. There are a few varieties of this fermented tea, the most famous being Pu'erh.

Rooibos Teas

Rooibos tea, or red tea, is made from a South African red bush. Rooibos teas can be delicious hot or iced. This is generally a mild tea and it takes well to many flavorings which explain why you can often find it in many exciting flavors.

Yerba Mate Teas

Mate tea is considered the coffee lover's favorite tea for some reason although I find it quite grassy and woody tasting. I first learned about it via fellow tango dancers, who came from Argentina where it is the national drink – just about. Drunk out of small gourds with special stainless steel straws (a bomba), which allows you to sip the tea without taking in the bits it's brewed from, Mate is an acquired taste but a lovely tea to add to your repertoire. Made from the leaves and twigs of the yerba mate plant, you can find all sorts of Mate teas

in most Latin food markets or via any tea purveyor offering a broad spectrum of teas.

Blooming Teas

Also called artisan or flowering teas, these teas actually bloom or disproportionately expand (many times their size)' as they steep. They are beautifully hand-twined by tea crafters or tea artists, include a flavor, flower or scent of note and feature a beautiful name (Lucky, Romance) to go along with their aesthetic presentation. These are romantic teas, perfect for Valentine's Day or when you want to impress. Just pop a blooming tea in a glass teapot and you have instant tea drama.

Tea Blends

Tea blends often have the best of both worlds since they combine more than one type of tea including mixtures of black tea with herbals, herbals and other botanicals, nuts, and dried fruit – you name it. You can purchase tea blends of course or start making your own. Just find a great tea purveyor (check the Source Guide) you prefer or stroll around your own town to find ethnic stores and try their teas. Alternatively, go on an online tea adventure or next time you travel, vacation or business, suss out some new teas to bring home.

Each type of tea has its own characteristics including a different taste and differing health benefits. One of the best ways to find out which teas you prefer is to taste many! Read, taste, explore teas in your neighbourhood, online, on vacation and be open to new things. Like coffee, tea is one amazing adventure that awaits. My only suggestion is that you choose leaf tea versus tea that comes pre-packaged in tea bags. Of course, many times, you'll find great signature brands of black tea or tisanes in pretty boxes with their requisite paper-wrapped sachets or tea bags. But leaf tea you can buy small amounts of, mix and match and then only invest when you find something that truly delights you. Last but not least, brew tea and coffee with pure spring water for the best taste.

Breakfast Tea, Civility in a Teapot

What tea traders might have referred to as Breakfast Blend tea was, at the onset, simply a tea mix created as the signature blend of early tea companies, i.e. their basic, blue-ribbon tea selection. The tea was blended to be consistent, i.e. a uniform bouquet of fragrance, flavor and brewing attributes. Like flour blending, which wheat and flour mills know well, blending a new year's harvest of tea to ensure reliable blends is a form of expertise and artistry. Weather affects tea as it does wheat crops. At one point, tea providers and blenders would even consider a town or city's water supply and then create the blend that best suited the brewing strengths of that particular water supply. And now? We dunk a tea bag in steaming water from an electric tap and say – tea is served.

Great Breakfast Blend tea is a hearty, well-planned blend of Indian black teas. Different companies do different blends (heavier on the orange Pekoe or Ceylon, a touch of Assam or even a dash of a smokier tea for bite and dimension) but it is a brisk breakfast tea, regardless of tea company or what they might name their breakfast blend. It is generally full-bodied, rich, and indeed, as the name implies, wakes you up. I also like it mid-afternoon if I am not drinking coffee for some reason and need a tea tonic. Breakfast blend can be drunk fresh, black, steaming hot with but a slice of lemon, but it is also strong enough to countenance milk and sugar.

Breakfast Blend teas can be brewed by the cup and are equally suited to a stalwart Brown Betty Teapot or any sort of ceramic, any color, and also do nicely in your best bone China. Vintage Royal Albert is a great match for this historical blend but then, so is a Japanese cast iron teapot or tetsubin, or a hand thrown potter's mug from New England.

Coffee Notes

You Don't Know Beans - A Walk in the Coffee Fields

Coffee - the quintessential wake-up call, the friendship break of coffee klatch, the soothing after dinner capper to a fine dinner or a homey supper. Whatever it is: coffee is always there, like a reliable and caring friend. Coffee comes pure and simple, pure and rich as in espresso, complicated with hot or steam milk, smoothed with cream or fortified with spirits and flames, as in the case of Irish Coffee and other fine holiday or gourmet concoctions. How many people drink coffee and how many are tea drinkers, and how many people are both? It's hard to say and certainly history and culture has a lot to do with it. But it's likely Americans became more partial to coffee as the aftermath to the Boston Tea Party.

Way before the fall-out in the Boston, it all started in warmer climes. Coffee comes from the coffee fields found on slopes and hilly mountainous regions, largely in South American, such as Brazil, Columbia, Costa Rica, Hawaii, Africa, Mexico, Jamaica and Indonesia, just to name some of the major coffee regions, of the best coffee. The beans, called cherries, for they look like small ripe berries and are either Robusta or Arabica (which are preferred). Once dried and curried the pulpy berry part gives way to the inner bean, which is, before roasting, a dull green. There are three major roast stages: light, medium, and dark beans and the tastes depend accordingly.

What's remarkable about coffee is like tea, depending on where it's grown, harvested and cured, the taste of your brew is vastly different. Blending various beans (versus a straight brew of just Columbian, or Kona) is one more art that adds dimension to a beverage that says hospitality with a capital H. You can blend all sorts of beans, like creating a perfume, in layers of flavor of velvety darkness or smooth brown velvet. When shopping for coffee in a coffee bistro, you can choose a few beans, black, brown and combine or rely on the establishment (or a line of fine coffee, see the Source Guide for some suggestions) for their legendary or signature blends. Each coffee house has a few standard blends but done as per their specs, as well as some particularly unique ones. There are also coffee blends referred to, as teas are, from 'single estate' that refers to blending of beans but the beans all come from one coffee growing estate. Most importantly, do choose beans that are from Fair Trade coffee farms. There are many great choices and it makes investing in coffee about taste and ethnics in one gulp.

Coffee Grinding

You can grind your coffee at home, for the freshest brew or at your favorite coffee store, in grinds that suit your coffee maker. Grinds can be as fine as flour (as per a filter maker or for Turkish or Greek Coffee) or more coarse for a Neapolitan flip pot, a Bodum, drip or percolator. If you do invest in a grinder, do consider a burr grinder wherein the coffee is ground between burrs, versus a blade grinder that merely hacks the coffee into fine bits. The flavor of burr-ground coffee is far superior.

Coffee Brewers

The choices in coffee brewers is yet another multi-dimensional world of coffee. You can boil ground beans in a pot over a wood fire as cowboys did, using egg whites to 'clean' the muddy (but good) coffee that results. But more likely, you will choose paper filters and plastic cones (as per the Melitta method), Bodum plungers, top of the range percolators, or state-of-art drip makers or toney, imported espresso cappuccino makers that not only prepare the coffee but store and grind beans. There are also classic vacuum coffee makers that look like science experiments. The bottom line in coffee brewers is generally about taste, speed of preparation and no coffee drinker I know of, is indifferent about their coffee brewer choice.

Baking Techniques

Bonus for Bakers

Baking Techniques

There's much lyricism about the seasons; merely writing about it is an artistic adventure. But one's baking foundation must built on sound recipes that are rich in taste and eye appeal, somewhat easy to do, and accessible, bound by solid baking techniques. We can wax poetic about sugar and spice, but the proving ground is in the kitchen, via the mixing bowl, the oven, and finally, drawing raves from appreciative eaters.

When I was in hotel school training as a pastry chef, one thing my teachers stressed was to think of the final person in the journey of that recipe, i.e. who will taste and enjoy what you've created? What experience do you want for them and how best to deliver it? This consideration is powerful and can also help to keep you inventive and mindful throughout the baking process. It's not "just dessert." Whether you're baking bread, a scone, or a cheesecake, it's all about that famed bliss factor – capturing someone's senses and spirits as they take a bite of something you've bake and suddenly enter the realm of magic. With care, as well as the incomparable trio of quality ingredients, tools, and equipment, you can create this magic.

Baking: Science or Magic?

How often do we hear things like: Baking is scientific! Baking is mysterious! These typical cautions can scare you off or convince you that great baking takes more time and expertise than you have. It's nonsense. Baking does respect science and chemistry, but it also gives back to you if you follow the recipe and appreciate that at its core, baking is simple. Great, high-performance recipes, wonderful flavors, prime ingredients, caring procedures and handling, a well-calibrated oven, proper tools and equipment – and an appetite for adventure - these are all you need to bake well. Of course, whether you're a new baker, a sometime baker, or competent pro, you also need the confidence that you will succeed. Baking is special, but it isn't sacred

If I could give one piece of advice, it's to have a sense of trust – trust in my recipes and trust in your efforts, your ingredients, your tools and your own hands. Expect *wonderful*. Proceed with respect and optimism – not fear or an insistence on perfection. Expect to get better with each effort. No one wins a race the first time they take the track. But somehow when we bake something, especially a new thing, and the results are less than perfect, we flee, assuming that either we or the recipe have failed. I implore you to have patience and treat yourself kindly. I assure you that however humble your first efforts, you'll eventually create some remarkably delicious things and/or hone what you already know. Baking, especially for family and friends, should be fun and relaxing. This said, I have some techniques and insights on ingredients that I think are important.

Ingredients, Tools, Techniques, and Terms

I think a few elements of baking of are of prime importance, and the first is flavor, whether in baking or cooking. While we might spend a lot of time looking for the best produce for a wonderful salad, when it comes to baking, I think we tend to assume the cinnamon is fresh or the vanilla is rich (even if it says "pure," that doesn't always mean it is rich and soulful in vanilla notes) and that a teaspoon of lemon zest is all that's needed. Flavor, fused to fragrance, is the anchor of food, with texture tied for second. Each additional flavor element takes you one more nuanced step toward incredible baking. That's why at times, my recipes have more than one extract in them or just a few drops of lemon and orange, with a touch more vanilla. It's why I use lemon juice as well as lemon zest, lemon oil, lemon extract, and extra sour citric acid in a dynamic, full-dimensional lemon recipe. I don't just want lemon on your tongue – that quickly fades until you have another bite of lemon loaf; I want it to be a many-splendored, layered experience. There exists so many ways to say "lemon" or "chocolate" or "vanilla," among other flavors – why not use all the ways at hand? Why stop at 1 tablespoon of fresh lemon juice when we can create a finely tuned piece of lemon art – an extravagance of flavor that is instantly memorable, even if you ate only one bite? Baking should positively sing and seduce, and flavor (as well as scent and texture) does that. That said, I am the first one to admire some things that are pure and simple, that rely on only the taste of butter, sugar, and flour. This trio is symphony enough.

Ingredients

You want to make your baking great from its very genesis, and that means respecting the ingredients and the planet itself before you spend a minute in the kitchen. If there is a fair trade, environmentally conscious, organic, in season, and/or local option for a particular ingredient, it pays to choose it. The results are wonderful tasting, healthful products for your efforts. As a baker, you're an integral part of a chain of choices and you have the autonomy to make great ones. It's not just about quality; it's about endorsement, in the broadest sense, through your purchase choices. Moreover, while you can get just about any fruit, any time, from somewhere and have it available in your supermarket. But flavor for flavor (and penny for penny), *nothing tastes better than fresh fruit, in season, near you.* There are exceptions, of course, as in the case of apples, when there are so many new and exceptional ones flooding the market and changing our apple palate. But overall, fresh, local and in season is the way to go.

Organically Speaking

One last note along the lines of: if you really want my opinion, buy organic as often as you can (or can afford). It doesn't matter in some things (bananas) as much as others (strawberries) but nothing beats the well-being you feel in not only creating wonderful homemade everything but using products that are as natural, and pesticide free as well. And then of course – choose Fair Trade or support your local farmers or co-op or plant your own.

To add another great dimension to your baking life, visit interesting, unique or new food stores. Whether you're in the middle of your own bustling city or snoozy suburbs or a rural area, you'll probably be able to find incredible food markets or ethnic shops that have ingredients to inspire you. New stores or approaches (even different packaging) spices your inner spirit before you even get into the kitchen. That said, nothing beats your local supermarket, open 24/7, if you need a block of butter and bag of unbleached all-purpose flour.

What do you need in order to bake? Baking is quite democratic; it calls for pantry basics: flour, sugar, butter, eggs, vanilla - simple things, mindfully chosen, with quality as the standard, careful handling as part of the process--that's the core. But there are things to be aware of, even in simple elements.

Wheat, All-Purpose Flour

Almost all recipes in this book use my go-to, unbleached all-purpose flour. For some of the yeasted recipes in this book, I recommend unbleached bread flour. Unbleached means the flour has been naturally aged whereas bleached all-purpose flour is prematurely aged with the use of bleaching agents. All-purpose flour is a blended and consistent flour of hard and soft wheat. It's created especially for home use (in professional kitchens, they

actually choose hard, soft, or blend the flours themselves). All-purpose flour is ideal for the recipes in this book that are essentially muffins, scones, cakes, or bars. I would choose one or two flours that you can stock easily and know to rely on. Even though most all-purpose flour, regardless of brand, is about 11.5 percent protein, if you're observant you'll notice slight performance differences. So get to know your floury friends and don't fluctuate brands too much, so as to have consistency in your baking.

In my home baking recipes, I rely on measuring versus weighing. To measure as I do, stir the flour a bit in its canister to loosen it. Then swoop in with a metal cup measure and scoop out a cup, using a knife to scrape flush across the top of the top and let the excess fall back into the canister. In industrial, high-volume baking, weighing is relied on for absolute accuracy, but at home, my recipes for me and my testers thrive on careful measuring.

Sugar

Granulated white sugar is the prime sweetener in this book. One thing about sugar, for all its detractors, is that it outperforms any substitute in all ways possible. Over the years, I've been open-minded as a professional, and tried substitutes of all sorts. Each promised to be healthier or better than sugar, had little or no calories, and hyped health benefits. Most, if not all, performed poorly in traditional baking, and many were not even truly better for you. That said, if granulated sugar intake is an issue for you or someone you bake for, some of these substitutes may be used. In that case, I would suggest books that specialize in recipes made with the substitutes. And as for sugar, yes, you can use a wee bit less at times, but it will affect the grain and taste of your baked goods. Some of my recipes are more "grainy" than other, more decadent recipes, but all my recipes are nutritious in their way. And some joyous, wonderful baked goods are special, once-a-year treats anyway and will hardly set your diet off its track permanently.

Baking is about enjoying sweet things in balance to all else in your day and diet. For myself, I am in a long-term relationship with one of the core ingredients that makes baking the thing we love so well. In baking, nothing shines through like pure cane or beet sugar. It not only sweetens, it helps with aeration (the crystals of sugar fluff up and aerate the butter), conservation, tenderness of grain, and browning, and of course it also supports the other flavors in the recipe.

Brown Sugar

Where my recipes call for brown sugar, by default it refers to light or golden brown sugar. If a recipe requires dark brown sugar for a recipe, it will be indicated. Brown sugar is granulated white sugar with traces of molasses on it. People think of brown sugar as perhaps healthier or more rustic, but really it just offers a distinctive caramel flavor hint in baking, especially in spice cakes or mixed in with apples. Measure brown sugar and pat it down firmly to ensure you have the right measurement.

Confectioners' Sugar

Confectioner's sugar, (known as icing sugar in Canada), is a pulverized sugar/cornstarch blend, used in icings, frostings, and for dusting cakes and pastries. It's also used for decorative dusting of cakes.

Honey

Honey – what a perfect name for an ingredient that is so natural and so naturally high-performing. And no wonder bakers love it. The words honey-dipped, honey-laced, and honey-sweetened never fail to conjure up goodness.

An ancient food treasure, honey comes from bees who manufacture it from the nectar (another gorgeous term) from flowers. Depending on what nectar the bees tote back to the hives, the honey varies in taste from mellow orange blossom or clover to heartier buckwheat honey, which is just the thing for a spice or honey cake (whereas milder honey suits a baklava, allowing the buttery pastry nut confection to shine). The dimension of a flavor in a particular honey depends on whether the hives are kept in one place or rotated from field to field so that the bees have access to different kinds of nectar. However, if you buy supermarket honey, chances are that it's pasteurized and blended in service to having a standard taste and color. Uniformity of ingredient, especially a sweetener, is generally a sought-after attribute, but the true delight of honey is in its diverse flavor. True honey aficionados become as adept at identifying honey as wine tasters can tell you vineyard, year, and decant. An especially flavorful wild honey anointing a cream scone is heavenly - and that's really where honey, served unadulterated and pure, commands center stage.

Just know that things baked with honey do tend to brown faster, so watch the cake or loaf as it bakes and do use doubled-up baking sheets, with the top one lined with parchment. Although honey is said to be sweeter than sugar, I've never really found that to be true. But honey is a liquid sweetener, so an exact ratio for substituting honey for granulated sugar is not possible. It's best to use recipes that are already calibrated with honey as the sweetener or part sweetener.

Like sugar, honey is not a storehouse of nutrients, but it does contain trace minerals, enzymes, and vitamins. Also, being liquid, honey is hydroscopic (water retaining), and thus recipes made with some honey tend to turn stale more slowly.

To measure honey, first spray the measuring cup with non-stick cooking spray. Once honey is measured, it will pour out more easily out of the greased measuring cup.

Maple Syrup

Maple syrup is a native American/Canadian sweetener, made from reducing the sap of sugar maple trees to a thick amber syrup. You can get varying qualities of maple syrup, but as long as it is *pure,* it is ideal for all the maple-using recipes in this book. Nothing beats pure maple syrup for flavor. Ironically maple is

harvested and produced in spring, but we tend to use it more in fall and winter baking, when its luxurious, lusty taste warms each and every recipe we put it to. You will find most maple recipes in this book in the spring chapter, but I would highly recommend you make maple recipes in fall and winter as well. Its heartwarming sweetness is always welcome.

Salt

Salt may seem strange to add to some baking recipes; why add salt to sweet things? Because salt balances the flavors and sweetness. I use sea salt or fine kosher salt for best flavor in the final recipe results. Fleur de sel is a popular salt these days; it has a delicate flavor and is lovely when put into recipes that have bittersweet chocolate or a lot of butter (such as shortbread). It is however, pricey and somewhat larger flake (versus fine salt). Use fleur de sel here and there but overall, the salt in this book is a fine baking salt, easily found in kosher sections or supermarkets. Sea salt is often from Greece and it is as good as a table salt as it is in the baking.

Butter

Unless otherwise indicated, unsalted or sweet butter is the butter for my recipes. Like sugar, nothing embraces flavor and holds it like butter. With its fat content, dairy component, and natural good taste, it is the consistent choice for home baking (versus shortening or neutral oils more often found in retail or commercial baking). Most butters in North America are equivalent in taste and nutrition.

If you can get hold of organic butter or a European (especially Irish) unsalted butter, it's interesting and rewarding to bake with.

Butter also freezes for months and months, so when you see a sale, stock up.

Margarine, usually salted, often whipped with air, water, and added chemicals, is not a recommended butter substitute in baking.

I measure butter in cups for my recipes (versus by sticks or weight).

2 cups = 1 pound butter = 4 sticks

1 cup = 1/2 pound butter = 2 sticks

½ cup = 1/4 pound butter = 1 stick

¼ cup = 1/8 pound butter = 1/2 stick

Oil

I use oil in some recipes and when I do, it's canola, corn, vegetable or another neutral oil such as safflower. Unsalted melted butter can be substituted with oil if you like, but you will lose some flavor in the recipe as well as some nice attributes of browning that butter contributes. Baking recipes that call for oil, such as a great bran muffin, however, are still highly flavorful and conserve a bit longer. And if a dairy fat, such as butter, is off your list, many of my recipes do very well with vegetable oil instead.

Eggs

Eggs, like flour, are part of the basic structure of a recipe, as well as offering tons of flavor, iron, and protein. Use grade A large eggs (not extra large or small or medium; my recipes are formulated to use standard large eggs). Brown eggs are visually nice to look at but within a recipe, they do not perform different from white eggs. Eggs keep well, a few weeks, refrigerated.

Dairy Ingredients: Milk, Buttermilk, Cream, Sour Cream

Dairy is a flavorful, healthy addition to any sort of baking, and it also assists with browning. You have choices too, from whole or 2% milk, to sour cream (light or regular), yogurt and buttermilk, and various creams (whipping or light cream). Each recipe specifies which dairy ingredient is the optimal choice.

Acidic dairy ingredients such as buttermilk also create some additional leavening when used with baking powder. Many baking books suggest you can taste the nice "tang" of buttermilk muffins or a sour cream pound cake, but personally I can't tell the difference. What I do notice is the great rise, tender crumb, and overall great flavor, plus I love the extra calcium in my diet.

I often use buttermilk powder, commercially available by Saco Foods, an especially helpful pantry ingredient to use in homemade pancake mixes and holiday muffin mixes. You can also replicate buttermilk by adding 1 or 2 tablespoons lemon juice to a cup of milk to sour it. But don't confuse sour milk with spoiled milk, past its due date, which should of course be discarded.

Yeast

There are really only two types of dry yeast: active dry and instant or rapid rise. A living organism, yeast is grown, harvested, and dried. Once solid, dry yeast is pressed through cast dies into fine shreds or granules. Active dry yeast is more granular. Instant and rapid rise yeast are different strains of yeast, with instant yeast having a finer shred (and a faster action).

Bread machine yeast is another label for instant yeast, so if you have that on hand, do use it for my yeasted recipes.

Yeast comes in jars, vacuum bricks, or packets. I prefer jars or bricks –yeast stores in the fridge a good few months and it is easier to measure yeast in spoons than rely on packets.

I create all my recipes with instant yeast. Brands I use include Fermipan, Red Star, Fleischmann's, and SAF. But my recipes will also work with your favorite active dry yeast if that is the yeast you prefer. My method of handling yeast is the same for both types of yeast (I whisk yeast with water always), but remember that the most important clue when working with yeast is the actual rise of the yeasted product (bread, coffee cake, or what have you). Differences in your kitchen conditions can cause variations in timing, so watch what's actually happening rather than eyeing the clock.

If you're adventurous and can find it, fresh yeast is another choice and one I use for my family when baking bread. It's less easy to find and doesn't really store that well (a week in the fridge, more time if frozen), and you cannot see it working (it doesn't foam as dry yeast might, showing it is alive and well). But fresh yeast does offer a fragrant and old-time yeasty scent and a gentler rise, and it can make you feel pretty empowered since it is far more old-school. Even big bakeries use it less these days. But as life is short and it's out there to try, I would suggest giving it a whirl, especially in bread baking. How bread dough seems to know it's being made with fresh yeast versus dry, I don't know, but it seems to be bouncier and more responsive to work with. That said, dry yeast is more reliable in sweet yeast baking (the yeast is heartier and suffers less yeast cell lost in the face of rich ingredients such as added butter and sugar), but fresh yeast for a fresh country bread is hard to beat.

Baking Powder

A wunderkind baking leavener, baking powder was invented around 1850. It is a mixture of baking soda and an acidic powder (various companies choose different acidic components). When moistened and then heated, baking powder creates carbon dioxide, which acts as a leavener. Baking powder is termed continuous action or double action, but it just means that there's one action when baking powder comes into contact with liquid in the recipe and another action when heat is applied. Commercial baking powders (once called yeast powders, incidentally) are generally all reliable, although I've found that Clabber Girl gives my baked goods a touch of added lift. Davis, Magic (in Canada), and aluminum-free baking powder such as Rumford are others I rely on.

What is most important about baking powder is that unlike baking soda, it does have a past-due date, so pay attention to the expiration date on its packaging. Old baking powder will absolutely ruin your quick bread or cake. So buy a small jar or tin, use it up, and then indulge yourself with a new, fresh can of baking powder potential.

Remember, the basic rule of thumb with baking powder is to use 1 teaspoon baking powder per cup of flour called for in the recipe.

Baking Soda

This is simply bicarbonate of soda, an alkaline, white powder that when mixed with acid ingredients in a recipe (buttermilk, brown sugar, natural cocoa) will create carbon dioxide, which helps a batter to rise.

The basic rule of thumb with baking soda is to use ½ teaspoon baking soda per cup of flour called for in the recipe, given the presence of acidic ingredients. If you see a lot of soda called for in any recipe, check the overall recipe construction (in this or any baking book!). Too much baking powder can cause exploding cupcakes, but too much soda just tastes terrible.

Pure Vanilla Extract

Foodies are fond of reporting vanilla as one of the most expensive ingredients from the high-end trio of vanilla, cardamom, and saffron. True, premier quality vanilla is not inexpensive,

but neither is it so unattainable that artificial vanilla is a reasonable option. Like true love, nothing tastes, smells, nor freezes like the real thing: pure vanilla. Artificial vanilla contains one compound from pure vanilla extract—vanillin—while pure vanilla has some 170 different components. Real vanilla comes from beautiful orchid vines that house the vanilla pods. Artificial vanilla is generally a byproduct from the pulp and paper industry and has a very heavy, sweet taste. Like pure cane sugar, pure butter, and simple wheat flour, vanilla must be pure. Buying the rest of your ingredients in pure and natural form and then anchoring them with artificial vanilla is like taking fine oak furniture and gluing it together with plastic. Choosing pure vanilla will elevate your other ingredients and make your baking worthwhile.

I often use Nielsen Massey Madagascar vanilla, and sometimes their Mexican and/or Tahitian, and sometimes combine them to take advantage of their unique nuances. If you have access to quality vanilla varieties, try blending them--a little Madagascar for pure, subtle vanilla taste along with Mexican or Tahitian for more warmth and sweetness. Such a combination would be ideal for biscotti or cookies. There is also McCormick (Club House in Canada) and other brands, both national and/or specialty items. I've also become acquainted with fine vanillas from the Hawaiian Vanilla Company and Cook's Vanilla.

When choosing vanilla extract, check the ingredients list to make sure it contains only vanilla, alcohol and sugar. And whatever vanilla you choose, be sure to taste, taste, and taste again to see if it has the flavor you should expect from a great vanilla.

Other Extracts and Pure Flavor Oils

With other extracts and flavor oils, it's just as important to choose the "pure" version, and remember to smell and taste your purchases before using them in your baking. Oils are more intensely flavorful than extracts, and extracts help to augment the overall flavor profile. In my recipes, I often use them in combination to create a many-tiered bouquet of flavor. Boyajian is a reliable purveyor of fine orange, lemon, and lime oils. There are more sources for extracts than oils, and and you'll be able to determine your own preferences from among them. Whatever you choose, baking with flavor oils and extracts allows you to add to the portrait of your baking, just as you'd paint with a wide palette of colors.

Chocolate

I group people into categories: fruit people, vanilla sorts, and the "anything chocolate" bunch. For them, and for me, there's nothing like the real deal of great chocolate, whether it's unsweetened, semisweet or bittersweet, milk chocolate or great white chocolate (which is essentially cocoa butter, sugar, and milk but still referred to as chocolate). Imported brands can be exceptional (I am thinking of Callebaut and Lindt in particular), but there are many wonderful brands in North America, such as Scharffen Berger. In chocolate, as well as cocoa, there are so many great choices to choose from and bake with. It is, as in all other ingredients, all about taste, but when baking with chocolate, pay special attention to your final results, from the grain and flavor of a cake to how the chocolate melts in a glaze or ganache. Learn what you like and can rely on. You might prefer one variety of semi-sweet for your brownies and another for lofty cakes, but that's part of the fun of baking and the excitement of working with this special ingredient. A bite of chocolate, like a sip of coffee, is a distillation of time, expertise, and cuisine immortal.

Spices

Long before spices were used to flavor and enhance food, they were used in medicines and cures, as well as spiritual traditions. Spices so enhanced the taste of food it was inevitable they would make the short leap from the domain of the shaman, alchemist, and pharmacist into the kitchen. Centuries before we had shaker jars and canisters, let alone mass-produced, prepacked spices in jars savvy bakers relied on their spice boxes. Indian, Asian, Middle Eastern kitchens all had various versions of spices boxes, with their particular assortment of favored spices. Colonialists traveled from Europe with hopes, dreams, and a precious personal cargo of spice boxes.

Today, with spices so easily available (no need to sit in the galley of a wooden ship and travel perilous seas or cross deserts on a camel), we don't always give them a second thought – shaking out cinnamon as indifferently as we pass a salt shaker. It's just so easy to pop a few canisters of cinnamon from the warehouse store in our baskets or visit a quality bulk food stores compared to buying smaller amounts of probably fresher spices from superb sources. If one prioritizes the role of spices in baking, (and who doesn't?) we seek out the best, freshest spices from the finest purveyors. Spices are aromatherapy of the first order, for one whiff of fresh allspice or nutmeg is totally uplifting. Choose great spices and your baking will thank you.

Nuts

Like spices, find the best and freshest. Taste them before buying (if the nuts are sold in bulk) or order them from a supplier you know and trust. There are definite harvest seasons for nuts, and it pays to find a great nut grower and packer for the absolute best and freshest nuts – no matter what sort.

Toasting Nuts for Extra Flavor

Gently toasting nuts in the oven also helps bring out their flavor (unless the recipe says not to). To toast them, double stack two baking sheets and line the top one with parchment paper. Spread the nuts on the sheet--don't crowd them--and gently toast at 300°F until they're just starting to turn golden and emit a gently nutty, buttery aroma. Take them out and cool before using in your baking.

Citrus Zest and Making Zest Sing

Orange, among other citrus zests, offers much added flavour to baking. A baker's tip to up the citrus boost is to mix the sugar called for in a recipe with the zest before adding the butter. Ordinarily recipes add the zest with the dry ingredients but adding it with the sugar makes more sense. The sugar crystals 'sand' away at the zest, helping those wonderful, fragrant citrus oils release that much more fully and into the baking (cake or cookie) at hand.

Fresh or Frozen Fruit

Fruit should be optimally fresh. Fruit that is too ripe fruit isn't for use in baking (unless you're talking about bananas, which should be very soft), because as with making preserves, in baking you can't get a better product than the ingredients you start with. When you bake in season, you'll have access to the best and freshest plums, pears, apples, and berries to work with. But as the months go by, frozen fruit (especially rhubarb and berries) can do the trick. It's a matter of remembering to stock up before you lose the opportunity.

Dried Fruit

Whatever the quality of your dried fruit, for the most part, it profits from plumping in boiling water for several minutes. In all my recipes, the term plumped and dried means to cover the fruit with very hot water for a few minutes, then drain, dry with paper towels, and use. This small but important step ensures that you won't have dried or otherwise wizened raisins haunting an otherwise moist, luscious cake or muffin.

While I didn't include recipes that call for dried star fruit, kiwi, or black raspberries, they (as well as many other varieties) exist and are quite fun to add to muffins or scones. Your mom and grandmother had dates, raisins, and dried apricots to choose from, but now the sky, when it comes to dried fruit, is the limit.

Tools

Baking Pan Musts

This is my baker's go-to baking pan list. I prefer basics in pans, mostly because inasmuch as I like novelty pans (and more so for seasonal baking when different shapes or themes making recipes shine), I tend to rely on classics in bakeware. But don't discount specialty baking pans, especially heart-shaped pans for Valentine's Day or pretty Bundts.

I advocate doubling up on your basic pans, especially if you do a lot of holiday baking. If you give away your holiday baking, often still warm, in the pan, you'll definitely need an extra loaf or layer cake pan while you wait for the other one to be returned.

I generally opt serviceable metal, such as plain old aluminum, bakeware. I don't care for non-stick (the dark surface tends to over-brown things) unless it's a Bundt pan, in which case, you cannot ever have enough release. Aluminum bakeware is fine, especially if you use parchment paper to line it with. That's something I often do, especially with tube or angel food cake pans. (Cakes just slip out when the pan is pre-lined).

Baker's Pan List

4 large cookie sheets (15 x 21 inch or 10 x 18 inch

Basic cookie sheets are indispensible for breads, cookies, squares, rolls—almost anything you can think of—and they're perfect to set another pan on for a double layer. I recommend buying sheets with rims, and do make sure the pans will fit your oven leaving room for air to circulate before you invest in them.

4 jelly roll sheet pans (15 x 11 inch) with rims

1 rectangular pan (9 x 13 inch)

This is your pan for coffee cakes and other casual cakes, and for brownies and squares.

1 square pan (9" x 9")

Another pan for coffee cakes, crumbles, squares, and casual cakes.

2 pie pans (9 or 10 inch)

For pies and tarts and even brownies or a corn bread. Aluminum is ideal in pie pans, but so is ceramic, blue steel, or enamel on steel (called graniteware). Pie pans can be decorative and part of the seasonal flair overall. Inexpensive, serviceable and fun, why not collect a few and choose whatever suits the season? Flea markets and yard sales are as usual, a great place to pick up some special pie pans.

2 springform pans (9 inch round or 10 inch round)

1 deep quiche pan (9 or 10 inch round) with removable bottom

I use springform and quiche pans for tons of recipes. The removable bottom solves a lot of problems, and although springform pans are obviously great for cheesecakes, they're another way to bake a rectangular cake (instead of a 9 by 13 inch pan) and do double-duty for yeasted sweet cakes. More than any other piece of bakeware, you need extra springform pans. Since cheesecakes are often the cakes you bring to parties and gatherings, the bottoms often 'get lost'. Sooner or later, you'll have rings without bottoms. So whenever you see a good deal on a solid springform pan, buy an extra one.

Note on Cheesecake Pans

High Cheesecakes and Low Cheesecake Pans Tricks

I love high-standing, dramatic cheesecakes. Once you are investing in all that cream cheese glory and no doubt, your cheesecake is destined for a special occasion, perhaps you, as I do, would choose tall too. So how to achieve height and not have any spill-overs? I just make a 'cake collar' – something I learned ages ago in hotel school as a pastry chef. Simply cut out portions of parchment paper and put them inside the cake pan, on the upper inside edge, using non-stick cooking spray or even some of the batter as 'glue' to make the paper stick. This collar effectively extends the height of the pan, offers support for the batter, and also prevents spill-overs while helping you get a nice tall cheesecake. It's like a 'girdle'

for cheesecake but cake collar sounds so much nicer. One last thing about cheesecake or spring-form pans, if you have any doubt their seals are snug, wrap the outer pan with aluminum foil paper to prevent any surprises and don't forget, like all my recipes, place the pan on a parchment paper lined baking sheet (unless it is a cheesecake recipe that calls for a water bath method).

2 loaf pans (9" x 5")

2 loaf pans (8" x 4")

These loaf pans take care of your needs for quick breads, sweet loaves, and small yeasted breads. Heavy-duty pans are best, but treated well, even light, aluminum loaf pans are fine.

1 tube pan (9 or 10 inch)

This pan, with a removable or non-removable bottom, is a terrific coffee cake baking pan. It features a wide tube in the center that helps hoist up a big cake. It makes for a great slicing cake or yeasted coffeecake. It's nice and roomy and tends, if prepped properly, to release any cake easily.

1 angel cake pan (9 or 10 inch)

Another great pan for coffee and pound cakes, with a narrow center funnel that helps hoist up a large cake and release it easily. This pan tends to make for a taller, more elegant cake. Originally created for angel food cakes (meringue-based cakes that few people make anymore), the pan has stuck around and is wonderfully serviceable (I use it instead of a Bundt pan). For some reason, I find the best angel food cake pans are found in old-fashioned hardware stores. A tall, cheap, but solid one is all you need.

1 Bundt pan (12 cups), aka fluted baking pan

A European-inspired American cake pan legend, a Bundt pan makes for gorgeous fluted cakes. Non-stick is definitely the way to go in Bundt pans and even then, brush a thick coating of shortening into the flutes of the pan to ensure total cake release. Nordicware makes the original Bundt pans; other manufacturers call them fluted baking pan, as Bundt is a trademark of Nordicware, one of the most innovative cake pan manufacturers around.

2 round layer cake pans (9 inch)

Your go-to pan for layer cakes, rolls, and small coffeecakes.

2 to 4 muffin or cupcake tins

I recommend heavy duty, professional muffin pans, coated with industrial glaze. Non-stick is another good choice, but whether I bake cupcakes or muffins in them, chances are I, and you, will use muffin paper liners, which ensure release. Unfortunately, in domestic bakeware, it's hard to find a standard size pan, so yield for recipes might vary by a couple of muffins, more or less.

My Favorite Baking Tools

Cookie, doughnut, and biscuit cutters

Always have both plain and fluted nested cutters on hand. You can find cutters in plastic or stainless steel, as well as specialty cutters for holiday baking. Use them for biscuits, cookies, scones, and doughnuts. Seasonal cutters are inexpensive and inspiring, so always be on the lookout for special ones. You can also create a wonderful gift by including a fun cookie cutter with your seasonal baking.

Knives

For general baking, I rely on one or two 8-inch chef's knives, an 8 to 10 inch bread knife, a thin serrated knife (for slicing cake layers), and a regular straight-edged paring knife as well as a curve paring knife called a bird's beak parer. Cutco's bird's beak parer is my go-to apple-peeling tool because it's unrivaled in its effectiveness.

Great knifes feature a certain heft, a full tang, and are made of stainless or carbon steel. Sharpen your knives professionally every few months, but in between, just hone them yourself on a knife steel. The sharper your knives, the fewer knife accidents you'll have.

Measuring Spoons

I prefer long-handled spoons so I can dig into spice jars and baking powder without fuss. As with bake ware and small tools, have extra measuring spoons on hand versus relying on one, too-busy pair.

Measuring Cups

Use Pyrex or glass for liquid measures (honey, milk, water, oil) and metal cups for dry ingredients.

Ice Cream Scoops

How do professional bakers get those nice caps on muffins and cupcakes? They use ice cream scoops. There, the secret is out. You can use regular ice cream scoops, but professional ones are heavy-duty and long lasting. Restaurant supply stores have them, or order online. Professional scoops are labeled by a specific number that tells you how many portions of ice cream per quart they furnish. For example, a #16 scoop produces 16 scoops of ice cream per quart. Scoops can be as large as a 10 or 12, right down to a melon baller size of 100 or 80 (excellent for cookies and meatballs). Sizes 12, 14, 16, are good choices for standard muffins or cupcakes.

Rolling Pins

So simple, so old-fashioned. What finer tool is there for cookies, pies, and pizza than a wood rolling pin? But all pins are not created equal. Thorpe or Banton are great choices in ball-bearing pins, but I tend to rely on tapered French rolling pins. This sort of pin, which has no handles, is perfect for almost all your baking needs, but if you're a newish baker you may prefer a heavier ball-bearing pin. Why not make a home for at least two pins, one tapered and one with ball bearings? That way, if you have kids or a friend drops by to bake, you have a spare. Baking is about hospitality, after all. A higher price usually indicates a better-quality wood, such as dense, northern maple versus softer, imported boxwood. Porous, soft woods in a rolling pin can cause the dough to stick, but a little extra dusted flour will fix things.

Shortbread Molds

These are usually made of clay and can be found at specialty suppliers such as King Arthur Flour, or in vintage and antique stores, or if you're very lucky, bequeathed to you. Shortbread molds are usually round and bear Celtic motifs, hearts, or traditional Scottish thistle patterns. They're for use with shortbread cookie dough only and make one large cookie that is segmented to be easily broken apart after baking. You can also find wood-like or wood replica molds.

Whisks

Although many home bakers prefer wooden spoons, whisks are my usual choice, for their pure versatility. I use a whisk for both wet batters and blending dry ingredients. Small ones are great for mixing up glazes or melting chocolate or honey and butter. I like traditional French whisks and also the Danish dough whisk, which looks like a rug beater, with a circular wire lollipop on a wooden stick. This odd-looking tool is still the best tool for mixing muffin, pancake, or carrot cake batter. It's wise to have an assortment of whisks in different sizes and shapes. Restaurant supply places tend to stock whisks that are NSF approved, which means they are anti-bacterial.

Zester, Traditional Citrus or Microplane

Traditional citrus zesters work great, but a Microplane is more versatile; it works on maple sugar, chocolate, and cheese as well.

Metal Dough Scraper or Bench Cutter

Use these to cut dough into sections and to clean your work surface. There are NSF-approved, dishwasher-safe dough scrapers, but almost any one you like will do the job. Just wash them well.

Parchment Paper

Parchment paper is heat and fire-proof, and I go through a lot of it in my kitchen; it rescues you from burned bottoms on cookies and cakes and helps to make clean-up easier. It's available in bakery or restaurant supply places in stacks of 1000 sheets; choose the size you will use most often and then just cut pieces to fit when necessary. Some parchment paper lasts a few bakes; some lasts only one bake and has to be chucked out. Parchment paper is usually kosher certified.

Paper Boxes, Paper Bags

Avid bakers like to share the results of their labors with others. If you're going to bake beautiful recipes, plan to also present your craftsmanship just as beautifully. Leave the foil, cling wrap, and plastic tubs at home. Visit a kitchen or bakery supply house or party center (such as Sweet Celebrations) and stock up on commercial cake boxes, bags, waxed paper sheets, muffin liners, and other odds and ends. Your baked goods will look better in commercial-style dress. Add a ribbon, gift card, or business card, and you have a gift like no other.

Plastic Bags

I am known for using large clear trash bags or leaf bags to cover rising dough, because they're ample enough that you can lay them over large baking sheets (for rising rolls, let's say) or drape them over a mixer where you have a yeast dough rising (saves you from dirtying another bowl). I also use Ziploc bags to store finished bread or cookie doughs or scone mix, or cookie doughs in the freezer.

Stand Mixers

I grew up without a mixer; my hands and a good wooden spoon worked just fine, at least for awhile. But a great mixer is really a kitchen road warrior; I try new mixers all the time and still rely on the 5- or 6-quart KitchenAid. It's similar to what I worked with commercially, mixers by Hobart, and I like the look and feel of a commercial mixer in my kitchen. What I like about the KitchenAid 6-quart mixer is that it's large enough to prevent overflow. KitchenAid comes out with some of the prettiest colors in mixers every other year. But brands such as Kenwood, Rival, Hamilton Beach, Viking, and Jenn-Air are also solid choices, and new brands seem to show up every year. A good mixer is an investment, so take the time to find one with the capacity and reliability you're looking for.

Food Processors

As with mixers, look for large-capacity food processors, which can take care of a ton of baking jobs, from mixing icing to making pie dough, streusel, or scones. KitchenAid offers 7-, 9-, and 12-cup models, and their processors are especially easy to use (no fighting with the feed tube or safety locks), have great capacity, and are incredibly durable. Again, take your time to find the food processor that's right for you—a good one isn't inexpensive!

Bread Machines

I never *bake* in a bread machine, but I do appreciate its ability to mix and rise dough seamlessly. I have Zojirushi in my test kitchen, but any 1-½ pound bread machine, even a basic one, is fine for that purpose. I once wrote a feature on using bread machines as auxiliary dough-kneaders, not as a replacement for your own hands, and the legendary Julia Child herself called me to say she agreed. I find that a bread machine is especially useful for sweet yeast and bagel doughs.

Special Baking Tips and Techniques: Professional Pastry Chef Methods for the Home Baker

I've spent hundreds of hours in hotel school and the professional pastry kitchen, and what's always amazed me is how many really easy tips and techniques seemed to stay state secrets of the professional chefs I worked with. You'll find some of these tips with individual recipes in this book, but here's some of my best general kitchen advice.

The term: "In a Mixer Bowl"

This is my umbrella reference to either a stand mixer bowl with a paddle attachment or a bowl on its own with which you use a wooden spoon, whisk, or electric hand-held mixer. If a specific tool or attachment is necessary, I say so.

Double Up Baking Sheets

Professional pastry chefs and bakers (at least the ones I trained with) always take one extra step that is a veritable baking miracle worker. They always place a baking pan on a baking sheet that has been lined with parchment paper. Sometimes, if the item being baked needs a long bake or is quite rich (which means the sides and bottom can brown faster than the top or middle), they use two baking sheets, stacked one inside or atop the other and line the top one with parchment paper. This makes for much more evenly baked goods and makes clean-up much easier if there is batter or streusel overflow. Cookies baked on double pans come out with lovely rolled edges and without burned bottoms or mushy centers. Plus, it's certainly easier to wrestle a baking sheet out of the oven than many other kinds of pans.

Yeast on the Rise

No matter which yeast you use remember that yeast is really quite alive and made of cells that want to multiply and thrive. Each time a little yeast cell perishes, the yeast will provide that much less rise. Ultimately, once yeast does its alchemic/physics dance in the oven, the baking structure is set and then the yeast has done its job.

Yeast really dislikes ice-cold water or other liquids, such as milk, sugar, and fat (such as oil) and salt dumped right on top of it. Salt and sugar in particular can "burn" the yeast and render it inactive. Cold milk, being both cold and a dairy product, also keeps yeast from doing its best work.

My best trick for working with yeast is to quickly whisk the yeast with warm water to activate or rehydrate it. (Don't expect the new instant yeast to foam and expand as active dry does.) Then cover it with a "shield" of flour (one cup of the flour called for in the recipe). This protects the yeast from inadvertent contact with its inhibitors.

Most of all, don't think of yeast as difficult to work with. Instead, think of yeast as a gifted, talented child that, given extra love and care, will become a star in whatever production it's in. Homemade, yeasted baking gives glorious, incomparable results—something the world needs more of, not less.

Raisins, Plumped and Dried

Who wants contracted, tight, dry raisins in the midst of a quick bread or muffin? You want an oasis of moist, chewy sweetness. When it comes to raisins and all dried fruit, my recipes say "plumped and dried." This means, cover the dried fruit with boiling water and let stand 1 to 3 minutes. This treatment makes the dried fruit plump and expand, and the flavor ups accordingly.

Seasonal Stocking Up

It's true that we can get almost anything these days, regardless of season or geography. But if you want piquant and fresh cranberries the northeast seems to grow so well, you'd best stock up in the fall when they're plentiful and prices are good. This is ditto for clementines or the best citrus – coming in mid to late winter – that's when oranges are sweetest, plentiful and priced for bakers. In cooler months, opening a freezer to bags and bags of blueberries, strawberries, slices of peaches, cranberries and any sort of plum is a baker's paradise of inspiration. And nothing perks up a storage-apple pie than a few cranberries and some diced rhubarb, courtesy of your own forethought and deep freezer.

Turn Up the Heat: About Your Oven

Over the years, I've received a lot of queries about ovens. Some bake fast, some slow, some have hot spots; some are too "modern" and too convective, some are stubborn old New York City apartment ovens that seem haunted by their very first residents. In short, you have to know your oven – get it calibrated and learn about its quirks and idiosyncrasies. Don't complain and be confounded – you're the mistress or master of the fire. When people had to bake using fires they'd built themselves, they knew how to tame the fire –how to bank it and work with wood and coals and get the most out of the flame. Today, we have infernos of marvelous construct and yet –for all the modernity, heat is heat. Good bakers are fire tamers. They how to get great results by working with and knowing their own ovens. So, I encourage you to get on intimate terms with your oven. Love it, respect it, pay attention to it, and respond accordingly in order to get the most out of your recipes.

In a way, we're no different from the pioneer bakers, who cozied up to their outdoor bread ovens or big log fires. We spend so much time finding the perfect recipe, buying the best ingredients, preparing them with attention, and then throwing up our hands in despair, as if our ovens are entities beyond our control. Your oven is on your team, but make no mistake – you are the captain. So get an oven thermometer, place it on the back of the middle oven shelf and see, when you set the oven to 350 F, exactly what temperature you have. You can work around inaccuracies of temperature once you know how 'off' it is or call someone in to recalibrate it.

Freezing Dough and Finished Baking

I am not keen on freezing stews and meals for some reason – I prefer fresh soups, spaghetti sauce, and main dishes and don't mind the extra time it takes to make a batch of those things. But I do appreciate frozen pie dough on hand, extra streusel mix, cookie dough, and frozen fruit, of course. Having basics like those around makes it easy to bake a quick pie. Even iced carrot cakes are handy (and my cheesecakes generally freeze well). To be a baking star, have a back-up of some elements you use often. It doesn't compromise the baking and provides tasty treats in ways that saves a bit of your energies.

Acknowledgements

There's so many people to thank when a book is finally ready to show and share with the world. This is particularly true about a cookbook on seasonal baking because the feeling of completion is fused to a certain nostalgia. Nostalgia, like the seasons, echoes a sense of time and unique passages in our lives. There's a unique beauty to be found in all this when one considers all those people who filled the pages of those passages. On book journeys in particular, there are loyal friends who help you stay the trek even as you fret, squawk and otherwise carry on each time they casually ask, 'How's the book going'? There's also volunteer editors, proof readers and recipe testers who I now count as friends. Of course, there's family, my three sons – who watch me go quietly into my 'bat baking cave' with each new cookbook and just let me do what I have to do.

Finally, there's the readers of my books and visitors to my website, www.Betterbaking.com who hear me chat about 'the book, the book, the book' for ages until it's finally released.

My family, friends and readers are the wind beneath my baking and writing sails.

So, as inadequate or as simple as two words can be, let me just say, thank you. Thank you from the bottom of my heart.

Recipe Testers, Editing and Proof-Reading

Senior Editors

Michele Meiner

Bev Solomon

Alison Rutherford

Deborah Racine

Additional Editorial Assistance

Betsy Carey

Margaret (aka Peggy) Carrol-Tornberg

Sue Epstein

Eugene Escherline

Susan Hatch

Ellen Gold

Janet Goldstein

Charla Gray

Jennifer Kaminski

Alana Lesueur

Sandi Pierce

Alison Rutherford

Tracy Slinker

Recipe Testers

Ellen Fuss, Test Kitchen Manager
Louise Allen

Janice Bell

Jane Batt

Sheryl Birenbaum

Marcia Blonder

Jackie Born

Eden Cantkier

Emily Carrara

Margaret Carrol-Tornberg

Betsy Carey

Joan Casey

Laurel Christianson

Regine M.Cineas

Valerie Darabaner

Marcia Emanuele

Sue Epstein

Melanie Freeman

Caroline Geller

Vicki Gensini

Ellen Gold

Janet Goldstein

Marla Gottlieb

Kathy Gourdin

Charla Gray

Janice Guimond

Samantha Haas

Susan Hatch

Susan Harding

Ann Harste

Wendy Hunt

Julia Hyland

Brenda Jackson

Candace Jones

Regina Joskow

Jennifer Kaminski

Barbara Kohn

Leone Lamb

Joyce Leitman

Alana Lesueur

Dana Martin

Hilary McGown

Michele Meiner

Janice Melendez

Myra Michaelson

Sheila Moore

Lisa Neumann

Renee Pearl

Theone Perloff

Sandi Pierce

Lori Rael Northon

Deborah Racine

Lorrain Rogerson

Joyce Rosenfield

Alison Rutherford

Dorothy Sandstrom

Stephanie Sedgwick

Debra Singer

Tracy Slinker

Bev Solomon

Joan Stamp

Cyndi Stollers

Amy Stromberg

Ilana Z. Toledano

Rosemary Varson

Ann Wallace

Beth Berman Wechsler

Eva Weisberg

Shelli Weisz

Sheli Witz

Marcie, Ali Wolfskehl

Corporate Thank You's

American Spoon Foods

Boyajian Inc.

Chapters Indigo

Chemex

Clabbergirl Baking Powder

Costco Connection

David's Tea

Dansko

Harney Teas

Jenn-Air Whirlpool

JS Public Relations

Kitchenaid

Kitchen Arts and Letters

Meyer Cookware

Nielsen Massey Vanilla

Simplex Kettles

The Spice House

Teavana

Upton Tea

Source Guide

Ingredients, Tools and Equipment

Included in this source guide are my most trusted and respected sources of suppliers of ingredients, tools, equipment, teas, and some scents. The Internet (including Ebay, Craigslist, Kijij and Etsy), is another treasure trove of companies and items to assist you in your baking and cooking. Don't discount local flea markets, vintage and antique stores (both for seasonal décor or old-fashioned, hard-wearing bakeware), and your local restaurant suppliers for great deals and inspiration. Keep your eyes open for table-top, seasonal elements – things that add to the culinary effort but can bring the seasonal outdoors, indoors – whether they are items to hang on the walls as decoration or a centerpiece for any holiday.

Most basic ingredients are easily found in supermarkets, with a wide range of quality and value. For specialty items or particularly endorsed items and brands, check out some of my recommended sources. Always keep your eyes open for a new apple or special plum or make a note, when you score with a place for exceptionally fresh, local, well-priced spices, nuts or extracts. And always – when butter is on sale – jump and stock up!

All-Clad Metalcrafters

www.allclad.com

Premier manufacturer of cookware and specialty, high-end bakeware.

J.K. Adams Co.

http://www.jkadams.com/

Solid hardwood rolling pins with plastic bearings, as well as pastry boards and spice racks.

American Spoon Foods

http://www.spoon.com/

Highest quality dried fruits and nuts for baking, as well as preserves, sauces, and chutneys as well as some of the best fruit butters to be found.

Ball Jar

http://www.freshpreserving.com/ (U.S. site)

http://www.homecanning.com/can/ (Canadian site)

Famed Ball preserving company, supplies, recipes. Ball is the company behind the famed Ball Blue Book, which had some of the best preserving recipes and information of all time.

Beehive Kitchenware

www.beehivekitchenware.com

Pewter culinary products

Bella Viva Orchards

www.bellaviva.com

Supplier of unique as well as classic, up-quality dried fruits, especially a variety of Californian baking apricots and pluots.

Boyajian

www.boyajianinc.com

Maker of pure citrus oils including orange, lemon, tangerine, lemon, lime, as well as natural maple extract.

Broadway Panhandler

866-266-5927

www.broadwaypanhandler.com

Bakeware, pots and pans

Bridge Kitchenware Corporation

www.bridgekitchenware.com

Commercial American bakeware, as well as imported molds and other small wares.

Brown Bag Cookie Molds

www.brownbagcookiemolds.com

Shortbread and cookie molds of clay

Bubble Tea Supply

http://www.bubbleteasupply.com/index.php?page=main.html

The Canning Pantry

http://www.canningpantry.com/canning-jars.html

Supplier of canning jars

Ceremonie Tea

http://www.ceremonietea.com

This Israeli company has some of the finest and most delicate of gourmet teas and unique tea bags you fill yourself. Beautiful selection of black, green and herbal teas.

Chef Revival

www.chefrevival.com

Best white aprons, professional style and cut

Chemex Coffee Maker

www.chemexcoffeemaker.com

Makers of glass coffee and tea carafes

Cook's Vanilla

www.CooksVanilla.com

Suppliers of fine, pure vanilla extract (in 4-5 choices), vanilla products such as vanilla paste and powder and other extracts such as chocolate, lemon, raspberry, and orange.

Cuisinart

www.cuisinart.com

Renowned for their food processors and many other upscale kitchen appliances including bread machines.

Cumberland General Store

www.cumberlandgeneral.com

Various country style baking pans and canning equipment.

www.Dansko.com

Wonderful stylish footwear designed to keep your hard-working baker's feet massaged and energized. The choice of professional chefs nationwide, these are only as great to look at as they are to wear.

Eden Foods

www.EdenFoods.Com

Quality organic foods, such as fruit butters

Fleischmann's Yeast

www.breadworld.com

National yeast company. Products available in the United States and Canada, offering fresh, as well as active dry and instant dry yeast products.

Green Mountain Coffee

www.GreenMountainCoffee.com

Fine coffees and organic blends from Vermont coffee roasters

Golda's Kitchen

www.goldaskitchen.com

This Canadian-based retailer offers bake ware, cookware, Kitchenaid mixers, Zojirushi bread machines, tools, small wares.

Hawaiian Vanilla

www.hawaiianvanilla.com

Supplier of Hawaiian vanilla essences and associated products

Home Canning

http://www.homecanning.com/can/ALProducts.asp

Supplier of canning products

Hearth Kitchen Company

www.hearthkitchen.com

This company offers a hearth baking stone for superior homemade pizza.

Hodgson Mill, Inc.

www.hodgsonmill.com

Excellent grains and multi-grain flours; also offers white whole-wheat flour.

House on the Hill

www.houseonthehill.net

Replica wood molds of historical and artistic cookie designs, used in shortbread, butter cookies, and gingerbread houses, etc.

Hulman Company

Clabbergirl Baking Powder

www.Clabbergirl.com

www.bakewithlove.com

Finest quality baking powder with the Clabber Girl, David, or Rumford brand name. Recipe booklets available on request.

www.Jivacubes.com

ingenious coffee cubes that are compressed gourmet coffee, with both creamer and sweetener built in. Drop it in hot water and you have instant coffee or café au lait.

Great taste always but especially good for camping or at the cabin.

King Arthur Flour Baker's Catalogue

www.kingarthurflour.com

A unique source for professionally inclined, dedicated home bakers, the company is a treasure chest of commercial bake ware, specialty salts, sugars, extracts, flour, malt powder, baker's caramel, mixes, yeasts, mixers, bread machines, and unique tools such as the Danish Dough Whisk. Whatever is of the highest quality or most recently on the market, King Arthur usually has it and everything is tested with a product review.

Kitchenaid

www.kitchenaid.com

Full line of stand mixers, as well as refurbished mixers, food processors, blenders, large appliances, electric grain mills, and more.

Kitchenwear Aprons

www.kitchenwears.com

Great, roomy, retro aprons circa 1940-1950. Custom embroidery is available

La Cuisine Kitchenware

www.lacuisineus.com

An excellent source for upscale bake ware, decorating equipment, and anything associated with the art and craft of baking and cooking. Many unique, imported items, and specialty chocolate for baking and extracts.

Lee Valley Tools Ltd.

www.Leevalley.com

Many fine cutlery products but in particular, a source for the original stainless steel rasp, also known as a microplane, used to zest citrus and grate cheese or chocolate.

Lehman's

www.Lehmans.com

Supplier to the Amish community and everyone else who appreciate for old-fashioned, durable bake ware and other items

www.Meyer.Com

Exceptional cookware, including the Cake Boss line of fine baking products.

Leon Neal

bowlman-neal@nc.rr.com

Authentic wooden bread or biscuit bowls.

New York Cake and Baking Distributor

http://www.nycake.com/

For the baker, the cake decorator, and home pro, all manner of everything associated with baking and decorating.

Nielsen-Massey Vanillas Inc.

www.nielsenmasseyvanillas.com

One of, if not the best, vanilla manufacturers in the United States, offering single and double strength vanilla in Madagascar, Bourbon, Mexican or Tahitian extracts and vanilla blends. They also offer pure chocolate, almond, lemon, and pure orange extracts.

Nordic Ware

www.nordicware.com

Renowned original maker of the trademarked Bundt pan; also makes many varieties of Bundt cake styles and sizes and specialty bake ware such as brownie and scone pans.

Peet's Coffee and Tea

www.Peets.Com

Wonderful coffee since 1966, a vanguard in quality coffee, meticulously roasted.

Penzey's Ltd. Spice House

www.penzeys.com

One of the best sources for quality spices with an unheralded selection. They sell Nielsen Massey vanillas and exceptional varieties of wonderful baking cinnamons. There are many retail shops around the country.

Red Star Yeast

http://www.redstaryeast.com/

National yeast company, specializing in fresh, active, and instant dry yeast for consumer and trade markets.

Robin Hood Multifoods

www.robinhood.ca

Canadian Flour Company and maker of Red River Cereal for specialty breads.

Rochow Swirl Mixer Co., Inc.

www.rochowcutters.com

The heaviest duty, most commercial biscuit, scone, and donut cutters to be found.

Rycraft Inc.

www.rycraft.com

An unusual source for unique, heirloom ceramic cookie stamps, suitable for shortbread and other holiday cookies. They also do custom stamps.

Saco Foods Inc.

www.Sacofoods.com

Buttermilk power as well as fine cocoa.

Scharffen Berger Chocolate Maker

www.scharffenberger.com

American chocolate company renowned for high quality chocolate in a variety of forms.

James Sloss/ French Butter Dish

www.frenchbutterdish.com

American pottery, French butter crocks in all sizes, as well as mugs, vases and ceramic pie plates.

Spices, Etc.

www.SpicesEtc.com

The Spice House

www.TheSpiceHouse.com

Quality spices, superior service, one of my favourite go-to places for spice, especially their cinnamons and pumpkin pie spice.

Stitch Thru Time

www.stitchthrutime.com

Specializes in vintage aprons. Lorraine makes roomy, old-fashioned smock style aprons.

Sur La Table

www.surlatable.com

This extraordinary mail order supplier has a baker's and cook's catalogue offering imported brands of bake ware as well as famed nested Matfer cookie cutters, heavy-duty aluminium cake pans, Kugelhopf molds, Zojirushi bread machines, and ceramic pizza stones for great bagels. There are also retail stores in many areas of the U.S.

www.ThanksgivingCoffeeCompany.com

Purveyors of artisanal roasted coffees

Thorpe Rolling Pin Company

Hamden, Connecticut

203-787-0281

Classic, quality hardwood rolling pins, ball bearings, available nationwide in culinary stores, or contact the company for the location of the nearest retailer.

Viking Range Company

www.vikingrange.com

Ranges, cookware, and stand mixers

Williams-Sonoma

www.williams-sonoma.com

Premier supplier of ingredients, tools, and kitchen appliances. There are many retail outlets.

Wilton Industries

www.wilton.com

Wilton offers a full line of specialty and standard cake pans that are suitable for a variety of baking purposes. Offers a few different lines, "Performance Pans", non-stick pans, anodised aluminium (a treated aluminium pan) as well as "Wilton Pro", a more heavy-duty baking pan. Available nationwide at cake decorating stores, gourmet shops, and house wares departments.

John Wright

www.jwright.com

Beautiful enamel on cast iron steamers, for steaming potpourri, fragrance oils and cinnamon sticks in your kitchen, as per season. Also offers cast iron and porcelain on cast iron seasonal bake ware and molds, including gingerbread house molds, and oven apple bakers.

Tea and Coffees Source Guide

The companies and their products here are some of the best and I have tried, and can endorse them all. It is by no means, a definitive list. If you are on the trail of great coffee and tea, you might start with any of these companies, and then browse the internet, and your own local coffee and tea venues which I encourage you to support.

R.C. Bigelow Inc.

www.bigelowtea.com

I have a fondness for Bigelow since their trademark Constant Comment was a favorite tea of mine while growing up. You can find Bigelow brand in stores but their mail order catalogue shows you their extensive line.

Capresso

www.capresso.com

A maker of very upscale, high design, high performance brewers of regular drip coffee, espresso and cappuccino makers or combination. Their burr grinder is one of the best I tested. Visit them at their website and they will direct you to retails carrying their product line.

Celestial Seasonings

www.CelestialSeasonings.com

One of the original companies as far as herbal teas goes, this company now offers, as a switch, black teas in with their regular, and ever evolving line. Their fruit and herb teas, as well as more 'medicinal' line (green teas, diet teas, ginseng, etc.) are beautifully packaged and tasteful in every way.

Chantal Cookware

www.chantalcookware.com

Chantal makes exceptional cookware but their whistling teakettle, in enamel on steel, or shiny, mirror finish stainless is pretty as a picture.

Chemex Corporation

www.chemexcof.com

This company has been quietly manufacturing its unique glass carafe for over 50 years.

David's Tea

www.DavidsTea.Com

Incredible black, oolong, green and herbal teas. A most exciting tea company that is known for its contemporary, imaginative and quality tea blends with exotic themes that update seasonally (although many become constant classics). Available online or kiosks world-wide (originated in Canada).

49th Parallel Roasters

www.49thparallelroasters.com

A West coast Canadian company, their Epic Espresso is indeed epic. Superlative coffee.

www.Gillies Coffee

www.Gillies.com

One of the oldest of American coffee roasters, this New York roaster offers choice beans as well as grinding and brewing products.

Green Mountain Coffee Roasters

www.GreenMountainCoffee.com

This Vermont company is environmentally oriented and offers a nice line of premium coffees, as well as some brewing and grinding equipment.

Harney Tea Company

www.Harney.com

One of my favourite tea companies of quality teas, hotel/restaurant tea purveyors, hands on service and attentiveness. Fine teas from around the world from a family that has incomparable expertise, respect and passion for tea. Harney has been consistently garnering respect, adoration and justified renown among tea fans. Full range of black, green, white, herbals, as well as the best Roasted Buckwheat Tea around.

Peet's Coffee and Tea

www.Peets.com

California-based, America's treasured coffee roasters since 1966. A legacy coffee company which was at the beginning of American's love affair with better coffee.

Phil and Sebastian Coffee

www.philsebastian.com

Exceptional coffee from Calgary-based coffee roasters.

Saeco USA Inc.

www.saeco.com

This world-wide company is one of the leaders in top of the line coffee brewers, primarily espresso and cappuccino, as well as combination units and grinders.

Serendipitea

www.serendiptea.com

One of the first mail order companies online at the forefront of the new wave of tea companies.

Simplex Kettles

www.simplex-kettles.com

A British based company that makes the most durable as well as beautiful stove-top kettles. Iconic design

Starbucks Coffee Company

www.Starbucks.com

Starbucks may be everywhere and is always a welcome coffee oasis (and their founder, Howard Schultz, is an inspiration). Coffee, Teavana tea, and coffee accouterments from the franchise that taught America about café latte and espresso.

Stash's Teas

www.StashTea.com

A broad and good line of variety teas.

Tazo

www.Tazo.com

Mail order or at Starbucks (at one point; now they serve Teavana) are known for their herbals and fruit teas

Twinings

www.Twinings.com

The venerable British company with tins of traditional tea blends.

Upton Tea Imports

www.UptonTea.com

Superb teas, service, and tea accouterments. Source for famed Sadler and Chatsford tea pots (Check out their River Shannon Tea – it's the best)

Index

Made in the USA
San Bernardino, CA
15 July 2015